BORDER THINKING

Border Thinking

· · · ·

Latinx Youth Decolonizing Citizenship

Andrea Dyrness and
Enrique Sepúlveda III

University of Minnesota Press
Minneapolis
London

Portions of chapter 1 were previously published as Enrique Sepúlveda, "Toward a Pedagogy of *Acompañamiento*: Mexican Migrant Youth Writing from the Underside of Modernity," *Harvard Educational Review* 81, no. 3 (2011): 550–72, and in Enrique Sepúlveda, "Border Brokers: Teachers and Undocumented Mexican Students in Search of *Acompañamiento*," *Diaspora, Indigenous, and Minority Education* 12, no. 2 (2018). Portions of chapter 2 were previously published as Andrea Dyrness and Enrique Sepúlveda, "Education and the Production of Diasporic Citizens in El Salvador," *Harvard Educational Review* 85, no. 1 (2015): 108–31; as Andrea Dyrness, "National Divisions, Transnational Ties: Constructing Social and Civic Identities in Post-war El Salvador," *Journal of Latin American and Caribbean Anthropology* 19, no. 1 (2014): 63–83; and Andrea Dyrness, "'*Contra Viento y Marea* (Against Wind and Tide)': Building Civic Identity among Children of Emigration in El Salvador," *Anthropology and Education Quarterly* 43, no. 1 (March 2012): 41–60. Portions of chapters 3 and 4 were previously published as Andrea Dyrness and Enrique Sepúlveda, "Between 'Here' and 'There': Transnational Latino/a Youth in Madrid," in *Global Latin(o) Americanos: Transoceanic Diasporas and Regional Migrations*, ed. M. Overmyer-Velázquez and E. Sepúlveda, 139–61 (Oxford: Oxford University Press, 2017). Portions of chapter 5 were originally published in Andrea Dyrness, "The Making of a Feminist: Spaces of Self-Formation among Latina Immigrant Activists in Madrid," *Journal of Diaspora, Indigenous, and Minority Education* 10, no. 4 (Fall 2016): 201–14.

Poetry by Aurora Levins Morales and Jorge Argueta is reprinted by permission of the poets. Previously unpublished poetry by youth poets is printed by permission of the poets.

Published by the University of Minnesota Press
111 Third Avenue South, Suite 290
Minneapolis, MN 55401–2520
http://www.upress.umn.edu

ISBN 978-1-5179-0629-0 (hc)
ISBN 978-1-5179-0630-6 (pb)
A Cataloging-in-Publication record for this book is available from the Library of Congress.

Printed in the United States of America on acid-free paper

The University of Minnesota is an equal-opportunity educator and employer.

26 25 24 23 22 21 20   10 9 8 7 6 5 4 3 2 1

To *los eternos indocumentados*,
in the words of Salvadoran poet Roque Dalton,
and to the young people in this book, poets all of them,
for inspiring us with their vision

Contents

Introduction

Rethinking Youth Citizenship in the Diaspora

THERE IS A MONSTER under my bed!" begins a children's book by Daniela Ortiz, a Peruvian who immigrated to Spain in 2007. "It is a really scary monster," continues the tale, which depicts in rich illustrations "the beast of the immigration office" as far more powerful and scarier than the monsters in other children's books. "And how is it this monster got into my bedroom?" the child narrator asks. She describes accompanying her mother to the immigration office, where they must wait in several long lines and then build a "huge tower of papers" to prove their worth and "usefulness" to European society. "Even though we brought a lot of papers, they said to my mama: 'NO!!!' The words were so strong and so hard that they built a bridge into my ear. That office worker managed to hide inside my LITTLE EAR. By hiding in my ear the monster managed to get under my bed" (Ortiz 2017).

In this tale Ortiz, a self-described anticolonial and antiracist activist and artist, highlights how immigrant children experience the violence of national borders and white racism, flipping the script on the "crisis of immigration" in Western liberal democracies. Subverting popular narratives of immigrants as beasts or monsters who invade and infest peaceful Western societies, the story graphically illustrates the "super violent power" of the European state over the lives of immigrants, a power that dates to colonial times when white Europeans "did awful, painful things to my people." In the book, the child's mother helps her drown out the monster of the immigration office by sharing the songs and stories of anticolonial freedom fighters, including bell hooks, Audre Lorde, Berta Cáceres, Julieta Paredes, "and many, many more." The story ends, "My ears, my room and my life were so full of these great words that there was no space for the WHITE MONSTER anymore."

Like Ortiz's children's book, this book attempts to flip the script on "the crisis of immigration" in Western societies by highlighting the experiences and perspectives of im/migrant youth around borders. In particular, it examines the citizenship experiences of young people growing up in the Latino diaspora: the messages they receive about membership and belonging in the various communities in which they participate and the cultural practices through which they create and imagine new forms of identity and belonging that transcend national borders. Like the child in Daniela Ortiz's book, immigrant youth encounter the state and learn about official notions of citizenship through their interactions with immigration agents, as well as with teachers and educators in schools and after-school programs and through encounters with the police. However, these encounters are mediated by their experiences in diaspora communities—extended networks of family and friends from the same country of origin, living in multiple places—which offer them alternative narratives, forms of belonging, and ways of making sense of and responding to dominant nationalist discourses. How does lived experience in the diaspora, and a diaspora consciousness, shape their citizenship formation? How does participation in transnational social fields give them new understandings of self, strategies of resistance, and resources for confronting the violence of nationalism? And finally, what pedagogies and methodologies can excavate and nurture these resources for democratic citizenship? These are the questions this book explores.

Daniela Ortiz's children's book is one example of a diaspora cultural product as an activist strategy—a resource to help other immigrants resist and overcome the violence of "the beast of the immigration office." In another children's book, by Dominican diaspora author Junot Díaz, a six-year-old girl is helped by the members of her Dominican community in the Bronx to recreate the island where she was born. Through dialogue with her grandmother, mother, and neighbors she learns about a country with "more music than air, fruit that makes you cry, beach poems, and a hurricane like a wolf" (Díaz 2018). In addition to nostalgic recollections of beaches where "fish jump from the waves into your lap, and at sunset sometimes the dolphins . . . come out of the water to bow good night," there is also a monster in this story. This monster, though unnamed in the story, is the dictator Rafael Trujillo, who ruled in a reign of terror over the island for thirty years. Díaz thus presents a multidimensional portrait of cultural richness, natural beauty, and violent state power in the Dominican Republic that shapes the diaspora's conflicting and ambivalent relationship to the island. Furthermore, the child protagonist learns that the monster was ultimately defeated by brave heroes who rose up, "strong smart young women just like you, and a few strong smart young men, too," and that she is descended from them. Like Ortiz's heroine, Díaz's Lola is encouraged to imagine herself as part of a tradition of resistance.

Díaz's *Islandborn* demonstrates how knowledge of and connection to one's home country is central to identity formation for diaspora youth, how this knowledge unfolds through relationships with family and friends who are also connected to the island (or home country), and that these relationships and communal knowledge are a key resource for countering deficit views of immigrants and exclusionary citizenship regimes. As Dominican scholar García-Peña (2016) writes, black Dominican migrants are exiles both at home and abroad; "They are symbolically and physically expunged from their home nation because they are black and poor, yet they remain unadmitted into their host nation for the same reasons" (2). García-Peña asserts that while "official stories of exclusion are influential in bordering the nation and shaping national identity . . . they are always contested, negotiated, and even redefined through contra-*dictions*" (3; emphasis in original). The children's book authors introduced above, offering their books to fill gaps in the official narratives told to and about immigrant children, engaged in such contestation. As Junot Díaz explained in an interview about *Islandborn* with National Public Radio, "When we look at the discourses around immigration, it's always this deficit model: 'We didn't have anything at home' or 'We had less at home, and so we came here for more opportunities.' OK, that's very, very comforting. There's also the fact a lot of people come because political realities have uprooted them, have driven them from their homes."[1] As they flesh out the countries from which migrants came, these books historicize the migrant experience "from the perspective of those who have been silenced in the nation's archive" (García-Peña 2016, 17).

In this book, we add the voices of Latino diaspora youths—from the Dominican Republic, Peru, Mexico, Guatemala, El Salvador, Ecuador, and Venezuela—to the archive of Latinx cultural critics, artists, and intellectuals who have commented on the diaspora condition. The young people in our research are both the authors and the children in the story. They are learning about themselves and their place in the world, and they are also sharp social observers, sophisticated cultural critics, and eloquent narrators of their experience. Some of them are activists, but most have not had the support or mentoring to translate their critical awareness into civic action. By accompanying these youths in three different transnational communities—in Northern California, El Salvador, and Madrid, Spain—we hope to learn from them what nurtures and supports their democratic citizenship formation: their ability to respond to and critique the forces that divide and leave them outside the bounds of nation, and to imagine and contribute to more expansive and inclusive communities of belonging. As Michelle Fine (2018) writes, young people marked as "Other," exiled within, "narrate their own lives but, as important, they refract back on the shape and policies of a nation designed, and regularly refashioned, to exclude" (26).

Young people in the Latino diaspora are coming of age in the midst of a contradiction between increasingly rigid nationalisms—with constricting definitions of national identity and citizenship—and fluid diaspora identities and experiences. Global communication technologies increasingly allow them to maintain relationships and affiliations in multiple national contexts, creating transnational social fields (Levitt and Schiller 2004). At the same time, discourses of citizenship and integration continue to insist on national identification and assimilation as a condition for membership and belonging in the host country. As we will show, in both the United States and Spain, popular, scholarly, and policy discourses of integration construct immigrant young people's transnational affiliations and ethnic communities as suspect and a threat to democratic society. The U.S. election in 2016 of a president who built his campaign around vilifying Mexican immigrants, and the policies of the early Trump administration, laid bare the extent of anti-immigrant and white nationalist sentiment in the United States. But the view of Latinos as "other" and a threat to U.S. society has a long history (Chavez 2008). In both the United States and Spain, common perceptions of Latino criminality, illegality, and cultural inferiority; fears of ethnic separatism; and violent state repression and policing of immigrants have created a hostile context for citizenship formation (Chavez 2008; González 2016; Massey and Sánchez 2010; Zavella 2011). In this context, it is critical to understand how diaspora young people, whose lives transcend national borders, make sense of and respond to discourses that frame them as outsiders and a threat to the nation.

The Political Context of Migrant Youth Citizenship

In spite of very different contexts of reception and histories of immigration in the United States and Western Europe, on both sides of the Atlantic, public anxieties and fears about immigrants who appear unable or unwilling to assimilate—those who remain attached to their co-ethnic communities and/or countries of origin—continue to frame the debate and policy about immigrant youth. Far-right politicians have risen to power across democratic states by stoking fears that their nations are under siege by migrants. The association of migrants with terrorism and violent extremism, a staple of anti-immigrant rhetoric that was once the purview of right-wing fringe parties, has now become mainstream. A 2016 European public opinion survey conducted by the Pew Research Center found that more than half of respondents believed incoming refugees would increase the likelihood of terrorism in their country (Wike, Stokes, and Simmons 2016). The survey also found that negative attitudes toward minorities were very common, with very few Europeans believing diversity has a positive impact on their countries. In 2018, an EU public opinion poll conducted by the European Commission found that immigration remains the leading concern of Europeans (European Commission 2018), even though the number of migrant arrivals was sharply down.

Increasingly, the political discourse around immigrants and cultural diversity in Western liberal democracies has mirrored (and fomented) negative public views of immigrants and suspicion of multiculturalism. In his speech before an international security conference in 2011, former U.K. prime minister David Cameron famously criticized "state multiculturalism," warning that it was fostering extremist ideology and contributing to homegrown Islamist terrorism. Arguing for the need for a stronger national identity to prevent people turning to extremism, he signalled a tougher stance on Muslim groups. "Frankly, we need a lot less of the passive tolerance of recent years and much more active, muscular liberalism," the prime minister said.[2] As Cameron's speech illustrates, when national security is perceived to be at risk, toleration of cultural difference is condemned as a sign of weakness and naïveté, not only by right-wing media outlets and populist politicians but also by liberal political and intellectual elites. In a review of the response to the *Charlie Hebdo* terrorist attacks in Paris, Mark Lilla, writing for the *New York Review of Books,* asserted that the multiculturalist perspective was "the least in touch with social and political realities today," because it "refuses to recognize" the radicalization in the Muslim *quartiers* (Lilla 2015).

Muslims are particularly targeted on both sides of the Atlantic as potential security threats, not only because of high-profile terrorist attacks but also because of the widespread public perception that they refuse to assimilate and "want to be distinct" (Wike, Stokes, and Simmons 2016). The treatment of Muslims in Western liberal discourse has received much critical scholarly attention (Abu El-Haj 2015; Ali 2017; Jaffe-Walter 2016; Maira 2009). While it is not the focus of this book, the construction of Muslims as violently opposed to the ideals of democratic citizenship reveals much about the inability of national citizenship regimes to absorb cultural diversity, and it deserves brief mention here. The same 2016 Pew survey cited earlier found that unfavorable views of Muslims were on the rise across Europe, and that for many Europeans, these negative views are tied to "a belief that Muslims do not wish to participate in the broader society. . . . The dominant view is that Muslims want to be distinct from the rest of society rather than adopt the nation's customs and way of life" (Wike, Stokes, and Simmons 2016, 5). In this view, Muslims are suspect simply for their maintenance of distinct cultural and religious practices and identities. In the United States, half of U.S. adults say Islam is *not* part of mainstream American society (Pew 2017). In the wake of the 2015 to 2016 presidential campaign and election, hate crimes and assaults against Muslims rose significantly to surpass 2001 levels, the previous peak following 9/11 (Kishi 2017). President Trump's executive order restricting travel from Muslim-majority countries explicitly targets Muslims as potential security threats.

In the United States, Latinx youth and their communities have also been targeted by immigration enforcement and popular and political discourses that construct them as a threat to American society (Chavez 2008; Zavella 2011). According to Chavez (2008), the "Latino Threat Narrative" is based on a pervasive view that Latinos, unlike previous immigrant groups who became part of the nation, are unwilling or incapable of integrating. Based on notions of Mexican criminality and fears of "reconquest" and separatist inclinations of Mexican immigrants, the Latino Threat Narrative casts U.S.-born Latinos as "'alien-citizens,' perpetual foreigners despite their birthright" (2008, 6). The Trump presidency is an iconic example of the Latino Threat Narrative undergirding a policy regime, as the president has repeatedly pointed to immigrant criminality to justify his get-tough enforcement proposals, even though the data on immigrant crime do not support his assertions.[3] In the early Trump administration, dramatically stepped-up immigration enforcement included the cancellation of Deferred Action for Childhood Arrivals (DACA) protections for "Dreamers" (later reinstated by the courts); the cancellation of Temporary Protected Status (TPS) for immigrants from El Salvador, Honduras, and Haiti; expanded deportation sweeps targeting lawful immigrants with minor criminal convictions and undocumented immigrants with no criminal background; and the "zero-tolerance" policy at the border that authorized criminal prosecution of anyone who crossed the border unlawfully, which resulted in the widely protested family separation policy in the spring of 2018. Although the research for this book was conducted before the election of Donald Trump, it is important to note that these policies, and the growing public hostility toward Latinos, build on two decades of escalating immigration enforcement that have had a particularly strong impact on Latinx youth in the United States (Coutin 2016; Massey and Sánchez 2010).

Migrant youth in the United States and Europe encounter the heavy hand of the state not only through immigration and law enforcement but also through educational programming designed to integrate and "liberalize" them (Jaffe-Walter 2016; Shirazi 2017). As we will see, state-led educational efforts to "discipline" migrant youth, to transform them into acceptable subjects of the liberal nation-state, work to criminalize migrants' cultural difference and connections to their homelands. It was no coincidence that in the aftermath of the *Charlie Hebdo* shootings in Paris, the French education minister introduced a vast program of education reforms, including civic education to expand the teaching of democratic values, "more emphasis on reasoning and the use of the French language, including for parents who do not speak it; [and] greater involvement of parents in the disciplining of their children" (Lilla 2015). Civic education was explicitly framed as an antiterrorist measure: the minister "made the case that educational reform was crucial for national security" (Lilla 2015). In the United States, Arshad Ali (2017) writes that Muslim students have been targeted for Countering Violent Extremism (CVE) programs by the FBI. "A CVE framework assumes any Muslim, at any moment, may be 'radicalized' to engage in acts of nonstate violence," and draws on "older epistemic traditions of Orientalism, in which Muslims are seen as irrational, enraged, and unpredictable simply because they are Muslim" (113).

Fears of "parallel societies" position migrants who maintain their cultural practices and ties to their homelands as opposing integration, leading states to adopt interventions that target migrant communities. In a revealing example, Denmark has instituted a number of measures directed at migrant "ghettos," aiming to minimize the contact migrant children have with their parents and families, and even criminalizing extended trips to their homelands, on the grounds that these hinder the process of integration (Jaffe-Walter 2016). A new law requires that "ghetto children," children born in neighborhoods where more than 50 percent of the residents are non-Western immigrants, must begin preschool at one year of age for at least twenty-five hours a week of instruction in "Danish values."[4] Other laws target "re-education trips," where parents send their children for stays in their home countries to learn their cultural values. Parents who "force" their children to make these visits may be punished by a prison term of two years and risk losing their residency permits. When announcing the tough new measures, the Danish immigration and integration minister, Inger Støjberg, said, "It's a serious breach of their duty of care when parents threaten and coerce their children into taking these re-education trips abroad. This tells us that these parents don't want any part of Denmark for themselves or their children."[5] The subtitle in the article reporting on this in the *Copenhagen Post* read, "Children from immigrant backgrounds are being sent abroad by their parents for indoctrination." Such measures—and the media discourse about them—stigmatize migrant parents' efforts to socialize their children according to their own values and uncritically associate migrants' desire for cultural preservation with opposition to the host society. As we will see, this discourse is echoed in Spain (chapter 3) and in the United States.

These examples of political discourse and policy interventions reflect widespread assumptions that schools in liberal democracies are sites of democratic teaching and that homeland influences are undemocratic. Pitting the "democratic" teaching of schools in Western liberal nations against "homeland influences," these interventions assume that migrants must choose one or the other, and that any attempt to preserve homeland attachments signals a threat to the host society. This book takes the perspective that such views are not new: efforts like Denmark's are not simply the result of recent immigration flash points such as terrorist attacks, the European refugee crisis, or the election of populist politicians. On the contrary, they are sewn into the fabric of Western liberal nationalisms and democratic citizenship itself. "Receiving countries" of Western liberal democracies are invested in constitutive processes of categorizing and expelling Others—those deemed different, less worthy, or dangerous—which began under colonialism and continue to this day. According to Abu El-Haj, Ríos-Rojas, and Jaffe-Walter (2017), "Discourses of modern liberalism are inextricably linked to colonial productions of 'liberal subjects' capable of full citizenship in democratic nations, and 'illiberal subjects' unfit for the full exercise of democratic citizenship—dichotomies that have in turn been 'naturalized' as distinct human groupings—i.e. race" (313). Their study of Muslim immigrant youth across three countries—the United States, Spain, and Denmark—found that despite significant differences in historic and contemporary approaches to immigration in the United States and Europe, "shared discourses of liberalism . . . work across these contexts to racialize and exclude people from Muslim majority countries and communities" (314).

We build on such critical studies of nationalism, and on theories of coloniality/decoloniality (Quijano 2000; Mignolo 2007, 2011), to understand the citizenship experiences of migrants from colonial and former colonial areas as "colonial/racialized subjects of empire" (Grosfoguel, Cervantes-Rodríguez, and Mielants 2008). Citizenship as a (Western) construct is built on a system of racial social stratification that was integral to the colonial project and that indelibly shapes the experience of migrants in the metropole today (Taylor 2013; Mignolo 2011; Grosfoguel, Cervantes-Rodríguez, and Mielants 2008). As Lucy Taylor (2013) urges, drawing on theories of coloniality, "We must consider how western epistemology conditions *the concept of citizenship* and how that concept works to sustain global racial-knowledge hierarchies. We might highlight its 'locus of enunciation' and ask how citizens are defined, and we might focus on the question of education, asking how citizens are 'made' " (598; emphasis in the original). We take up this call here, adopting a critical analysis of state power and diaspora subjectivities among Latinx youth in educational spaces in California, El Salvador, and Spain. Interrogating Western citizenship as a (colonial) cultural product clears our lenses to view migrants' experiences through terms other than the nation-state optic, to observe the ways in which migrant youths actually experience their membership and belonging in different national and cultural communities. Most important, shedding our nationalist lenses opens up our analysis to the democratic possibilities of their transnationalism and hybridity, of lives lived between multiple national and cultural communities. It is to these possibilities that this book turns, in an effort to rethink and decolonize citizenship in an era of globalization.

This book explores the citizenship implications of Latinx young people's transnational experiences, and advances a methodology that aims to expose and support the democratic possibilities in diaspora young people's hybrid identities. The title of the book, *Border Thinking: Latinx Youth Decolonizing Citizenship*, captures our dual focus on diaspora young people's transgressive citizenship practices (i.e., transcending the nation-state) and research methodologies and epistemologies that assist in the decolonizing project, including critical ethnography and participatory action research, to support young people in the development of their own critical consciousness. Drawing on research with Latinx youth in three different locations, we analyze how dominant regimes of citizenship—discourses of nationalism and integration—construct diaspora youth as outsiders and erase their multiple identities; how diaspora youth make sense of and respond to the contradictions of their multiple memberships and exclusions in ways that create new possibilities for democratic citizenship; and how participatory research methodology engages this. Corresponding to these questions, the book makes two central claims. First, diaspora young people's multiple connections to home and host countries offer them a critical perspective on national citizenship that lends itself to the development of democratic civic identities. Their multiple experiences of *belonging* and *exclusion* across multiple national contexts at once sharpens their awareness of and commitment to democratic citizenship and nurtures a border epistemology that delinks this from the nation-state. However, these experiences must be tapped by critical educators or cultural workers to support and develop active citizenship formations. Second, making young people's in-between location a central object of inquiry and reflection becomes a powerful educational and citizenship tool, and contributes to the project of decolonizing citizenship.

Without romanticizing the possibilities of transnational identities, for our analysis also attends to the hegemonic forces that interpolate the third spaces where diaspora youth carve out their identities, we unapologetically embrace the goals of decolonizing citizenship, and put our analytical tools toward the work of excavating the subjugated knowledge of diaspora communities. In the remainder of this introduction, we outline the conceptual framework that informs this book. First, we review existing research on immigrant integration and transnationalism to examine how it informs or challenges popular assumptions that pose transnational identities as a threat. We argue that dominant research on immigrant incorporation, in taking for granted the perspective of the nation-state, too often reproduces binaries of assimilated or oppositional im/migrant youth. These binaries obscure the often undemocratic teachings of nationalism as well as the democratic learnings of transnationalism—that is, the possibility that migrant *refusals* of national identity might be informed by, and contribute to, democratic sensibilities (Dyrness and Abu El-Haj 2019). We introduce frameworks of coloniality/decoloniality and borderlands feminist theories to highlight the alternative ways of being found in the space between nations, the diasporic third space.

Immigrant Education and Incorporation

The late Harvard political scientist Samuel Huntington famously spear-headed the view that immigrants who maintain a distinct cultural identity represent a threat to American civil society, in his works *The Clash of Civilizations* (1996) and *Who Are We? The Challenges to America's National Identity* (2004). Since then, a variety of social science research on immigrant integration has challenged these claims, but Huntington's main concern—about the impact immigrants and their children have on American national identity and society—continues to drive and frame this research. We engage critically with a dominant strand of research on immigrant youth that focuses on their adaptation and incorporation into the nation-state, high-lighting the assimilation processes and mobility trajectories of the second generation (Portes and Rumbaut 2001, 2005; Portes, Vickstrom, and Aparicio 2011; Kasinitz et al. 2008). Much of this research focuses on school performance and the extent to which immigrant youths adopt behaviors and identities that facilitate success and assimilation into nation-state institutions. In taking for granted the nation-state as the horizon of immigrant aspirations and the unit of scholarly analysis, this research exhibits what has been called "methodological nationalism" (Wimmer and Glick Schiller 2003). Assuming assimilation to the nation-state as the goal or expectation for immigrant youth, research informed by methodological nationalism bolsters the binary logic that poses immigrants as *either* assimilated into the American (or host-nation) mainstream *or* separatist and oppositional. For example, sociological theories of segmented assimilation posit that immigrant youth could assimilate either upward into the white middle class or downward into a poor urban underclass of U.S.-born minorities (Portes and Rumbaut 2001; Portes and Zhou 1993); "downward assimilation" generates the concern that immigrant youths will "add to the social pathologies that have been the bane of American urban life" (Portes and Rumbaut 2005, 986). As a third path, immigrant youth could experience "selective acculturation," in which they retain key elements of their home cultures while selectively adopting aspects of the white middle class to enable upward mobility. In this pathway, the focus is on immigrant youth's use and appropriation of their ethnic cultures and communities as resources for upward mobility, taking for granted the ultimate goal of assimilation into the host nation's dominant culture.

Along with segmented assimilation, theories of "reactive ethnicity," in which immigrants are seen to construct a "reactive, anti-American identity" in response to experiences of discrimination and exclusion (Portes and Rumbaut 2001; Massey and Sánchez 2010), lend themselves to popular discourses that pose unassimilated immigrant youth as a threat. Even when such research aims to highlight the role of a hostile context of reception in creating anti-American identity (Massey and Sánchez 2010), or to show that immigrant youths are, in fact, assimilating (Portes, Vickstrom, and Aparicio 2011; Kasinitz et al. 2008), the effect is to reinforce the binaries that pose continuing transnational and panethnic identities as problematic. In their study of immigrant identity among Latin Americans in the United States, for example, Massey and Sánchez (2010) found "a negative process of assimilation in which the accumulation of discriminatory experiences over time steadily reinforces an emergent pan-ethnic 'Latino' identity while promoting the formation of a new, reactive identity that explicitly rejects self-identification as 'American'" (2). This reaction against constructing an American identity, in their view, suggests "the potential for future conflict" (247). Theories of reactive ethnicity pose cultural and ethnic identities as existing only in response to discrimination, and in an ideal world these would disappear or be "optional" (Rumbaut 2008). Such views make it hard to see the meaning of cultural attachments for migrant youth, as well as the value of deep, affective group bonds for engaging in a democracy.

Other research that aims to show that immigrants are joining the mainstream portrays the hybrid realities of the second generation as an "advantage" that helps them do better than their parents. Immigrant youths are constructed as objects of hope, to the extent that they are leaving their parents' communities behind. For example, Kasinitz and colleagues (2008), in their study of U.S.-born children of immigrants in New York City, admit that their research was "initially motivated by worries of second generation decline"; that the children of immigrants might be "at risk of downward assimilation as they become Americans" (342). But they happily report that their comparison of second- and 1.5-generation immigrant youths with native-born peers of the same race on a variety of outcomes led them to be "guardedly optimistic about the second generation" (16). The reason for their optimism is important: "The children of immigrants have not achieved these successes by clinging to the networks and enclaves of their immigrant communities. Instead, they have joined the mainstream" (16). Pitting success against "clinging" to ethnic networks and enclaves, such research reinforces fears of parallel societies that drive draconian measures like Denmark's.

Similarly, Leo Chavez (2008) aims to counter the Latino Threat Narrative by presenting data showing that Latinos are integrating: they are intermarrying with non-Latinos, speaking English (and losing Spanish), buying homes, participating in U.S. civic institutions, and making non-Latino friends. Data on home ownership and income show that Latinos are buying more homes and acquiring more income with each generation. The answer to popular fears of the Latino Threat is "they *are* assimilating"; the absence of threat is predicated on their worthiness as consumers and their similarity to other Americans. "They are just like other folks" (68). Indeed, Chavez and others have shown that immigrant activists themselves have sought to contest narratives of their Otherness and advocated for inclusion on the basis of their good behavior as model citizen-subjects, proving themselves to be self-reliant, entrepreneurial, neoliberal subjects (Chavez 2013; Baker-Cristales 2009). These responses to the immigrant-as-threat narrative, emphasizing immigrants' conformity to neoliberal citizenship models, leave open the question of whether nonconformity to mainstream citizenship ideals poses a threat. Do Latinos who continue to speak Spanish, for example, or who don't buy homes, still belong? The emphasis on assimilation leaves unchallenged the exclusionary politics of neoliberal citizenship, and unexplored the possibility of other kinds of citizenship.

We extend critiques of "methodological nationalism" by showing the ways that studies of immigrant incorporation in this framework not only miss transnational spheres of influence on Latinx young people's identities but also reify the structures of nationalism and are complicit in the harms of nationalism on migrant young people's lives. In our view, research and policymaking driven by nationalist concerns obscures the social and political construction of "nation" and "immigrant" and the formative role of transnational and diasporic communities on young migrants' developing identities. Whether immigrant cultures are seen as a harbinger of future conflict or as commodities for migrant young people's individual advancement in American society, a focus on how they affect national assimilation obscures the ways *nationalism* disciplines and shapes migrant subjects, and, alternatively, how transnational belonging might constitute a resistance to the violence of nationalism.

Challenging Methodological Nationalism: Transnationalism and Diasporic Citizenship

We refer to the youths in our research as "diaspora youth" to widen the lens beyond immigrant-receiving nations to include sending countries and multiple receiving contexts in transnational circuits and to allow us to interrogate the construction of "immigrant youth" and "nation" as political categories that do the work of nationalism (Lukose 2007; Villenas 2007).[6] That is, "immigrants" do not exist except for where they are so labeled by nation-states, whose labeling processes and integration regimes are constitutive of their national identity; immigrants are the "Other" that make possible the definition of "us." In seeking to understand how transnational youths forge a sense of self and connection to a civic community, then, we refuse the perspective of the nation-state and take an approach that aims to challenge "methodological nationalism."

Border Thinking answers a call to bring the anthropology of immigrant education into more explicit dialogue with diaspora studies, by considering the "transnational cultural politics of home, belonging, and identity in the context of migration" (Lukose 2007, 406) and the possibilities of hybrid identity formation. Diaspora, according to Lukose (2007), "refers to the cultural productions and identity formations of migrant communities that have become important and salient for the larger political, economic, and cultural transformations that mark contemporary globalization" (409). Acknowledging the significant overlap between notions of *transnationalism* and *diaspora*, Lukose argues that "diaspora studies is less focused on actual movement across [national] boundaries and more focused on the imaginative worlds and cultural productions of migrants, whether they actually and continually traverse these boundaries . . . or not" (409). Thus, while scholars of transnational migration have focused on the webs of relationships and exchange networks linking people in multiple locations (Glick Schiller, Basch, and Blanc Szanton 1992; Levitt and Glick Schiller 2004), diaspora offers a useful lens for analyzing the subjectivities of migrants in these networks—the ways they imagine themselves and their belonging in relation to multiple cultural and political communities. Anthropologist Lok Siu (2005) defines "diasporic citizenship" as "the processes by which diasporic subjects experience and practice cultural and social belonging amid shifting geopolitical circumstances and webs of transnational relations" (5). At the core of this citizenship lies a tension between affinities and affiliations with multiple sites and awareness of "only partial belonging and acceptance by them" (2005, 11). This awareness is similar to what Patricia Zavella (2011) calls the "peripheral vision" of Mexicans on both sides of the U.S.–Mexico border, who experience "feeling at home in more than one geographical location" and simultaneously a sense of vulnerability and marginality in both places, "feelings that one is neither from here nor from there, not at home anywhere" (8–9). In highlighting the subjectivity of migrants and decentering the perspective of the nation-state, a diaspora citizenship framework allows us to witness the agency of transnational and diasporic subjects in responding to processes of globalization.

Anthropologists have been at the forefront of pointing out complex, hybrid identity formations, cultural practices, and skills that migrant youths develop through their participation in multiple national contexts (Abu El-Haj 2007; Hall 2002; Jaffe-Walter 2016; Lukose 2007; Maira 2009; Ríos-Rojas 2011; Sánchez 2007; Trueba 2004; Villenas 2007). Within the anthropology of education, however, most of the research on transnationalism has focused on the implications for educational achievement. Research on transnational youth conducted by Patricia Sánchez (2007), for example, highlights the cultural learning that occurs on students' trips to their parents' hometowns in Mexico and how this could be tapped by schools to support more relevant instruction in the global era (see also Sánchez and Kasun 2012). Others have pushed educators to consider how processes of diaspora and transnationalism impact the education of Puerto Rican (Rolón-Dow and Irizarry 2014), Dominican (Bartlett and García 2011), and Mexican binational students (Zúñiga and Hamann 2009). A burgeoning literature on transnational literacies points to the ways that students' transnational experiences contribute to robust literacy learning and practices (Lam and Warriner 2012). This research goes far toward countering deficit views of migrant youths' home cultures and transnational ties, but the focus on educational achievement, a marker of national assimilation, stops short of challenging the association between national identity and democratic citizenship (Dyrness and Abu El-Haj 2019).

Other research documents the benefits of migrants' transnational ties for civic participation (Reed-Danahay and Brettell 2008; Miller 2011; Chavez 2008; Jensen 2008) and economic mobility in the host country (Portes, Guarnizo, and Landolt 1999). Arpi Miller (2011) draws on long-term research with Los Angeles–based Salvadoran activists to show that in the process of transnational political organizing, Salvadoran immigrants became embedded into host-nation civic and political institutions. Lene Jensen's (2008) research with immigrant youths from El Salvador and India found that a concern for their country of origin, and a comparison of conditions between the United States and their home country, was a positive source of civic engagement in the United States. We build on this research, but rather than focusing on the benefits to host-country incorporation, we inquire into the impact of transnational experiences on democratic citizenship more broadly, understanding that this may or may not align with the objectives of the nation-state. We view diaspora as an important socializing agent for citizenship because, as Siu (2005) argues, "Being diasporic entails active and conscious negotiation of one's identity and one's understandings of 'home' and 'community'" (11). The studies in this book examine and capture this negotiation among Latinx diaspora youth, to illuminate the meaning they make of their multiple belongings and dominant citizenship discourses.

We also expand studies of transnationalism beyond U.S. immigrant communities, which have dominated the literature, to include analysis of the transnational practices of Latinx and Caribbean youth in Spain and the children of migrants in El Salvador, and to include transnational practices that are not identified with the nation-state of either the sending or the receiving country. It is here that we find the concept of diaspora most useful. Examining the experiences of Latinx young people in multiple national contexts—different nodes of the Latino diaspora—necessarily dislodges the nation-state as the dominant unit of analysis and decenters the United States as the locus of Latino transnationalism (Overmyer-Velázquez and Sepúlveda 2017). Comparative research shows, for example, that the term *Latino* as an identity category and cultural identifier exists and flourishes in contexts as diverse as Spain, Italy, Israel, and Canada, in addition to the United States (Overmyer-Velázquez and Sepúlveda 2017). The Latinx young people in our research in Spain both identified as and *were identified by others as* Latinos, as well as other identities based on national or regional origin (e.g., Caribeño/Caribbean). Thus, while U.S.-based scholars might think of *Latino* as a U.S. construct, it has become a global, diasporic construct. We use the construct of diaspora as a unifying frame, despite its complications, because focusing on Latin American diaspora opens up new possibilities to see cultural formations and affinities that transcend and are not tied to the nation-state.

Much of the research on transnational migration, while widening the analytic lens, is still conducted for purposes of nationalism—for example, to assess the effects of transnational ties on host-country incorporation, examining the relationship between transnational practices and national assimilation (Haller and Landolt 2005; Levitt and Waters 2002). Fouron and Glick Schiller (2002) advance the concept of "long-distance nationalism," which they define as "ideas about belonging that link people living in various geographic locations and motivate or justify their taking action in relationship to an ancestral territory and its government. Through such ideological linkages, a territory, its people, and its government become a transnational nation-state" (173). This view of transnational civic practices— consisting of efforts at building or rebuilding the homeland from the diaspora—runs the risk of substituting a focus on one nation-state for a focus on another. Our approach expands the concept of transnational citizenship beyond "long-distance nationalism" by considering the range of ways diaspora youth engage in citizenship practices that resist and transcend national identification and animate other forms of belonging and identity. Most importantly, this approach allows us to explore processes of identity formation that are *critical of the state,* and to see these as not necessarily animating opposition or disengagement, but often motivating *engagement in democratic social change* across borders.

For example, research on immigrant civic engagement suggests that experiences with discrimination and social exclusion are linked to diminished social trust and confidence in the state (Jensen 2010). Within a nationalist framework, such distrust of the state or ambivalent attitudes toward the host nation are equated with oppositional identity, as in the theories of "reactive ethnicity" cited previously. The image of the rioting young immigrant, burning cars and looting stores, as happened in Paris in 2005, looms large in national imaginaries and in scholarly discourse on immigrant integration; it is the prospect that "unemployed, underemployed, and alienated youth" will engage in "criminal behavior as a challenge to a racist society" (see Kasinitz et al. 2008, 344). However, in the context of increasingly repressive citizenship regimes with racially motivated police brutality and militarized immigration enforcement, distrust of the state might be necessary to fuel activism for social change. Research on immigrant youth activism and the undocumented student movement in the United States shows that the experience of exclusion, and in particular the contradiction between their exclusion from legal citizenship and their subjective sense of belonging to the nation, mobilizes many young Dreamers to get involved in activism (Negrón-Gonzalez 2014; Jensen 2010; Seif 2010, 2011). As Seif (2011) puts it, "Rejected by the nation-state, undocumented youth understand that their life chances and those of their loved ones depend on social change" (457). The burgeoning literature on immigrant and undocumented student activism underscores that ambivalent identities and the *liminality* that comes from living in between can be a motivating force for positive civic engagement (Coutin 2016; Negrón-Gonzalez 2014; Flores-González and Rodríguez-Muñiz 2014). These studies further upend the notion that critique of inequality in the host society is maladaptive or obstructive to integration. Migrant youth are uniquely poised to recognize the contradictions between national rhetoric of democratic equality and the reality of unequal rights (Abu El-Haj 2015; Flores-González and Rodríguez-Muñiz 2014; Coutin 2016); this consciousness of contradiction, we argue, can be a resource for democratic citizenship formation (Dyrness and Abu El-Haj 2019; Dyrness and Sepúlveda 2015).

A diasporic citizenship perspective recognizes that critique of the state can coexist with multiple forms of belonging and attachment in both home and host nations, and that these multiple attachments, far from posing a threat to democratic society, cultivate sensibilities that lend themselves to democratic citizenship. These include, for example, a critical awareness of inequality across borders, responsibility for the plight of family members in faraway places, sensitivity to the connections between oppressions in multiple parts of the world, and aspirations for greater inclusion, justice, and equality in and across their multiple communities (Dyrness and Abu El-Haj 2019). This perspective helps us understand how Guatemalan activists in Madrid (chapter 5) could feel a deep responsibility and attachment to Guatemala while being highly critical of the Guatemalan state, which has been responsible for genocide and ongoing repression, femicide, and violence against indigenous communities. This type of transnational activism, which is not captured by notions of "long-distance nationalism," represents a transnational alliance of feminist and indigenous communities in resistance to state repression, which can best be defined by a decolonial, transborder perspective (Trinidad Galván 2014). A decolonial transborder perspective illuminates practices of belonging and activist strategies that reject national identity categories in both home and host nations as animated by transnational cultures of resistance that are deeply democratic (chapter 5).

Studies of transnational activism and citizenship conducted within a framework of nationalism miss the ways that transnational experiences can provide both compelling motivation and cultural resources for resisting oppression. Seeking to assess the impact of migrant activism on Western liberal citizenship, and often relying on national institutions and identity categories to report this activism, scholars conflate a "strong homeland-orientation" with violence and "migrant extremism." For example, in a study of migrant political claims making in five Western European countries, Koopmans and colleagues (2005) found that in all five countries, "homeland-directed activism" took violent forms more often than did other types of claims making. One explanation they offer is that the "action repertoire" of migrants "is likely to strongly mirror the cultural repertoire of mobilization of the country of origin. Many of these homelands are characterized by high levels of repression and political violence, and therefore homeland-oriented claims making will often display similar radical features" (137). But such an analysis conflates the activity of the homeland state and national political culture with the "cultural repertoire" of migrants. Even when migrants' homelands are characterized by high levels of state repression and political violence, there may also be deep traditions of nonviolent resistance to state repression, as is the case, for example, among indigenous communities in Guatemala (Warren 1998, 2001). Migrants in the diaspora might choose to identify with and draw on cultures of resistance from their homeland in opposition to the state's history of repression, as described in chapter 5. The point here is not that Koopmans and colleagues did not see violent forms of activism, but rather that an approach characterized by methodological and conceptual nationalism will "see" only certain behaviors and not others. Significantly, the primary source of data for the above study was media coverage of migrant claims making—incidents of migrant activism as reported by "major national newspapers." National news media coverage might be strongly biased against migrants and likely to focus on violent activity, as we found to be the case in Spain (chapter 3). The practices of transnational belonging of the young people in our research would not appear in major newspapers, and indeed would not be visible through dominant nationalist lenses that look for assimilated subjects. They become visible when we center the lived experience of young people in the diaspora.

We draw on and align ourselves with ethnographic studies of the cultural production of identity, citizenship, and nationalism in a transnational context (Abu El-Haj 2015; Hall 2002; Jaffe-Walter 2016; Maira 2009; Ong 1996, 1999; Siu 2005). These studies take an anthropological perspective on citizenship as lived experience rather than juridical status, highlighting cultural processes of "subject-ification," in Aihwa Ong's (1996) words: "a dual process of self-making and being-made within webs of power linked to the nation-state and civil society" (738). A cultural citizenship perspective is especially important for social groups who are excluded from legal citizenship (e.g., undocumented youth) or for whom legal citizenship is not enough to guarantee protection under the law, such as Muslims and Puerto Ricans in the United States and other racialized minorities (Maira 2008, 2009; Abu El-Haj 2009, 2015; Flores-González and Rodríguez-Muñiz 2014). Focusing on the everyday experience of national belonging allows us to explore the "disjunctures" between legal structures and lived experience for diaspora youth, as well as the creative ways youth are responding to these (Abu El-Haj 2015; Coutin 2016; Rubin 2007).

Critical ethnographic research in this vein illuminates the cultural production of immigrant subjects through public discourses and everyday interactions in schools and communities, unmasking both the exclusionary politics of nationalism and the alternative forms of belonging and participation found in migrant youths' transnational lives. A primary example is Thea Abu El-Haj's (2015) compelling study of Palestinian American youth after 9/11, *Unsettled Belonging*. Her ethnographic account shows how the production of U.S. nationalism in schools serves to exclude these youth, constructing them as enemy-outsiders or "impossible subjects" (Ngai 2004) of the nation, and at the same time, how young Palestinian Americans are producing multifaceted citizenship practices that creatively respond to transnational social fields. The Palestinian American youths in her study made a distinction between their legal citizenship as U.S. citizens, which gave them access to a set of rights and opportunities, and their sense of belonging to Palestine, which instilled political consciousness, civic purpose, and social responsibility. Far from creating oppositional identities, the combination of these two types of citizenship led them to be involved in efforts for democratic social change across borders. Abu El-Haj argues that the experience of rights-bearing citizenship in the United States juxta-posed with the youths' experience of the denial of rights in Palestine sharp-ened their commitment to democratic citizenship for all. "This complex, fluid, 'flipping' sense of belonging," she writes, led many Palestinian Ameri-can youths "to develop social, cultural, and political commitments and to enact active citizenship practices in relation to both the United States and Palestine" (41).

As Abu El-Haj's work suggests, transnational youth are in a unique lim-inal space as insider-outsider members of multiple national communities. Their own experiences as "second-class" or suspect citizens of the nation, and the experiences of their family members in countries on the receiving end of U.S. imperialist military aggression and/or corporate abuses, give them a critical awareness of the limitations of national citizenship and the contradictions of Western democratic discourses of freedom and equality. At the same time, they are appreciative of rights and advantages they enjoy in their adopted country that family members back home do not have.

This space between nations, we argue, with frames of reference that encompass multiple experiences of rights-bearing privilege and rights depri-vation across different axes of inequality, resembles what Chicana/Latina feminist scholars have termed the "third space" (Pérez 1999; Sandoval 2000; Anzaldúa 1987). The diasporic third space is richly generative of critical con-sciousness and imaginative possibilities, but seeing these possibilities requires a conceptual lens dedicated to dismantling the binaries and hier-archies of colonial thinking.

Coloniality/Decoloniality and Borderlands Feminisms

Theories of coloniality/decoloniality and borderlands or transnational feminisms offer complementary frameworks for analyzing the subjec-tivity of people in between—in between nations, social categories, and knowledge systems—as a resource for democratic social change. These frameworks foreground the epistemic potential (Mignolo 2011) of border consciousness—the potential to usher in new ways of knowing and being that challenge Eurocentrism and the legacies of colonialism on the land, bodies, knowledge, and ways of knowing of colonized peoples. Walter Mignolo (2011), drawing on Peruvian sociologist Aníbal Quijano, articu-lates coloniality as the *colonial pattern of power* based on the racial and patri-archal foundation of knowledge established during European colonization, which was the "dark side of modernity." Decoloniality, then, means "confronting and delinking from coloniality" or the colonial pattern of power, which highlights the decolonization of knowledge—"the analytic task of unveiling the logic of coloniality and the prospective task of contributing to build a world in which many worlds will coexist" (54). Among other things, European colonizers assumed the right to classify and rank people, categorizing those they encountered in the Americas as "Others" (*anthropos*), outside the realm of humanity, and themselves as *humanitas*. Those who were classified and had to live with the systems of classification imposed on them developed a unique form of consciousness Mignolo calls "border gnosis" or "border epistemology": "Border epistemology emerges from the exteriority (not the outside, but the outside invented in the process of creating the identity of the inside, that is Christian Europe) of the modern/colonial world, from bodies squeezed between imperial languages and those languages and categories of thought negated by and expelled from the house of imperial knowledge" (20).

Drawing on Gloria Anzaldúa's notion of the borderlands as a colonial wound—"The U.S.–Mexican border *es una herida abierta* where the Third World grates against the first and bleeds" (1999, 25)—Mignola argues that border thinking emerges in all of those places where, through the expansion of Western civilization, "modernity grates against coloniality and bleeds" (xxi). Borderlands are places where the fictions of Western categorizations that divide, separate, and rank come up against the daily lives of those who live in between and among them, whose lives defy the categories. The spectacle of family separation at the U.S.–Mexican border in the spring of 2018 was a dramatic manifestation of the border as colonial wound. The media was flooded with images of young children separated from their parents and detained in cages while their parents were taken into criminal custody. They were symbols of the government's effort to police and secure the nation by removing those deemed undesirable, in spite of the histories that connect us (see chapter 2); the aim was not only to punish the trespassers but also to shape public understandings of "citizens" and "noncitizens" (Chavez 2008). The Mediterranean Sea is another colonial wound: in June 2018 Italy's new right-wing government turned away two rescue boats filled with hundreds of refugees from Africa. The enforcement of borders by physical removal and detention is only the most visible and violent mechanism through which liberal nation-states constitute themselves; coercive assimilation and benevolent liberalism, as efforts to police migrant identities, achieve the same ends (Jaffe-Walter 2016). As Anzaldúa writes, "Conventional, traditional identity labels are stuck in binaries, trapped in jaulas (cages) that limit the growth of our individual and collective lives" (Anzaldúa 2015, 66). Decolonial thinking calls us to address not just border policy but also the colonial logics undergirding these policies, the mental as well as the physical cages.

Borderlands feminism, or *mestizaje* feminism, emerging from the lived experience of women in the borderlands, breaks down binaries and embraces notions of hybridity and difference as critical to *la conciencia de la mestiza,* "the consciousness of the 'mixed blood' . . . born of life lived in the 'crossroads' between races, nations, languages, genders, sexualities, and cultures" (Sandoval 2000, 60). As Gloria Anzaldúa wrote, "The new mestiza copes by developing a tolerance for contradictions, a tolerance for ambiguity. . . . She learns to juggle cultures. . . . Not only does she sustain contradictions, she turns the ambivalence into something else" (1999, 101). Key to this theorizing is understanding how these insights emerge from Anzaldúa's queer Chicana feminist standpoint. Chicana/Latina feminists and other U.S. feminists of color building on *la conciencia de la mestiza* imagine a decolonial feminist praxis as a "third space," a "bridging house of difference" (Sandoval 1998, 358), in which the experience of difference and being in between could cultivate a disciplined mode of resistance to dominant social hierarchies (Sandoval 1998, 2000). As Chela Sandoval suggests, the differential consciousness comes from the activity of "weaving 'between and among' oppositional ideologies" (2000, 57). Based on the experience of intersecting oppressions and global solidarities across different inequalities, third-space feminism refuses any one ideology, identity, or meaning system, but makes use of all of them in the creation of new, decolonizing subjectivities (Villenas 2006; Sandoval 2000).

Homi Bhabha described the third space as a process of cultural hybridity that "gives rise to something different, something new and unrecognizable, a new area of negotiation of meaning and representation" (1990, 211). Chicana postcolonial theorist Emma Pérez, citing Homi Bhabha, describes the third space as the distance in between the colonialist self and the colonized Other, which she reframes as "*decolonizing* otherness" (1999, 6; emphasis in original). In the quest for liberation from the colonial imaginary, she writes, "perhaps our only hope is to . . . knowingly 'occupy' an interstitial space where we practice third space feminism to write a history that decolonizes the imaginary" (20). Postcolonial scholars of many disciplines have embraced the notion of the third space as a space of creative cultural production, insight, and critique, made possible by exclusion from recognized social categories of citizenship, race, nation, or sexuality (see Hall 2002; Lukose 2007; Siu 2005; Pérez 1999; Sandoval 1998, 2000).

Mignolo (2011), as an Argentine of European descent, draws parallels between "immigrant consciousness" and the decolonial concepts of "double consciousness" articulated by W. E. B. Du Bois (1903) and Anzaldúa's (1999) "mestiza consciousness"; all of these arise from "the experience of the displaced in relation to a dominant order of the world to which they do not belong" (107) and consist fundamentally in the "awareness of coloniality of being" (109). Just as coloniality is hidden behind modernity, and constitutive of modernity, so the oppression and inferiorization of immigrant and indigenous subjects is constitutive of modern nation-states. "Epistemically disavowed colonial subjects" are now migrants in the United States and Western Europe (80). As they negotiate the tensions in embodying contradictory identities and meaning systems and interrogate the disjunctures between imposed categories and lived experience, they engage in decolonial thinking and being.

Decoloniality and borderlands feminism invite us to join with diaspora youth in reading their world for the purpose of working toward "epistemic decolonial democratization" (Mignolo 2011, 92). Mignolo argues:

> Decolonizing is nothing more and nothing less than taking democracy seriously instead of using it to advance imperial designs or personal interests. We cannot leave the word *democracy* only in liberal and neo-liberal hands. If used, it will belong to all of us, to the anthropos and the humanitas, as that is precisely what democracy means. . . . We (the anthropos) are working toward decolonizing knowledge and therefore decolonizing Western interpretations of democracy. (92)

In the studies in this book we collaborate with Latinx diaspora youths to interrogate the interpretations of democracy to which they are exposed and to put these in dialogue with their own experiences of belonging across multiple spheres. Discourses of Western democratic citizenship are imbued with narratives of progress, development, and freedom. In Western (Northern) democracies, these narratives of progress call for assimilation of the immigrant/native Other. In neocolonized countries of the Global South such as El Salvador, narratives of progress call for emigration to the neocolonizing power (chapter 2). In both cases, these discourses of citizenship socialize Latinx youth away from their native communities, cultures, and identities—dispossessing them of prior cultural knowledge and ways of being—in the interest of adapting to the needs of the market and global capitalist expansion. For example, just as the children of Latino/a immigrants in the United States are required to speak English and divested of Spanish through "subtractive schooling" (Valenzuela 1999), youth in many Latin American countries are also required to learn English in school, socializing them into a neocolonial relationship with the United States (Hurtig 2008; Dyrness and Sepúlveda 2015).[7] The imposition of English throughout the Latino diaspora, carried out by state actors in the name of promoting "success," progress, and development (now defined as producing consumer-entrepreneurs for the global market), is the clearest example of the hegemony of market interests as the latest stage of coloniality and U.S. empire. A decolonial perspective allows us to see the continuity between discourses of civilization/modernization from past periods of colonial domination and current discourses of neoliberalism, economic development, and educating for the free market. These continuities and the colonial logics behind them are more easily unveiled when we cross borders and examine citizenship practices from the space in between.

Excavating Transnational Cultural Knowledge

This book draws on decolonial thinking to subvert hegemonic discourses of immigrant integration that focus on the challenge immigrant youth pose to the liberal nation-state. Rather than inquiring into how they are adapting or assimilating to their host nation-states, we engage young people's border crossing—cultural, national, figurative—as a central object of inquiry and epistemological frame. As ethnographers, cultural brokers, and pedagogues, we seek to excavate the cultural knowledge and border thinking of diaspora youth as a means to decolonize and rethink citizenship in a global era. That is, we seek to decouple citizenship from the nation-state and its attendant colonial cultural constructs, and to recognize young people's in-between location as a source of insight, critique, and radical possibilities. What does it mean to accompany young people in the space between nations, the liminal space between belonging and exclusion, between here and there, between no longer and not yet? What can we learn from their efforts to narrate their selves and their lives in this space?

This book contends that diaspora young people's democratic citizenship resources have been buried, hidden from public view by discourses of nationalism and national integration that pose young people's transnational connections as a threat. Schools, as instruments of the nation-state, silence or ignore young people's transnational experiences even as they communicate impossible terms for national belonging. We use critical ethnography to unveil the cultural production of national identity and the disciplining effects of nationalism on immigrant subjectivity in daily life. We also use a variety of participatory methods with young people—video, *testimonio*, poetry, participatory research, role play, interviews, group dialogues, identity mapping, and more—to engage them in reflecting on their relationships to multiple communities and to facilitate the expression of complex, fluid, multiple identities. These methods allow us to excavate and bring to light histories, experiences, and yearnings that dominant discourses of integration disregard or erase.

What do we learn from young people's transnational experiences? We learn about what it is like to endure family separation—to wonder about what a brother looks like after so many years of not seeing him; to miss having coffee with your mom. Long separations from siblings, parents, and grandparents across borders mark diaspora young people's lives, as sometimes do reunifications, joyful and painful, reminding them that lives have changed and things aren't what they were before. For some, trips home during summer vacations or at Christmas remind them what it is like to be surrounded by extended family, to laugh with old school friends who understand your sense of humor. Young people speak longingly of the communal life in their home countries, of birthday parties with extended family, of music and dancing, of spontaneous trips to the beach with cousins. These self-affirming social relations provide a respite from the racialization and stigmatization in the diaspora (Jaffe-Walter 2016). Then there is also the land—the jungle, the rain, the beach, the taste of particular tropical fruits, the joy of walking barefoot. These visceral memories connect diaspora youth to the land, sustain them through cold northern winters, and make up who they are and how they want to live. The experience of scarce resources in the lives of their families back home also shapes their awareness—the lack of running water, the run-down outhouse eventually replaced by indoor plumbing with help from remittances sent by their mother, though you still can't drink the water that flows from the tap. Each of these experiences creates a corresponding appreciation, a valuing of resources that other young people (nonmigrant Spanish or American) take for granted.

Young people's concern for the plight of family members in their home country and their comparison of conditions in the host country and home country are prime cultural resources for democratic citizenship that could be tapped by educators. Transnational young people are aware of and deeply affected by conditions of violence, insecurity, and precarity that threaten the lives of their family members in countries of origin, and they often feel a strong sense of responsibility to alleviate these conditions (chapters 4 and 5). But it is not only scarcity that moves them. Some who are exposed to activist and intellectual circles in Latin America, or who had the chance to learn from and reflect on indigenous and peasant communities, are inspired and motivated by traditions of solidarity, organizing, and resistance there (chapter 5). They draw on cultures of *convivencia* (joyful togetherness) in their efforts to build community in their new homes. Perhaps the motivation and skills to build new social networks, necessary to survive and overcome isolation in a hostile context, are the most important outcome of social dislocation.

Transnational youth also develop tremendous linguistic flexibility as they move in and out of and combine different languages and language varieties in their daily lives. With each language comes a different way of understanding and being understood, different humors, different lexicons for cataloging human love and grief. This linguistic flexibility grants them participation in but also partial exclusion from multiple cultural communities, because their speech and manner mark them as different from insiders who have not crossed borders. Diaspora youths become adept at "navigating multiplicity" (Naber 2012) as they broker and negotiate the perspectives and judgments of multiple Others across a transnational social field. For Dominican immigrant youth in Spain, for example (chapter 4), the Others whose views they broker daily might include friends and family members in their hometowns in the Dominican Republic; Dominican family members in the United States; other Dominican youth and families in Spain; majority-group Spanish youth; other Latino immigrants in Spain; and immigrant youth of other national origins (e.g., Moroccans and Chinese) in Spain. Youth in El Salvador (chapter 2) are in dialogue not only with local Salvadoran peers and adults but also with Salvadorans and other

Latinos in the United States and white Americans, to whom they are connected through popular and social media.

Just as these young people understand that each language, by itself, involves some loss—some part of themselves that can't be expressed or understood—so they feel deeply that no single place with a single language and set of cultural rules can fully embrace who they are. Diaspora young people's hybrid identities and linguistic flexibility are perhaps the strongest critique of the exclusionary and racialized boundaries of current regimes of national citizenship—regimes that are increasingly ethnocultural and monolingual—and the greatest resource for imagining new forms of belonging that embrace multiplicity. As they come to experience transcultural friendships and solidarity in their new home cities with immigrants of other national origins and sometimes with dominant-culture youth, they revel in the richness of diversity and "the bridging 'house of difference,'" as Chela Sandoval describes the third space (1998, 358).

All of this and more lies just beneath the surface of transnational young people's performance for national actors and institutions. While these lived realities are known and understood by transnational youth of many backgrounds, they are often invisible to the agents of the state most responsible for "integrating" them, including teachers, social workers, after-school educators, and the police. Seen only through the lens of terrorism, extremism, or criminality, transnational experiences are the very realities that national integration regimes aim to curtail, as exemplified by Denmark's move to criminalize extended homeland trips. So it should come as no surprise that studying them is difficult, that young people might not be immediately forthcoming about these realities to an unknown outsider.

Integral to our conceptual lens, therefore, is a methodological approach open to diasporic subjects' complex experiences of belonging and based on relationships of trust and mutuality, in which young people are invited to participate as experts and coresearchers of their own experience. Participatory action research (PAR) is uniquely suited for studying diasporic citizenship because it engages research participants in examining and reflecting on their own realities. A critical decolonizing methodology that emerged from the Global South, PAR maintains a focus on critical recovery of histories and experiences that have been subjugated by official knowledge (Fals-Borda 1996; Fals-Borda and Rahman 1991; Nabudere 2008; Ayala et al. 2018). Michelle Fine, in describing her decision to use participatory methods in a study of Muslim American youth (Sirin and

Fine 2007), relates that participatory methods were necessary to complicate binary distinctions and either/or notions of identity: "Working against this dominant literature that's fixing and arguing opposition" required a methodological approach that "seeks messiness rather than sterility," a "certain comfort level with ambiguity and complexity," and "a high degree of flexibility" (Ravitch and Riggan 2016, 102, 104). Like Fine, we believe that participatory research methods provide the space to wrestle with complexity, to allow for hybridity, heterogeneity, intragroup variation, contradiction, and change in the lives of diaspora youth.

Building on the legacy of Brazilian educator Paulo Freire ([1970] 1999), PAR asserts that ordinary people, including youth, have the capacity to analyze their social realities and generate the knowledge they need to become agents of change (Cammarota and Fine 2008; Cammarota 2007). While the types of research activities participants engage in might vary, a key feature of all participatory research is dialogue, based on Freire's notion of praxis, defined as collective reflection and action on the world in order to change it. In the United States PAR has been embraced by educators working with youth of color, who have shown that engaging marginalized youth in a critical examination of their reality can promote critical consciousness, school achievement, and active citizenship (Ayala et al. 2018; Cammarota 2007; Cammarota and Fine 2008; Irizarry 2011; Morrell 2006; Sánchez 2007). Jennifer Ayala and colleagues (2018), arguing for an approach to PAR *EntreMundos,* in the borderlands, describe how the methodology emerged from the Southern Hemisphere and has been adapted to address the needs of Latinx students in U.S. schools. They describe PAR as a research approach and an epistemology based on "enactments of multiplicity and bridging, residing among the in-between spaces of self and other, and the psychological, social, cultural, sexual and structural boundaries we move between daily" (30).

Our approach to PAR explicitly troubles national boundaries and national identity categories, moving to multiple locations in multiple national contexts to better understand the transnational worlds Latinx diaspora youth inhabit. As diaspora scholar Jorge Duany argues, "Methodologically, transnationalism calls for multisited ethnographies and other forms of fieldwork in the points of origin and destination, as well as for the comparison of different groups, localities, and periods (see George Marcus 1995)" (2011, 9). Combining this multisited sensibility with a PAR approach, we engage Latinx diaspora youths in remembering and recalling their lives *over there*—in Mexico, for undocumented youths in California (chapter 1), and in the Dominican Republic, Venezuela, Guatemala, or Ecuador, for Latinx youths in Spain (chapters 4 and 5)—and reflecting on the lives of their loved ones and possible lives over there (in the United States for youths in El Salvador, chapter 2), exploring together how identities are shaped by both places, how lives over there and here overlap and affect each other. These are the histories and experiences that have been silenced by schools and national discourses of integration and neoliberal development. In excavating them, we counter the dispossession and dismemberment wrought by colonial histories of migration. As Susan Coutin (2016) suggests, "re/membering" is a way of countering the dismemberment that the violence of war, emigration, and immigration laws has caused in the lives of transnational Salvadoran youth. As an effort to "overcome disjunctures by reassembling nations, persons, and histories," Coutin writes, "re/membering troubles distinctions between origin and destination as it revisits the past in order to account for the present and to advocate for more just and inclusive futures" (207). Thus, in the context of transnational migration, recalling and narrating histories and lives that have been fragmented is a process of restoring wholeness. In this context of PAR, the change that emerges from the research process might be one of personal and collective healing, which is integral to the struggle for social change (Dyrness 2011). As Ayala and colleagues observe, PAR can be a way of healing ourselves and our communities by "wholing" the fragmentations imposed upon us (2018, 30).

We submit that in the context of transnational migration, PAR provides a space to articulate notions of citizenship that are not tied to assimilation or the nation-state (Abu El-Haj 2009; Villenas 2007). As we will show in the chapters that follow, PAR can both investigate and help create spaces and processes that support displaced youth to analyze how they are positioned within multiple identity categories and create their own identities from a place of difference and resistance. We call these spaces and processes a form of *acompañamiento* (accompaniment), accompanying young people in their citizenship formation. As participants collectively bear witness to the effects of migration, nationalism, racism, and xenophobia in their lives, they also simultaneously create new communities of belonging and new terms for identification. We choose to address these findings to a discussion about democratic citizenship rather than educational achievement for immigrant youth. While there is no doubt that young people's intellectual engagement and academic skills can be improved through PAR, more important are the lessons for the nation-states they call home, which need to radically refigure the terms of belonging if we are to create inclusive and sustainable futures. In this sense, the processes migrant youths adopt to reconcile and overcome the contradictions of their divided lives can point the way to new futures. As Coutin (2016) writes about the process of re/membering, "If successful, youths would not only overcome and make sense of the disjunctures that they and their families had experienced, but also help to make the nations that they were part of whole" (208).

We end this introduction with a note about ourselves. We are the children in the stories, having grown up in transnational social fields, nurtured by what is not near us, striving to keep it close. Like Lola in Diaz's *Island-born*, we create this book as an effort to piece together what has been fragmented and (almost) lost, to give voice to parts of ourselves that daily life in U.S. institutions would erase. Through dialogue with our young interlocuters in the diaspora we find the deepest form of community and affirmation of our call as educators to accompany those who cross borders on their journeys.

Andrea: As a Costa Rican–born transnational, raised by a Costa Rican mother and a North American father between multiple countries, I have been intensely interested in questions of cultural and national identity from my earliest days. For my first eight years we lived in the Philippines, where my parents were missionaries. "Missionary Kid" is a fraught identity, and for most of my schooling back in the United States I did not admit that I was one. It wasn't until as a PhD student at Berkeley I was asked to write a paper for my proseminar on the question "Why am I in graduate school?" that I realized the seeds of my academic interests were planted as a Missionary Kid, and they were not only academic. For me, growing up a Missionary Kid meant the experience of living between worlds, coming face to face with contradiction, disparity, my own privilege, and cultural difference on a daily basis, as well as being exposed to a life of faith-based social action fueled by the values of service, solidarity, and fellowship across difference. These values have stayed with me and shaped the way I approach research.

After my family settled in Berkeley, California, beginning when I was eight years old we took regular trips to Costa Rica during summers and Christmas vacations to visit my mother's large clan of siblings, cousins, and of course my *abuelitos* before they passed. I grew to love these trips for the ways they rooted me to my family, to the land, to the language, and to ways of being in community that I missed in the States. The rhythm of spontaneous family gatherings, family stories, daily tropical downpours during the rainy season, and the smell of black beans and rice made me feel home. When I was of age I submitted the paperwork for my Costa Rican citizenship, and I have been a dual citizen ever since. It's important for me to recognize the privilege that dual citizenship allows, the legal as well as class privilege that allowed my family to travel back and forth without worry, which was not afforded to many of the youth in this book.

Enrique: I am Chicano, the son of Mexican migrant farm and cannery workers, and I grew up between the California Central Valley and the Mexican–U.S. border states of Coahuila and Texas. At the time of my birth my father, Enrique II, was away *en la pisca* picking sugar beets in a northern U.S. state, and my mother, Romelia Sepúlveda, was living on the Mexican side of the border. When her waters broke and the birthing contractions began she crossed by foot the international bridge spanning the Rio Bravo that both divides and connects the two nations. As she crossed the old river, I crossed her birth canal and was born in Eagle Pass, Texas. A few days later my mother and I returned to the Mexican side to await my father's return from the north. Both sides of my family have been living in this border region going back many generations. The Spanish of this region is our mother tongue.

I spent most of my childhood in low-income and subsidized housing in Stockton, California, where my father found regular employment. My best friends were African Americans, Filipinos, white Americans, and Mexican Americans who didn't speak Spanish. Learning to be urban in multiracial and multilingual Stockton was punctuated with hot summer days and nights and Christmas seasons in rural South Texas and Northern Mexico. I credit my parents' decision to send us to the border regularly throughout our upbringing as a counter to the worst aspects of U.S. socialization of Mexican children. I cherished my time with my favorite uncle, Tío Beto in Tejas, and my *abuelitas/os* and *primas/os* on both sides of the border. It was in those moments, surrounded by kin who loved and accepted us unconditionally, that we heard our family's stories. It was at those loud and boisterous family gatherings, and sometimes in quiet moments too, where the alchemy of love, belonging, and storytelling worked its way through my consciousness like a healing balm for my bordered dismembered wounds. The *conocimiento* and *La Facultad* that I learned from my own struggles with borders and displacement, conflict-filled identity formations, and academic institutional failure have led me to examine and engage with the struggles of modern-day migrant youth as they come to terms with their own existential concerns of belonging, transgression, complex sociocultural formations, and negotiations of new lands.[8]

Both of us worked with and conducted research on Mexican and Central American immigrants in California before coming together for the research in this book. Our respective experiences with migration and cultural displacement have shaped our research questions and allowed us to approach migrant subjectivities from different, nonhegemonic vantage points, bringing out a special type of engagement with our participants that is communal, based on shared exploration of the liminal space we occupy in between nations and cultural communities.

A Note on Terms

In this book, we use the terms *Latinx* and *Latino* or *Latina* interchangeably to refer to our research participants from the Latin American and Caribbean diasporas. We use *Latinx* as a gender-neutral and inclusive term, referring to male, female, and nonbinary and transgender individuals. However, this term was not used by our research participants to refer to themselves or others. For that reason, we also use the terms *Latina* and *Latino* to recognize that these were the identifiers used in everyday speech by the participants in our research. Our shifting use of these terms reflects the shifting terrain of our research and these signifiers across time and space. Likewise, we also use the terms *migrant* and *immigrant* interchangeably throughout this book. Although we prefer the term *migrant* because it encompasses transnational and two-way movement beyond receiving states, we recognize that *immigrant youth* is the identity assigned to our research participants by host nation-states and that this category carries political weight in their daily lives.

CHAPTER 1

Acompañamiento in the Borderlands

Toward a Communal, Relational, and Humanizing Pedagogy

Enrique Sepúlveda

ARI WAS A JOVIAL TEENAGER, skinny and wiry at fifteen years old, with a thick shock of shiny, fluid black hair that stood straight up, defying gravity. He was a dark-brown kid from the state of Guanajuato with big eyes and a smile a mile wide. But his automatic smile and joyful demeanor masked inner struggles and a deep melancholy as he made his way through a twenty-first-century world marked by the fiction of borders. His mother had to leave him behind in Mexico when he was eleven as she embarked on a journey north to the United States in order to provide for him and his grandparents. After four years of separation, Ari, then fifteen, decided to make his own journey north in search of her. When the moment finally came that he saw her again, he held her strongly and buried his face in her, crying "*demasiado* [a lot] on her shoulders." He said both of them cried, "no sé, de alegría y tristeza al mismo tiempo" (I don't know, out of joy and sadness at the same time). On reuniting with her, Ari instantly felt the simultaneous and contradictory feelings of joy at seeing her and the deep pain of his years of separation from her; both emotions were present. Longing for his grandparents, cousins, and old neighborhood friends was also now part of the emotional and psychological landscape for Ari. It was the paradoxical moment of a migrant's life, characterized by loss and gain, reunions and separations, and the thrusting, integrating forces of a global order built on expulsion, rupture, and exclusion.

Ari's new high school teachers, who were predominantly white and monolingual English-speaking, didn't know—and by and large didn't care to know—his story of migration and border crossings nor that of his family. The social distance between him and his teachers was immense, and their indifference and lack of curiosity about migration only exacerbated the situation. They were oblivious to the fact that Ari lived in poetic times. To live and think poetically, writes Jackson (2007), "is a way of keeping alive a sense of what it means to live in the world one struggles to understand" (xii). Ari, like many of his migrant classmates, was living a life of radical change, dispossession, and dislocation, always on the verge of something new and transgressive. His poetic writings on crossing the border reflected this when he wrote, "El siguiente día, en la noche, estabamos listos para brincar la barda y cruzar al otro lado" (The next day, at night, we were ready to jump the fence and cross over to the other side). He knew viscerally what it meant to live in globalized times, and yet, like many of his peers, he was alienated and failing his high school's English Language Development (ELD) classes. He was experiencing a profound sense of displacement, and he skipped school regularly. Ari's school, Bosque High School (a pseudonym), in Woodland, California, was situated squarely in the middle of a dynamic transnational social field, but his teachers and the sanctioned curriculum they curated, based on abstract liberal ideas and values, were out of sync with this reality despite facing the awesome spectacle of modern, transnational lives revealing themselves right underneath their noses.

It is from this context that I document and analyze the insurgent and communal actions of a small group of Chicanx educators at Ari's public school in a Northern California town, all of whom came from families with border-crossing experiences. This group of educators deliberated, independently of each other, to act and move into the social void that migrant youths were experiencing at Bosque High, first by rebelling against and departing from the official curriculum to engage transnational Mexican youths from a different sociocultural standpoint, a borderlands viewpoint. Based on what Anzaldúa (1987) has called "border *conocimiento*" (knowledge, awareness, and understanding), these insurgent educators acted from an episteme that emerges from everyday life in the borderlands—of border-crossing, transnational lives in which migrant subjects learn to maneuver, make do, create new ways of being, and improvise complex cultural negotiations of oppressive, racialized bordered spaces embedded in multiple, contrasting linguistic systems and spaces, all the while searching for family, community, and dignity. I call these insurgent educators "border brokers," and their alternative practices of cultural engagement with migrant youth, acts of *acompañamiento* (accompaniment)—communally oriented, relationally based, and dialogical approaches driven by a border gnosis and solidarity with the migrant Other, with the aim of examining collectively the unfolding forces of globalization that thrust families and migrants into a dizzying socioeconomic order that renders them expendable.

U.S. Imperialism in the Amerikas: Laying the Groundwork for Mexican Migration

In the United States' route to global ascendancy, Latin America in general, and Mexico in particular, became the staging ground for the United States to practice its imperial ambitions before becoming the leader of the colonial world system in the twentieth century, or as Washington likes to say, the "leader of the free world." The taking of land, the displacement of peoples and communities, the extraction of natural resources and exploitation of labor, and the profits earned on the territories and on the backs of colonized and globalized populations continued under U.S. hegemony as it did in the early days of the colonial world system. Stoll (2017), in his work on American settler culture, argues that U.S. history is one long history of outright possession and dispossession of land and bodies. He writes that "Americans tend not to think of ejectment and enclosure as central to the history of the United States" (xiii–xiv). Through his scholarship, Stoll came to realize that "the idea of historical progress required taking land away" (xv). Grandin (2006) writes that by the end of the 1800s, "the dynamism of American capitalism and a growing sense of racial superiority had fortified the missionary impulse on display. . . . The 'world is to be Christianized and civilized,' wrote the Reverend Josiah Strong in his 1885 best seller, *Our Country,* 'and what is the process of civilizing but the creation of more and higher wants. Commerce follows the missionary'" (17–18). In the late 1840s the United States, convinced of its own cultural and racial superiority and divine ordination, waged war against a weaker government in Mexico and took half of its territory. Between 1869 and 1897 the United States "sent warships into Latin American ports a staggering 5,980 times . . . to protect American commercial interests and, increasingly, to flex its muscles to Europe" (Grandin 2006, 20). By the late 1800s the United States had taken Puerto Rico, the Philippines, Guam, and Cuba. This happened alongside the ethnic cleansing, dispossession of their lands, and cultural genocide of native, indigenous populations of the continent (see Lowe 2015, 191, 192n34; Wolfe 2006).

The missionary zeal combined with military might and control, followed by commerce, investment, and trade, proved to be the signature marriage of sociopolitical forces that would reproduce the neocolonial order for the twentieth century and beyond, with the United States at its summit. In the case of Mexico, it attracted more than a quarter of total American foreign investment, rendering the border meaningless to U.S. financial houses by the early 1900s (Grandin 2006, 17). In short, "by the late 1920s, the United States had apprenticed itself as a fledgling empire in Latin America, investing capital, establishing control over crucial raw materials and transit routes, gaining military expertise, and rehearsing many of the ideas that to this day justify American power in the world" (Grandin 2006, 23).

It is this outsize, imperial role of the United States in the Mexican economy and politics that set the stage for Mexican migration to the United States. More to the point, Gonzalez (2011) describes the period between 1876 and 1924 as having laid the groundwork for Mexican migration to the United States. Gonzalez, building on Chicano social scientist Ernesto Galarza's earlier work, writes,

> Galarza's words objectively emphasized that the push-pull model, which is repeated without question, fails to incorporate the critical role of U.S. imperial economic expansionism into Mexico and its far-reaching social consequences . . . [and] that the United States simultaneously initiates the uprooting of Mexico's citizens, the push, and then recruits and/or opens the door to migrant workers, thereby constructing the pull, in essence a single, unbroken process. (30)

Gonzalez's work illustrates how U.S. imperial economic dominance in Mexico and Latin America "has resulted in one hundred years of legal, undocumented, and temporary contract labor migration from Latin America" (288). Thus, as Overmyer-Velázquez (2011) subsequently describes it, Mexican migration to the United States is the "world's largest sustained movement of migratory workers in the twentieth and twenty-first centuries" (xix).

Works by Grandin (2006), Gonzalez (2011), and Overmyer-Velázquez (2011) bring into sharp relief the profound and consistent involvement by the United States in Latin American affairs, broadly, and in Mexico, specifically. It was this involvement that laid the groundwork that triggered, fostered, and sustained Mexican migration to the United States for most of the twentieth century and later, benefiting the coffers of U.S. captains of industry and positioning the United States to lead the modern neocolonial world system in the post–World War II era. And yet, as Massey (2011) has written, "U.S. immigration policies and public attitudes have thus undergone a steady evolution toward greater repression, moving from official acceptance and legal accommodation before 1965 to grudging tolerance through 1986 to rising hostility during the 1990's and culminating in an outright war on immigrants after September 11" (260).

Mexican Transnational Migration to Northern California

One influence on large-scale Mexican migration to the United States can be traced back to the early 1900s, when U.S.-financed railroads infiltrated deep into Mexico and connected with existing railway systems in the United States (Cardoso 1980). U.S. labor recruiters looking for workers for the markets up north used these railways to go far into Mexico and found considerable numbers of candidates in the west-central states of Jalisco, Michoacán, and Guanajuato (Durand, Massey, and Zenteno 2001, 109). Most of my students at Bosque High and their families came from these states. This sustained migratory trend undergirded the establishment of transnational ties between sending communities in central and western Mexico and established Mexican migrant communities in the United States, particularly California. Woodland, the setting for this study, is a semirural town located in the Sacramento Valley. According to Trueba and colleagues (1993), the Mexican presence in the region predated the Mexican–American War of the 1840s, though at the time, few Mexicans had settled in the area. With the development of an agriculturally based economy in the early 1900s, this Northern California region began to attract large numbers of Mexican workers and their families. This migration flow gained strength between 1910 and 1930 and would continue for the rest of the twentieth century.

It was in this context of twentieth- and twenty-first-century hemispheric, transnational migration that is structural to globalization, not incidental, that I engaged Mexican undocumented youths in a Northern California high school. This engagement was dialogical and reciprocal, aimed at examining, interrogating, and critiquing their transnational lives. In this chapter, I highlight and analyze how migrant subjects' borderlands thinking led to the organic emergence of a communal, dialogical, pedagogical, and cultural space for and with undocumented Mexican youths at a Northern California high school. I borrow from Anzaldúa's concepts of *conocimiento* and *La Facultad* (Anzaldúa 1999; Anzaldúa and Keating 2002) and Mignolo's (2000) idea of "border gnosis" (border thinking) to explain the alternate ways of thinking, feeling, and being in the world that compelled some Mexican American educators to claim space at Bosque High and deploy an alternate pedagogy of *acompañamiento* based on border epistemology. Asked to work with a group of marginalized undocumented Mexican boys who were having trouble in school, I engaged them in discussion and analysis of their border-crossing experiences. Together we read and discussed poetic works by borderlands authors in order to narrate and write/speak back to the forces of the modern neocolonial world system from its bottom, or as Enrique Dussel (1996) puts it, from the underside of modernity. From this examination and poetic writing, migrant youths' multiple and nuanced identities, experiences, and perspectives emerged.

My theorizing focuses on the local, experiential knowledge that emerges from the historical and cultural conflicts of migrants who are positioned as "Others" who don't belong to the established order of things, and who cocreate identities in the liminal spaces of society. From this engagement, we fine-tuned a pedagogy of *acompañamiento,* a decolonizing cultural practice deployed by border subjects for the purpose of helping undocumented migrant youths find passage in the U.S. borderlands to realize their full humanity.

From Achievement to Poetics: An Ethnographer's Turn

I came to Bosque High after having been a bilingual elementary school teacher and secondary school administrator in the same town from 1989 to 1999. I arrived with a reputation of having successfully mentored and worked with Latino male youth. This time, I was coming in as a researcher examining the relationships between Mexican immigrant students and their Mexican American counterparts and how these relationships affected school achievement. But the multiple border-crossing experiences of migrant students and the way they framed their schooling experiences within a transnational context (both "here" and "there") at Bosque High pointed to a larger and more profound reality that my education researcher's achievement lens failed to see initially. Early on, I was concerned with the achievement gap. But the discourse of achievement is largely framed by the technical acquisition and mastery of academic and linguistic skills, ignoring the fundamental needs of students in the learning process: the need to belong, the importance of durable and supportive relationships, and the development of a healthy sense of self.

I spent the entire academic year, from September 2004 through June 2005, observing, interacting with, and interviewing transmigrant students and their teachers in multiple locales on the Bosque High School campus and in the community. The school had a total of 2,001 students. The two major ethnic groups were Latino (48.3 percent, 966 students) and white (45.3 percent, 906 students). There were 414 English-language learners, and 94.9 percent of those were Spanish speakers (393 students). Of seventy-seven teachers, 12 (11 males and 1 female) were classified as Latino (California Department of Education 2005). I made contact with students through faculty, staff, and sometimes opportune chance encounters with curious students wanting to know about me and what I was doing there. These encounters developed into deeper bonds as I hung out and ate lunch with students in the cafeteria or played soccer with them during their lunch recess. Over several months, I became a fixture in their lives, and they in mine; this was especially the case with Mexican migrant students. These relationships formed in downtime moments afforded me valuable insight into their social worlds, migration stories, and border-crossing challenges related to being outsiders. These stories would later serve as the basis for future pedagogical reflections and discussions.

My exposure to the lives, dreams, concerns, and voices of transmigrant youths in liminal campus spaces, and those who accompany them, dramatically changed my original role. I had been a somewhat distant researcher and observer of their school lives, focusing on narrow technical achievement constructions dictated from above. Over time, I went from a peripheral participant observer to an ethnographer, educator, and fellow poet. I became totally immersed in their educational and social worlds as I developed dialogical and poetic activities, gave advice, listened to their stories, played soccer, organized field trips to the local university, and wrote poetry with them.

Local Context and Historical Designs: Migration, Youth, and the Liberal Nation-State

Ari and the other transnational, border-crossing classmates in my study would reteach me a valuable lesson, one I had already learned a generation earlier from my own experiences with U.S. schooling: namely, that to be Mexican in a U.S. school was to be seen as a problem in need of fixing, a member of the "needy" populations whose language and cultural ways had to be excised or corrected before they could be included.[1] These realities are not just historical legacies from another era but active ideologies that continue to have currency in many U.S. institutions and policies. They are part of the ongoing, evolving historical colonial narratives of those cast as different and distanced from the liberal view of humanity (see Lowe 2015, 3–8).

Schooling at Bosque High was primarily concerned with each student learning English at all costs and acquiring technical skills, and with "grade advancement." This, combined with the erasing of students' other languages and the silencing of their pasts, meant that it was not an education intended to explore and examine the social and material conditions and predicaments of migrant lives. Nor was it aimed at interrogating what it means to be a member of a community, transnational or not. In short, it was an education that was devoid of addressing the most pressing human and existential concerns of modern life. Leanne Betasamosake Simpson, a Native Indigenous scholar and writer from Canada, puts it simply and eloquently: "We learn how to type and how to write. We learn how to think within the confines of Western thought. We learn how to pass tests and get jobs within the city of capitalism. If we're lucky and we fall into the right programs, we might learn to think critically about colonialism" (2017, 14).

Mayela, one of the campus security officers at Ari's high school and a daughter of migration herself, *had* been expressing major concerns about the welfare of Mexican migrant youths at Bosque High. She shared how these students came from faraway places against all odds, often through hot parched deserts and gang-controlled territories (neighborhoods and towns), to reunite with long-separated family members and embark on creating a new home for themselves. But when they arrived, teachers didn't know what to do with them. "¡Y ahora qué!" (And now what!), she added exasperatedly, suggesting a woeful lack of understanding on the part of educators. It was schooling but not learning. Leo, a migrant student, succinctly captured the vacuous nature of much of his U.S. schooling: "It's interesting, because here you have everything—books, pencils, classrooms, buildings, and teachers—everything but learning!"

Outside "formal education" and the hallways of his new school, Ari *was* learning. He was learning in very concrete terms what it meant to be a transnational, globalized subject experiencing the profound cruelty of being torn away from family and community, forced to uproot, cross, and transgress militarized borders and build community elsewhere. Unbeknownst to his teachers and contrary to the goals of contemporary forms of education, Ari's life of *cruzando al otro lado* (crossing over to the other side) in a brown body was fertile ground for learning and interrogating the grand pillars and narratives of the modern liberal nation-state and coloniality, with its notions of democracy, citizenship, justice, national belonging, and culture and identity. The lives of Ari and his fellow migrant students were centered around negotiating globalized, transnational borderlands, while the majority of the educators—institutional agents dedicated to the liberal enterprise of schooling for a capitalist world—lived in an oblivious, parochial parallel universe. Sánchez (2007) writes, "As educators, we often completely overlook the fact that many of our nation's students are already steeped in processes connected to a global world where they are making their own interpretations and experiencing the learning of this phenomenon outside of school" (490).

While increasingly diverse (particularly Latino and Asian) student bodies can be traced back to transnational migratory flows (Cellitti 2008), the fact remains that U.S. students of Mexican origin have maintained a continuous presence in U.S. schools throughout much of the history of public schooling in the United States (Donato, Guzman, and Hanson 2017; Overmyer-Velázquez 2011). And yet, the woeful lack of awareness and understanding of their minoritized and transnational Latinx students on the part of large sectors of public school educators, who are predominantly but not exclusively white and monolingual, is astonishing. This lack of awareness and understanding is not coincidental—it is only the tip of the iceberg in the marginalization of brown bodies—nor is it an innocent function of simple cultural myopia, as much of the "diversity talk" has us believing. Rather, it is by design. Paris and Alim (2017) speak of the "many ways that schools continue to function as part of the colonial project" (2). Not knowing about communities of color or claiming sociocultural "shelteredness" is part and parcel of larger, historical colonial designs and processes in which black/brown bodies, their stories (both his- and her-stories), experiences, knowledges, languages, and cultural practices are segregated, erased, and negated intentionally, not accidentally. This is the colonial difference (Mignolo 2011; Lowe 2015). Concerns about growing diverse communities in U.S. society have been marked by competing discourses of tolerance, coexistence, and respect on the one hand, and fear, demagoguery, and hatred of the Other on the other hand. But for those on the periphery of society, where vast numbers of poor migrant students of color live, concerns stemming from living in a diverse society are fundamentally different from the mainstream. As Jesús Martín Barbero (1997) puts it, their concern has to do primarily with how they can keep from losing themselves, from dissolving into the heavy sea of globalization where cultural references have been dislocated and where identities and homes have been destabilized (88).

Social Locations and Neocolonial Perspectives: White Teachers' Responses to Their Mexican Students

On campus, educators of all stripes and backgrounds repeatedly expressed concerns about what they saw as the profound disengagement and academic underachievement of their Latinx (primarily Mexican-origin) students. Academic failure, absenteeism, fighting between student social groups, and a general malaise and disinterest were commonly perceived, experienced, and documented. The responses to these dynamics from mainstream white, English-only-speaking teachers (who comprised the vast majority of teachers on campus and in the Woodland school district) ran the gamut from blaming larger and more powerful institutions such as the legislature or district administrators, who, they felt, placed unrealistic expectations on teachers, to blaming students who were readily framed as having short attention spans and being lazy and ill-prepared to receive a "traditional school education," much less participate in college-preparatory courses. But white teachers' most pervasive explanation for their Mexican-origin students' academic failure and general disinterest in things academic had to do with culture. Numerous teachers at Bosque High School believed in the cultural deprivation of Mexican parents and their culture (see Valencia 2010). It was common to hear teachers blame Mexican parents' lack of parenting skills, or their lack of "drive" and ambition to succeed in a country that offered them plenty. One of the most common beliefs among white teachers was that Mexicans, and especially their children, urgently needed to assimilate at all costs into mainstream American, mono-lingual (English-only-speaking) culture. For many teachers, an inability to assimilate was at the core of Mexican-origin students' social and academic dilemmas. A math teacher, discussing his Mexican migrant students, shared that "many are absent on a regular basis. They probably skip class to go to second period lunch and play soccer. I don't know. They don't have any drive. Nobody shows them at home."

The vast majority of teachers in the ELD program were not certified to teach English as a Second Language (ESL). The main ESL teacher, an elderly white woman and former language arts teacher who was enticed to come out of retirement to teach in the ELD program, had never trained to work with emergent bilingual students. For her, the problem with Mexican students was with their culture and language. In an interview, she freely and unapologetically shared her perspective on the underachievement of her Mexican students:

> The problem with these students is that their whole world is in Spanish. They're not immersed in English. There's a lot of absenteeism, and they come from a macho culture that treats females with disrespect—especially me, a gringa. Part of the problem is culture, 95 percent of it is. It's all about assimilation time. Some kids need more time to assimilate. They need to speed up the process of assimilation. They need to be integrated more.

Assimilationist and integrationist processes in the United States continue to be viewed as positive "modernizing and progressive" dynamics in U.S. society (De Genova 2005, 80). However, assimilationist paradigms are consistently grounded in deficit views of the Other. Thus, for Mexican migrants, incorporation into the U.S. social order, from the start, means "incorporation into a racial order." They are integrated and "reracialized—as 'Mexicans'—a specifically racialized category within the U.S. social order" (De Genova 2005, 3). Espiritu (2003) calls this "differential inclusion," a process of inclusion that integrates vulnerable populations of color into subordinate standings and positions (47).

When he heard that I was looking for teacher perspectives on Mexican-origin students for my research, Mr. Derek, a white, middle-aged science and vocational education teacher at Bosque, sought me out to share his version of cultural deprivation ideas about Mexicans and their "culture." His eagerness took me by surprise and revealed to me the deeply entrenched, seemingly commonsensical, and unquestioned racist views of Mexicans, which are found among many white educators. Mr. Derek shared that his students (both white and Mexican) self-segregated and sat in specific areas in class, never mingling or integrating. And yet, he faulted only the Mexican students for this dynamic, not the white students who were also self-segregating. Mr. Derek felt that Mexicans were unable or unwilling to assimilate and integrate into U.S. mainstream culture. He said they were

> too segregated, too clingy to their culture. They need to take
> ownership of their own segregation and become part of the larger
> community. I tell Mexican students, rather than tag [graffiti] a
> school, why don't you become part of the school? They don't
> challenge themselves. They only associate with themselves. They
> have all of their services in their native language; the curriculum in
> their native language; their immediate network and community is
> in their native language. From PG&E utilities company and
> banking services to voter guides, all in their language. There is no
> incentive to learn English. (Sepúlveda 2018, 9)

Mr. Derek saw Mexicans as "Mafia-like" in their clinginess to their culture. The vast majority of white, mainstream, English-only-speaking teachers, including Mr. Derek, weren't able to see (or didn't allow themselves to see) the stark, dynamic social realities facing migrant Mexican students in and around campus. Teachers' perspectives, based almost exclusively on surface-level classroom behavior—that is, students' inability or unwillingness to do schoolwork or behave appropriately—shifted the blame for their students' academic failures to parents or to the youths themselves, or to something larger, like Mexican culture and identity, youth culture, or the broader culture of permissiveness. Many others, like Mr. Derek, voiced concerns about the underachievement of Mexican students but tended to express these concerns within cultural and linguistic assimilationist and deficit-oriented paradigms.

It was evident from my research that teachers like Mr. Derek were living in a parallel universe, beside their Mexican students' multiple transnational worlds. Their social location as members of the dominant class in racialized, classed, and gendered hierarchies prevented them from seeing the processes of change and dynamism of becoming that Mexican students were undergoing (Harvey 1989). These teachers were conscripted into reproducing old colonial arrangements that called for brown, black, and cultural Others to be integrated into the margins of school life, producing a marginality predicated on the sacrifice and dispossession of their languages, cultural practices, and ways of being in the world (Valenzuela 1999; Valencia 2010; Spring 2018). They were not interested in the diversity, complexity, and imaginary self-constructions of their students. Where Mr. Derek and most of his white colleagues saw "self-segregation" and a "clinging to the past," Mexican migrant students were actually coming to terms with reconstructing a new home, changing identities, and finding and internalizing new meanings and multiple perspectives in a dynamic social landscape. Equally revealing was the fact that the teachers' privileged positioning as members of the dominant group prevented them from seeing what was directly in front of them—that Bosque High was one site within the transnational borderlands where change and multiple perspectives were requirements for survival and adaptation for those on the periphery and borders of society.

Acompañamiento in the Borderlands: Theorizing from Life on the Margins

Saldívar (2006) posits that to understand a people in all their diversity, complexity, and imaginary self-construction, we must "feel the materiality of their presence in the cultural geography of the landscape. It is there that the significance of their history will reside" (145). Following Saldívar, border brokers felt different from their white, monolingual teaching counterparts about the predicaments of Mexican-origin students, and they, along with their migrant students, acted and moved within the liminal social and physical spaces of their school, Bosque High, in search of the "significance of their history." Border broker educators understood intimately that the multiple issues facing Mexican migrant students were not academic or technical in nature, such as poor grammar, reading comprehension skills, or vocabulary in the English language, which they allegedly didn't get from their parents and/or community. Rather, border educators knew that what was plaguing Mexican migrant students was also plaguing them—namely, the ongoing negotiation of a conflictual, neocolonial past shaped by conquest and complex global economic violence on both sides of the border, and a present where social, political, and economic marginality positioned them as the Other, dispossessing them of their language, cultural moorings, and economic security and negating their stories and connections to a past filled with relations, histories, and memories of a ruptured and disappearing world.

These border educators tore free from the dictates of officialdom to chart their own course for engaging with and addressing the needs of Mexican-origin students (both migrant and second-generation Mexican American) by confronting the "materiality of their presence" head-on. At different spaces on campus and independent of each other, the border brokers threw out the sanctioned curriculum and sidestepped their job descriptions to convene dialogue groups with migrant youths to address issues of belonging on the margins, their identities as border crossers, racial discrimination, and cultural displacement, as well as the ever-pressing search for a new home and place in the world. In their insurgent moves, border broker educators operated with a different cultural logic that stemmed from their own experiences of navigating and crossing borders and from bearing the brunt from mainstream institutional gatekeepers policing those borders, be they physical/political, racial, gendered, cultural, or linguistic. Anzaldúa (2002b) calls this "border *conocimiento*," a cultural gnosis that is "skeptical of reason" and logics of mainstream society and "questions conventional knowledge's current categories, classifications, and contents" (541). Border gnosis is, in part, a nuanced sensing and awareness that goes beyond surface-level behavior, beyond the technical and rational understandings and explanations of social context and realities by official institutional agents. Border *conocimiento* is a multileveled awareness that comes from being positioned as outsiders, as transgressors, which requires a finely attuned awareness of one's "surroundings, bodily sensations and responses, intuitive takes, emotional reactions to other people and theirs to you" (542). Whereas white mainstream teachers saw the delivery of the educational enterprise as technical and transactional, as well as assimilationist, requiring all students to bend to institutional demands, border brokers saw themselves in their migrant students' lives. They saw Mexican youths as part of their community or even family. They exemplified that a "community is defined by such intersubjective relationships" (Goizueta 2001, 75). They knew that the malaise, disconnect, and general disinterest in things academic and institutional were only symptoms of deeper issues in need of excavation and examination, which were found within larger social, global, and historical forces and designs. Their deployment of border *conocimiento* would "challenge official and conventional ways of looking at the world, ways set up by those benefiting from such constructions" (Anzaldúa 2002b, 542).[2]

Mayela, a member of the campus security team and one of the border broker educators, moved around campus with ease. Many students flocked to her. I often saw her in deep laughter with students or in serious conversation with them. She was the daughter of immigrants. Her mother was Mexican and father Guatemalan. Mayela articulated Anzaldúa's notion of profound awareness and *conocimiento*. Whereas others saw laziness, unwillingness, low skills, self-segregation, or cultural deficiency on the part of Mexican students and their culture, Mayela saw the warnings and signs of young people in search of home and belonging. Globalization had dispossessed them and rendered them economic exiles; and Bosque High and the city of Woodland framed them as outsiders and transgressors. Mayela, on the other hand, felt deeply and understood that what Mexican youths at Bosque High needed was passage and accompaniment through multiple worlds.

Mayela's ability to "see" and "feel" more deeply comes from a borderlands experience (gnosis) where all of a person's human faculties are recruited to make sense of the world and the people around them. Anzaldúa (1987) calls this *La Facultad,* a deep capacity "to see in surface phenomena the meaning of deeper realities . . . an instant sensing, a quick perception arrived at without conscious reasoning. It is an acute awareness mediated by the part of the psyche that does not speak, that communicates in images and symbols which are the faces of feelings, that is, behind which feelings reside/hide" (Anzaldúa 1987, 38). Mayela's border *conocimiento* prompted her to sidestep, and thus exceed, her narrow job description as a campus security guard and go above and beyond to start an after-school dialogue group with Mexican female students to discuss collectively the various issues impacting them. She observed that Bosque High was full of "lonely boys and girls with heavy hearts and heavy accents" and that "identity issues had to be addressed because as Latinas, as *mujeres,* we're in a crisis." She contended that by coming together and dialoguing on their lives as Mexicans, as *mujeres* "they balanced and helped each other out. They fulfilled each other's needs by hearing and supporting each other. It was their needs that brought them together, not my agenda."

On the other side of campus, the school principal, Mr. Rosales, a Chicano educator with strong migrant roots, had his own alternative ideas of engaging with disaffected Mexican youths. There had been a running conflict at the school between Mexican-origin social groups. One group consisted of second- and third-generation Mexican American youths, many of whom were bilingual or English-dominant and privileged speaking English. The other group was comprised mainly of recently arrived Mexican migrant youths who were Spanish-dominant. The conflict was typically (but not exclusively) manifested in the local youth gang phenomena between Norteño and Sureño street gangs. In many instances, speaking either Spanish or English became a social marker that indicated the group to which you belonged and whether you had any social status. The Spanish language was often targeted for derision by English speakers (both white and Mexican American students), and Spanish-speaking Mexican migrant students regularly bore the brunt of ridicule, pranks, and other forms of social exclusion.

Learning English as a second language at Bosque High was a complicated, perilous, and emotionally draining effort. For English Language Learners (ELL), a classification that all Mexican migrant students were given, the English language was so close and yet so far. Indifferent white students, antagonistic Mexican American youth groups, unqualified ESL teachers, and the larger political narrative of illegality were constant sources of displacement and Othering, and they all hampered the learning process. For Mexican migrant youths, learning English was not a linguistic problem or a lack of ability problem, but a problem of subject position (Kramsch 2004). Their status as Mexican migrants in a field of unequal power relations where ELLs were spatially and socially segregated, mocked, and positioned as intruders conditioned a severely degrading learning environment that created barriers to learning English, or any other subject, for that matter. In this social context, it was the norm of devalued Mexican migrant social identities, not an individual's lack of effort, that prevented academic learning. Angelika Bammer (2005) sheds light here: "Selfhood is a communal property. We are who we are in the connections we make in the spaces we share with others," and the "search for self-in-community is linked to language" (154).

Mr. Rosales would deploy his own version of border *conocimiento* and bring together in dialogue two sets of students, Mexican American and Mexican migrant males. The group called themselves the "Hombres Nobles"

(Noble Men) and engaged in a series of grand conversations about their lives as youths, as Mexicans, becoming men, and about what kinds of futures they imagined and wanted. They also engaged in extracurricular activities. They did team-building activities and went on field trips together, but mostly they just talked a lot about life and how to be honorable men.[3] Some of the topics included how to deal with racism, peer pressure, and being profiled and stereotyped by police, how to stay out of trouble, and how to handle academics and graduation. When I asked whether Hombres Nobles had significantly helped them, they together gave a resoundingly affirmative response. A participant named Arturo talked about Hombres Nobles as a place where he could learn "how to have respect and be respectful." He added bilingually, "Tener respeto, ayudar uno al otro, never to put anyone down, tener corazón en lo que vas a hacer y cumplir con tu palabra" (To have respect. To help one another. To have heart in whatever you do and to honor your word). Arturo said he had learned how to resolve conflicts without violence and was now motivated to help his younger brother, who was drifting toward gang life. He said he could now think about important things such as what career he wanted to pursue.

Spanish-speaking Mexican migrant students had the bulk of their ELD program classes in classrooms on the outskirts of the Bosque High campus, spatially separated from the main classrooms in the original, permanent buildings. ELD classrooms were in portable, temporary structures sandwiched between a warehouse for vocational education equipment and a temporary fenced-in area containing large machinery owned by a private construction company. These structures were also adjacent to the large expanse of athletic fields (soccer, softball, etc.) that lay beyond the center campus. The average English-speaking student did not visit this part of campus. ELD students came to call this area of campus "El Barrio."

Four and a half months into the academic year two border broker educators convened an emergency meeting in one of the portable classrooms and plotted a radical, insurgent move to engage with their migrant Mexican students from a different vantage point. They were fed up with the scripted curriculum handed down by the district office, having determined that it was useless, so they threw it out. Like Mayela and Mr. Rosales, they felt that something different had to be done. The discarded curriculum, called "High Point," was intended for elementary school–aged English-speaking students who were having difficulties with literacy in their native

English tongue. In the eyes of Mrs. Orales and Mrs. Ávila, this curriculum was misapplied to fully Spanish-speaking students who simply didn't know English. To these teachers, it was another sign of the miseducation of Mexican students.

Mrs. Ávila and Mrs. Orales agreed that they needed to approach their students within the context of their lives as Mexicans and migrants on the margins of school and society. They decided to use their sixth-period classes once or twice a week to engage their students in life lessons aimed at discussing and dissecting their individual and collective experiences as Mexicans in the United States. They felt that identity issues, cultural displacement, and conflict were the true issues plaguing their students— not academic disaffection and underachievement, which they considered symptomatic—so they mobilized to act and address these conditions surrounding their school life. And Mrs. Ávila and Mrs. Orales factored me, the researcher, into their plan. They had determined that I would take their male students, and they would take their female students. They understood intimately that the "significance of our history" was to be found in examining the liminality and materiality of this social landscape, the cultural geography of the borderlands. It was border *conocimiento* in action.

For the next five months I worked with twenty-four Mexican migrant young men twice a week in one of the portable classrooms, addressing the pervasive issues and themes that surrounded and marked their/our lives on the margins. Our work together was dialogical, poetic, and communal. We spent two hours a week from January to June 2005 dissecting issues, examining identities, and writing back to society about who we were, where we came from, and our never-ending crossing of borders. This new dialogical arrangement came on the heels of four and a half months of observing them and getting to know them in their classrooms, at lunch times in the cafeteria, in the hallways, and on the soccer fields during lunch recess. I conducted formal structured interviews and focus groups. I also took field notes of countless hours of observations in school as well as in the community, in neighborhoods and homes. In some cases, I interviewed their parents.

Poetry and dialogue were at the center of my work with Mrs. Orales's twenty-four Mexican boys. I brought in poems and narratives by authors who wrote about the things my students were experiencing—migration, exile, separation, not belonging, changing identities, and persecution. My students and I discussed these issues collectively and wrote individual poetic responses. Our weekly gatherings in cold, unused classroom spaces were transformed by intimate and fragile dialogues about our lives as border crossers constructing a new home. In these dialogical and poetic moments, the dispossessed narrated their lives, claimed space and territory, and staked out "an impossible home" (Alexander 2009, 32).

What started out as a teacher/researcher-student relationship ended up as migrants and interlocutors talking to each other, reading and writing poetry together, accompanying each other, and sharing and interrogating our human condition so that we could touch and ameliorate with words and thoughts those contours and conditions that seek to dehumanize us. As Goizueta (2001) wrote, "To be abandoned is to be nobody; to be accompanied is to be honored, a person. The people's accompaniment symbolizes a new honored status as a full human being" (75). In the following section I highlight and synthesize our poetic work together.

Acompañamiento: Border Poetics in Globalized Times

In our weekly class sessions, the twenty-four transmigrant boys and I began to discuss and examine, through poetry, storytelling, and dialogue, the multiple realities, identities, and meanings of being border crossers and outsiders in this land and school. Together, we developed a process and refined a method of working collaboratively and individually. I selected poems or narrative excerpts, mainly by Chicanx migrant authors, that spoke to the reality of their lives as border crossers. The students were instructed to visit stations where they were to individually and quietly read poems or excerpts written on large easel paper, then write down their thoughts or reactions. After a few minutes, we gathered to have group discussions about our reactions. Following a thirty- to forty-minute class-wide discussion, they each wrote their own poetic or narrative responses to our readings and discussions.

One of the first poets we examined together was Jorge Aigla (1995), a Mexican migrant himself. The first poem was "Una carta" (A letter):

Mamá,
las cosas por aca son diferentes.
La gente ya no hace lo que hacía antes y ni dice lo que seinte

ya no se dan los buenos días
ni lloran cuando miran el presente.

[Mamá, things here are different.
People do no longer what was done before nor speak of what they feel
they don't greet each other at daybreak anymore, nor do they weep
when beholding the present.]

The second poem had no title, but the students called it "El problema":

es que
a ratos
me atrevo
y contemplo lo nuevo y siembro sombras
y termino
por enterrar amuletos

[The thing is that at times I dare and behold the new and I plant
shadows and end up by burying amulets]

Following my instructions, there was some initial rustling of chairs and
desks, along with joking and laughter, as the students went to the different
stations in the classroom. They took pencils and notebooks with them
and quickly settled in to silently read the poems. I was intrigued by their
earnest intentions, which were contrary to the common view of disen-
gaged, apathetic, and unmotivated Mexican youth. I walked around the
classroom and stood next to them, shoulder to shoulder, looking at the
poems over their heads, rereading the texts, and absorbing the moment
with them. It was a moment of thinking, remembering, making connections, and trying to make sense of what was in front of them. Slowly, one by
one, they returned to their desks to write their thoughts down on paper.
I remember how one student scratched the side of his head while looking
up; another had the eraser part of the pencil resting on his lips as he
closed his eyes in deep thought. One student, Jesús, called me over to ask
me about the "Problema" poem. He said he was a little confused about
the word *atrevo* (I dare). I asked him, "What does it mean for you?" He
replied, "Quizá, significa iniciar una nueva vida o una nueva etapa en tu

vida en otras tierras" (Perhaps, it means to initiate a new life or a new stage in your life in other lands). I then asked him, "What else does it make you think of?" He said, "De mi pasado. De mi vida en mi tierra" (Of my past. Of my life in my land). I replied excitedly while pointing to his paper, "Entonces, escribe sobre eso" (Then, write about that). During this exchange, I noticed from the corners of my eyes other students in different parts of the classroom looking and listening intently to what Jesús and I were saying, genuinely interested in the conversation about our past and present lives. This led to other, quieter exchanges in smaller groups.

During the large-group discussion, a student named Jaime said that while he was not separated from his parents, he had many friends who were here in the United States working or going to school away from their mothers, fathers, and grandparents. He said many were living with uncles, aunts, godparents, or friends of the family. Others shared that sometimes they lived with their fathers because their mothers stayed back in Mexico or were in another U.S. state. Jaime said, "Tengo muchos compañeros que necesitan de ese apoyo, de ese amor" (I have many friends who need that support, that love).

Ari also chimed in. Though typically jovial, he was serious this time. He told the group that he had been separated from his mother for four years when she left him and his brothers with his grandparents to come up north and work *sin papeles* (undocumented). Throughout those years he missed her, he said, and when he came of age he decided to come up north to reunite with her. He added that it was a great reunion but that he missed his grandparents, uncles, aunts, cousins, and friends in his old neighborhood. He shared that he could write multiple letters home expressing *la falta de muchos abrazos* (the absence of many hugs).[4] There was a brief and heavy silence in the classroom. Ari looked the other way.

Then Jesús, in his typical quiet and resolute manner, asked to speak. He came from the state of Michoacán, from a small town near the capital of Morelia. He had been in the United States for a year when I met him. He said, "Mi poema se llama 'Me acuerdo'" (My poem is called "I remember"). He began to read slowly from his already crumpled piece of paper:

Me acuerdo de mi tierra,
contemplo la tierra donde estoy,

me acuerdo mi vida en mi tierra,
y creo que termino olvidando quien soy.

[I recall my homeland,
I contemplate the land where I am,
I remember my life in my homeland,
and I think I end up forgetting who I am.]

The dialogues, discussions, and resulting poetics allowed these migrant youths to "manage the often harsh and potentially overwhelming conditions they confront—the battle for survival and more, dignity, love, freedom—by deploying the most powerful weapons in their arsenal: signs, myths, rituals, narratives, and symbols" (León 2004, 5). Love was always at the core of all of our discussions. Migration is, if anything else, an act of love. And the presence and absence of it marks every stage of the migration circuit. For the first time in school since their arrival, these migrant youths were examining and coming to terms with the heavy emotional and physical toll of globalization on their identities and social realities in creative, poetic, and communal ways. In beginning by examining the human drama of family relations and separations and recalling the significance of spaces of belonging, the group privileged and centered their stories, their experiences, and began laying the ground for transformational possibilities.

Solomon was sixteen years old when I met him at Bosque High. He was from Mexico City. A year earlier, he, his mother, and sister decided to leave their city and reunite with his father in the United States. Solomon's family had been enduring the hardships of globalization for several years when their father left them to work in the United States without proper documentation. Even though the father's regular remittances home saw them through hard economic times, the emotional and psychological costs of separation proved overwhelming for the young family. So, they, like many of their compatriots, decided to follow the migration paths constructed by U.S. railroads a hundred years earlier.

In one session, Solomon wrote about his thoughts on the eve of departing Mexico City. He titled his piece "Dando vueltas":

Esa noche mi cabeza daba vuelta. El siguiente día era el día en que
dejaba una hermosa etapa en mi vida e ir en busca de nuevas
metas y nuevos triunfos. La hora ha llegado. Mi familia refleja

alegría y ánimo pero en el fondo una gran tristeza en sus cora-
zones. Después de todas las despedidas es hora de marchar y en
mi madre veo un gran temor. Durante el viaje, mi cabeza vuelve a
girar. Pienso en salud, trabajo, felicidad, y ser mejor. Algo me dice
que no será fácil pero creo que valdrá la pena sufrir y esforzarme.
Mis herramientas serán mi familia, el espíritu de superación, y
unas ganas de poner en alto mi identidad y mi familia.

[That night my head was spinning. The following day was the day
I would leave a beautiful chapter in my life in search of new goals
and triumphs. The hour has arrived. My family reflects a cheerful-
ness and enthusiasm, but deep down a sadness is in their hearts.
After all of the goodbyes, it's time to depart, and in my mother,
I see a great fear. During the long journey my head begins to spin
again. I think of health, work, happiness, and becoming someone
better. Something tells me that it won't be easy, but I think it will
be worth my efforts and suffering. My tools/strengths will be my
family, a spirit of achievement, and an enthusiasm for displaying
my identity and family.]

Solomon's poetic reflection is, on the surface, about his family's journey
from Mexico City to *la frontera* and eventually to *el otro lado*, echoing Ari's
poem quoted at the beginning of this chapter. But, it's also about the struggle of *dándole vueltas a la problemática de cómo crear una familia en un mundo
globalizado donde se tiene que vivir y mover en dos o tres países a la ves* (of making inroads into the problematic of how to create and maintain a family in a
globalized world where one has to live and move within two or three countries at a time). These new transnational experiences and existences conjure
up old and new insights on how to live in community with love, dignity, and
justice.

Solomon's mother, Sra. González, later recounted and added to their
migration *testimonio* in conversation with me one late afternoon in their sun-
lit living room on the agricultural outskirts of Woodland, California. The
family's migration objective was to reunite with her husband, the children's
father. During their journey north they encountered all sorts of characters,
from the most destitute and vulnerable to the indifferent and exploitative.
But what stood out for her in this life journey north with her children was
the presence of what she called "angels" in the borderlands. She was talking

about not heavenly, cosmic beings but everyday folk who lived on the border and felt compelled to accompany migrants in their midst who passed through the borderlands.

In Sra. González's border-crossing story she highlighted the individuals who came to her aid, accompanying her in critical moments of her journey. In the middle of the desert, she said, they encountered signs of humanity in the form of plastic gallon bottles of water left by someone who knew the importance of water in the open desert borderlands, as well as actual people who weren't "coyotes" but good Samaritans who appeared out of nowhere to point them in the right direction.[5] For Mrs. González, these instances were like small miracles of *acompañamiento* that occurred at the most vulnerable moments of their journey. She finished her *testimonio* by reaching over to me and putting her hand on my arm to emphasize a key borderlands insight: "Vinieron a acompañarnos y a ayudarnos a navegar lo peligroso del viaje y terreno" (They came to accompany us and help us navigate the dangerous journey and terrain).

Mrs. González's story of love and migration, transnational hardships, and *acompañamiento* at key moments in their journey illustrates multiple critical insights into contemporary global migration: (1) the presence of human agency in attempting to meet globalization's demands; (2) the unequal, unjust, and dehumanizing conditions imposed on migrants by larger global, structural forces; and (3) the presence of subjects/mediators in the borderlands who deploy what I call *acompañamiento*—a cultural practice of solidarity, of relationship and community building, of claiming space and bearing witness in an unjust, dehumanizing, and fragmented world.

This last point reflects Goizueta's (2001) critical insight he discovered while working in a Mexican American Catholic parish community in San Antonio, Texas—that *acompañamiento,* human action in the service of others, serves as the basis of life *in* community, and that an understanding of the self is a relational, intrinsically social understanding, rooted in our interactions with others (77). Sra. González's emphasis in her story, along with Goizueta's Latino theological ruminations and other *testimonios* I encountered, all served to help me to understand the critical, alternative work of insurgent border broker educators more deeply, and with a different lens. Their deployment of border *conocimiento*/gnosis in the form of accompaniment framed educational processes not as the acquisition of technical skills and content mastery but rather metaphorically, as journeys of becoming and belonging, of continual, daily border crossings and transgressions through and within bordered terrain where the acts of *accompañamiento* address both the individual and collective sociocultural, physical, and existential concerns of establishing a community of relations and a new home. Anzaldúa (Anzaldúa and Keating 2002) writes that "with the loss of the familiar and the unknown ahead," migrants struggle to regain their balance, reintegrate themselves, and repair the damage from displacement and discrimination as outsiders (547).

In the following piece by Samuel, a sixteen-year-old undocumented migrant youth in my group, he captures a key dimension of life in the borderlands. He wrote,

> Soy uno de los tantos inmigrantes que día a día
> van a sus trabajos con una sonrisa de alegría en sus bocas,
> pero con una intensa preocupación y tristeza en sus ojos,
> sabiendo que sus mejores deseos están lejos de sus cuerpos
> pero tan cerca de sus corazones.

> [I am one of the many immigrants who day after day
> goes to work with a happy smile
> but with an intense worry and sadness in their eyes,
> knowing that their deepest desires are far away from their bodies
> but so close to their hearts.]

Samuel articulated in poetic verse the paradox of a migrant's smile and his eyes exuding sadness and worry. After he had read his piece to the group, all of us seemed to know exactly what he meant. As we sat there silent, awed by the power and beauty of his work, Samuel broke the silence and added, "Todos nosotros," gesturing to all of us in the room, "All of us are happy to help and contribute to our families, but why can't we be together?" Globalization dictates that we live lives marked by ruptures and separations.

In the following piece, Salvador, also sixteen years old, writes a letter to his best friend back in Mexico, who is thinking of making his own journey north to the United States. The letter captures key points from a group discussion on hypocrisy and the contradictory nature of life in the United States, critiquing one of its most cherished narratives and political values: freedom. He calls his piece "La jaula de oro" (The golden cage):

> Hola amigo, he decidido escribirte estas pocas líneas cuando supe que
> soñabas venir a este país de lujos, de oportunidades, comodidades,

y de mejor posición económica. Pero lo que no sabes es que
también hay mucho sufrimiento. Sufres una soledad que te puede
llegar a afectarte. Donde las tentaciones están a la vuelta y donde
tendrás más obligaciones que derechos. En este país uno se siente
como un delincuente que tiene que cuidar lo que hace. Si quieres
que te diga como veo a este país te diría que es como una jaula de
oro, donde tienes todo pero encerrado al mismo tiempo.

[Hello friend, I've decided to write you these few lines upon
learning that you dreamed of coming to this country of luxuries, of
opportunities, comforts, and of better economic positioning. But
what you don't know is that there's also much suffering. You suffer
a loneliness that can come to affect you. Where temptations are
around the corner and where you will have more obligations than
rights. In this country one feels like a delinquent who has to watch
his every move. If you want me to tell you how I see this country
I would say that it is like a golden cage, where you have everything
but are imprisoned at the same time.]

In this letter, Salvador gives advice to his friend while providing a description and social critique of U.S. society. He captures the false, illusory aspect
of "freedom" in the United States, where you will have more obligations than
rights. He touches on the discriminatory and oppressive police state that
many immigrants, particularly Latinx communities, live and suffer under in
the United States. Salvador speaks truth to power: immigrants and people of
color know all too well that for them, law enforcement isn't about protection
of their bodies or their civil and human rights, but about curtailing, surveil-
ling, policing, and rounding them up. Coates (2015), writing to his son about
his black community and the larger social order, puts it succinctly:

To be black in the Baltimore of my youth was to be naked before
the elements of the world, before all of the guns, fists, knives, crack,
rape and disease. The nakedness is not error, nor pathology. The
nakedness is the correct and intended result of policy, the predict-
able upshot of people forced for centuries to live under fear. The
law did not protect us. And now, in your time, the law has become
an excuse for stopping and frisking you, which is to say, for
furthering the assault on your body. But a society that protects

some people through a safety net of schools, government backed loans, and ancestral wealth but can only protect you with the club of criminal justices has either failed at enforcing its good intentions or has succeeded at something much darker. (17–18)

For Samuel and his migrant peers living in the "golden cage," they understood that this way of life was not accidental, but intentional.

Leo, a newer student, having arrived undocumented from Mexico only a few months earlier, had another perspective about life in the United States. He had spoken little and hardly wrote anything in our sessions since his arrival. Nevertheless, in a short amount of time, he had commanded the respect of the other migrant Mexican youths. He was older than the others and was considered the best soccer player among them. Beyond that, his quiet nature disguised a long history of tough, urban street life in the central state of Guanajuato, Mexico, which he began to reveal when he spoke for the first time. He would later tell me that as he listened to the other boys' *testimonios* of real, everyday examples of the lack of freedom in the United States (a notion with which he agreed), he was thinking of how to contribute to the discussion without offending anyone. Without warning, and to our surprise, Leo stood and announced to the group, "Yo tengo otra perspectiva de la vida aquí" (I have another perspective of life here). He began by saying that in "his Mexico" there was no freedom. His Mexico was filled with not only family separation but also gangs, crystal drugs, constant fighting and unimaginable violence of all sorts. His life was one of *inseguridad* (insecurity), he said. Leo shared that he had come in search of his father and older brother, who had been working on a farm in a region just north of Woodland. He went on to say that he found freedom in migration itself, and that migration was an opportunity for renewal. He felt solace out among the tomato and corn fields of California, where he could think, reflect, and analyze his life back home. Finally, he talked to us about his "solitude out in the *campo* . . . where you could see far off into the horizon, literally in the middle of nowhere." He said that this was exactly what he needed to cleanse his spirit and body, *cuerpo y espíritu*.

Crossing the Border Together

My students responded to the poems and discussions in powerful ways. There was something significant and healing about the public sharing of intimate experiences and feelings associated with displacement, migrations, and border crossings. The young men's expressions and exposures of vulnerability created an emotional release, an opening of some kind that deepened our relationship and furthered our fledgling sense of community. This vulnerability was expressed by Pedro, one of the migrant students at Bosque, when he wrote, "Cruzamos la línea en Tijuana en carro. Pensé que la vida iba ser fácil aquí. Pero en realidad uno sufre mucho trabajando para ganar dinero" (We crossed the line in Tijuana by car. I thought life here was going to be easy. But in reality, one suffers a lot working to earn money). A third space for reinterpreting our lives had been formed through direct confrontation and radical acceptance of our illegality and our transgressions as border crossers, in poetic, collective terms.

After several weeks, we began to develop a stronger bond. We sought each other out for conversation or advice on any number of things. Sometimes they helped me understand youth culture and school life—for example, how the significance of baggy clothing differed between them and their Mexican American counterparts. I helped them with their homework or with navigating institutional channels. At other times, more serious discussions emerged during lunchtime, after school, and even on the sidelines of soccer matches, on topics such as loneliness, missing their mothers or grandparents back home, or the difficulty of crossing the U.S.–Mexican border illegally.

From the beginning, the students called me *maestro* or *profe*. The literal translation is "teacher," but the English word does not convey the same sense of respect and distinction that it has in Spanish in Mexican or other U.S. Latino communities. This sense of respect and legitimacy engendered a feeling of trust that helped me begin the process of facilitating conversation and examination in the classroom. However, equally powerful were the non–teacher/student dimensions of our relationships, which were developed outside of the classroom. For example, on the soccer field I was another player and opponent vying for control of the ball. After the initial excitement of a teacher playing soccer with students wore off, the other players attacked me with the same fierce determination they attacked the rest, and I was substituted in and out like my teammates. At other times, students invited me to their homes to watch soccer matches of the Mexican national soccer team. I often found myself sitting on a couch in front of a big TV, sipping soda and eating chips, enthralled by the soccer match drama and the youthful antics and verbal gymnastics of my young interlocutors.

Recovering Meaning

We continued to meet and discuss the idea of remembering our past lives, our reasons for coming to the United States, and the moment of crossing the border. During our time together, they seemed to become more confident, as if they had a new or renewed sense of purpose. On seeing me in the hallways or from the other side of the quad, they would yell out in public, "Oye profe cuándo se junta el grupo?" (Hey prof, when is the group meeting?). Perhaps their confidence and pride came from the power of narrating and "remembering oneself within a community of the past" and of claiming "that small stubbornness of voice that insists on its own story and that reconstructs the past in a register that claims ownership of the past, especially when ownership of the present is endangered" (Padilla 1993, 29).

The youths' poetic renderings and Leo's *testimonio* are emblematic of life in the borderlands. The departure from liberal mainstream thinking and institutional practice by border broker educators (including me) to engage students was insurgent because we tapped into a deeper *conocimiento* about cultural liminality, border existence, and what it means to be in community while in mobility. It was our borderlands imaginary that compelled us to act, to depart, to rebel against authorized pedagogies and *acompañar* youths in a dialogical and poetic interrogation of migration through oppressive structures and social realities. This poetic form of *acompañamiento* allowed stories of migration to be told in a way that broke "free of the past into a new understanding" (Jackson 2002, 59). This work and dialogue with undocumented Mexican male youths who became "my students" was, more accurately, a dialogue between interlocutors who bared our lives communally with trust and respect, cocreating a poetic space, home and episteme in the process.

Conclusion

In those first months of my ethnographic research project at Bosque High School in the Northern California town of Woodland, I kept hearing stories in the hallways and on the soccer fields of transmigrant youths sleeping on cold desert floors in the middle of winter, crossing international borders with "coyotes" or on their own, getting caught in a volley of shots, and living in the interstices of nation-states. Jesús, one of the migrant youths, captured the poignancy of their lives in one of his poetic works. He wrote, "Sueños perdidos. He perdido muchos sueños, muchas ilusiones en el desierto. Tantos años he perdido sin mi familia por buscar una vida mejor para ellos" (Lost dreams. I have lost many dreams, many illusions in the desert. So many years I have lost without my family in search of a better life for them).

Jesús's poem lays bare the paradoxical predicament of many modern-day migrants divided by political borders. He unmasks a bitter truth, that to love and provide for his family in this globalized age means to be without them; it is the paradox of full stomachs and empty hearts. Jesús was thirteen and living in rural Michoacán when he felt the pull to head north in order to contribute to his family's well-being and reunite with his father and older brother, who had left Mexico to work in the farm fields in Northern California four years previously. He missed them terribly. In his poem, which distills Mexican transnational migration, uprooting, and social dislocation, Jesús illustrates the heavy emotional and psychological toll of the ruptured lives of migrants, the "radical dislocation of things, images, even sensations" (Alexander 2009, 6). Jesús's dreams and illusions of the future are intimately wrapped in the fibers of his relationships and his people, yet these relations and this community were the first to suffer during his journey north to California.

These experiences were rarely noted in official school curricula or classroom discussions. But for certain educators at Bosque High School, and for me, challenges like the ones Jesús experienced and eventually wrote about prompted us to engage youths in a different way, to deploy different methods of instruction, learning, and relating to one another. These methods built on the students' own everyday social experiences to dialogue, reflect, and write. Building positive relationships with them and creating alternative spaces on school grounds where identities were validated, but also examined, were critical pillars. Their ways of being in the world forced us to rethink and reimagine pedagogies, citizenship, and belonging in a twenty-first century marked by movement, displacement, and global inequality. This process of *accompanying* youths in a more holistic manner—combining the arts, the cognitive, and the affective—transformed aspects of Bosque High into cultural spaces that supported both personal and intellectual growth as well as community development

(Freire [1970] 1999). What emerged from the cultural practice of *accompañamiento* was the transformation of the borderlands from a physical place to a poetic device of belonging and narration.

My students' cultural poetics bring into sharp relief the experiences of the subaltern in the borderlands, essentially those who have been left out of official, national narratives of citizenship and belonging (Saldívar 2006). Mayela was the first to illustrate for me how we, border-crossing Mexicans, the ordinary people, were collectively experiencing and imagining our social surroundings within a transnational field. Invariably, this meant imagining and addressing issues of belonging to multiple locations, changing identities and languages, and all while negotiating oppressive social and economic structures of dominance. This is something that was not readily grasped by mainstream teachers. Through her keen sociocultural lens and actions (border gnosis), Mayela was able to cut through the localized academic "achievement" jargon and morass of the liberal institution to pivot and focus on "the ways people imagine their social existence" and "how they fit together with others." Saldívar, building on Taylor's notion of social imaginary, frames this as a "transnational imaginary" in action (Dyrness and Sepúlveda 2015, 114–15). From Mayela's standpoint, Mexican-origin students of various backgrounds and cultural formations were in need of *acompañamiento*, dialogue, and a sense of community as a way to ground themselves, deal with the vagaries and instabilities of migration, find their voices, and see themselves within the larger social imaginary of mobile peoples. A by-product of this encounter and movement toward building authentic community is, "thus, the birth and development of free and unique human persons," and that "community does not extinguish but enhances individuality" (Goizueta 2001, 75). This encounter and subsequent forms of *acompañamiento* represented a community in the making.

It was through this border engagement that the writing of poems became "a ritual of cleansing," a way of imposing order (Alexander 2009, 28) and making sense of the "lethal puzzles and strange perils" (Coates 2015, 21) of colonial and neocolonial histories and a globalized social order. *Acompañamiento* was both a response to globalization and a cultural resource for fostering authentic webs of relations (Glissant [1990] 2000, 8). It was a sociocultural practice of solidarity, not unlike the actions of the individuals in Mrs. González's testimonial who came to assist migrants' passage through the Mexican–U.S. border desert. At Bosque High it was Mayela,

Mrs. Ávila, Mrs. Orales, Mr. Rosales, and myself who broke away from sanctioned institutional practice to engage with migrant youths in the "borderlands" of their high school and town.

For the border broker educators at Bosque High, this represented an epistemic shift away from hegemonic liberal institutional thinking, what Mignolo calls "delinking" from coloniality (Mignolo 2007, 502). Inherent in this epistemic shift is the critique of the liberal institutional project, with its eliminatory logics and erasures of students' histories and its practices of dispossession of land, languages, cultural ways of being, spiritual traditions, communal livelihoods, and so on. Spring (2018) calls this "an educational process that aims to destroy a people's culture and replace it with a new culture" (201). For me, the scholar/researcher, it was a crucial moment and "process of re-education" (Mignolo 2002, 250) in my own journey in realizing how U.S. schooling was part of a larger historical, global design to incorporate migrant workers and their children into a subcategory of exploitable, precarious, and expendable subjects—in short, marginal, non-English-speaking noncitizens. It is this legacy that has always been central to U.S. education as "part of European imperialism which involved not only the colonization of the Americas but also . . . Africa, Asia, and other parts of the world," and where, "in their quest for control of foreign lands many of these imperial powers attempted to impose their schools, culture and languages on local populations" (Spring 2018, 5). But this process of re-education was also a *testimonio* to how those migrant subjects moved within and around global structures to find their own meanings in the context of physical, economic, and cultural displacement and dispossession; to find coherence out of social and cultural ruptures and fragmentation; to find community in the context of separation and dislocation; and to find dignity and justice in the context of a criminalizing, destructive, and dehumanizing bordered world. These are found at home in Mexico, in transit on the migrant trail, and in the places of migrant destinations in the United States.

It was at that point of re-education and self-discovery that I began to see borderlands subjects as agentic individuals deploying border epistemologies and cultural practices that connected relationship and community as a way of responding to the sociocultural, historical, and political predicaments of our migrant life and times. The educators in this unfolding drama ceased to see themselves as teachers just propping up a system with a penchant for ranking, classifying, and sorting students along discriminatory, fictional hierarchical lines. They came to realize that they "belong to a world that, paradoxically, they do not belong [sic]" (Gordon 2011, 97). Gordon continues, "These people have been aptly described by W. E. B. Du Bois as 'problems.' . . . Such people are treated by dominant organizations of knowledge as problems instead of people who face problems. Their problem status is a function of the presupposed legitimacy of the systems that generate them" (97).

With the crossing of legal, racial, linguistic, and cultural borders, my students entered a world marked by multiple discontinuities. At the core of this is a seeming loss of identity as one experiences it in a contained self, which was so eloquently expressed by Jesús in his poem "Me acuerdo." As Jesús sees it, he is caught between a past that is still very present and a present that has not revealed itself. The youths' poetic and autobiographical narratives and discussions explore *and* expose a transmigrant experience that is defined by the "continual play between loss and gain" (Bammer 2005, 152). It is a world that Mayela, Mrs. Orales, and Mrs. Villa understood intimately, prompting them to act with deep empathy and to recruit me to work with their male students. They were, in effect, attuned to those spaces in between and to the very human feelings of being cast as outsiders. These are paradoxical spaces that exist *within* educational institutions yet *beyond* their authority and understanding, to be understood only by those whose lives are also in between, such as border-crossing subjects who carry "the burden of the meaning of culture" (Bhabha 1994, 38). Bhabha explains that "culture only emerges as a problem, or a problematic, at the point at which there is a loss of meaning in the contestation and articulation of everyday life" (34). I would add that identity also becomes a problem in those in-between spaces where "meaning and symbols of culture have no primordial unity or fixity" (Bhabha 1994, 37).

Chicanx educators and Mexican migrant youths at Bosque High transformed themselves into subjects working within a liberal institution of learning but not of it, as they searched to find their footing and voice, construct a new home, and create a deep sense of belonging within a community of relations. These educators became border brokers who tapped and deployed a border gnosis to illustrate Anzaldúa's notion of praxis as self-transformation and self-reintegration toward a "coherent whole," and in the process they illustrated, for us, the potential of the radical democratic possibilities of *acompañamiento* in the borderlands (see Alarcón 2013, 191, 197).

CHAPTER 2

In the Shadow of U.S. Empire

Diasporic Citizenship in El Salvador

Todos nosostros tenemos familia en los estados unidos. El que no tenga familia en los estados unidos no es salvadoreño.

[All of us have family in the United States. The one who doesn't have family in the United States is not Salvadoran.]

—Jorge, high school student, El Rio

[Ser] Salvadoreño para mi es luchar contra viento y marea.

[To be Salvadoran to me is to struggle against wind and tide.]

—Elías, high school student, El Rio

T HESE WORDS, spoken by two young male high school students in the urban marginal community of El Rio, San Salvador, evoke the complexity of being Salvadoran amid powerful currents of cross-border movement and ties. In an elite private school across the city, another student explained her identity in terms of the American music, American movies, and American clothes that she consumes, saying, "It's a mix, I think, for all of us Salvadorans. I don't think we can only call ourselves Salvadorans anymore because we're not." For young people in El Salvador, the ties to the United States are many and varied. Young people in El Salvador are exposed to life in the United States and are recruited into the diaspora even before they have left the country. As we will argue, they are participants in a diasporic social imaginary that connects them with Salvadorans and other Latinos in the United States, whether they have actually traveled across borders or not. What new subjectivities are offered and created in this diasporic space? If we conceive of citizenship, following Ong (1996), as a "dual process of self-making and being-made within webs of power linked to the nation state and civil society" (738), then what identities are made *for* young Salvadorans, and what identities do they attempt to fashion for themselves? How do they define themselves in relation to Others both within and outside of El Salvador?

This chapter begins with the premise that understanding the effects of transnational migration, the forms of displacement and new cultural formations that both precipitate and follow mass migration, requires crossing national boundaries, conceptually and methodologically as well as geographically, to include so-called sending communities in countries of origin in our ethnographic lens. Once our lens is widened to encompass the transnational circuits within which bodies, media, money, care, and love circulate (Sánchez 2007), points of "origin" and "destination" become blurred. Is El Salvador origin or destination? Numbers tell only part of the story. Salvadorans comprise the third-largest Latino group in the United States, after Mexicans and Puerto Ricans, and they were the fastest growing Latino group through 2013.[1] During the "border crisis" of 2014, El Salvador was one of three "Northern Triangle" Central American countries that sent more than fifty thousand unaccompanied migrant children to the United States; 16,404 of the unaccompanied minors apprehended at the U.S. border were from El Salvador.[2] At the same time, deportations to El Salvador, a country of approximately six million, skyrocketed between 2001 and 2013, making El Salvador the fourth most common destination for removals from the United States (Coutin 2016). Given the high percentage of Salvadorans in the United States who are undocumented and living in the shadows, the official numbers do not represent all of the Salvadorans who have migrated.[3] Nor can numbers capture when one story ends and another begins, when a story of leaving becomes one of return, or how origin and destination are connected in the lives of transnational migrants. Perhaps the poet Jorge Argueta said it best in "Journey": "And how many of us are we? / The question is not important anymore / The pain of each one / is 21,000 km^2 / where love and sadness / fit exactly" (2017, 126).

A bounty of ethnographic research has documented the love and sadness of Salvadoran transnational migration and how these are bound up with U.S. immigration and security policies, processes of neoliberalism and globalization, and the racialized and gendered social, political, and economic contexts in communities of settlement and origin (Abrego 2014; Coutin 2007, 2016; Mahler 1995; Menjívar 2000; Zilberg 2011b). Most of this research focuses on the migrating subject, the Salvadoran immigrant in the United States, and traces ties back to El Salvador, sometimes following deportation journeys (e.g., Zilberg 2011b; Coutin 2016). We began our research in 2008 with a different objective: to understand how migration was affecting education and citizenship formation in communities within El Salvador, among youth who have not (or not yet) migrated. We selected for our ethnographic fieldwork two schools where transnational ties were highly visible in distinct ways: an elite private school that sends many of its graduates to colleges and professional programs in the United States, and a public school serving an impoverished urban marginal community in San Salvador, where undocumented migration, gang violence, and deportation shape daily life. These two communities represent the two faces of Central American transnational migration today: the cosmopolitan elite (Sassen 2006) who travel to the United States to take advantage of superior higher education opportunities; and low-wage labor migrants, usually undocumented, who move to the United States seeking economic opportunities and find work in the informal economy (e.g., domestic work and day labor) or minimum-wage jobs (food and hotel service, landscaping, construction, etc.). Following Bradley Levinson (2005), who defines democratic citizenship education as "efforts to educate the members of a social group to imagine their social belonging and exercise their participation as democratic citizens" (336), we wondered what forms of social belonging and civic participation are offered and encouraged in El Salvador, where transnational migration is radically reshaping communities. How is the civic role of schooling being redefined when so many young people will leave?

To begin to answer these questions we must see the challenges to national identity and democratic citizenship in El Salvador as part of a larger history of U.S. imperial and neocolonial domination in the region. Transnational migration is but one part of this history; in other words, it is not a cause of (or not *the* cause of) but rather a response to larger processes of economic, political, and cultural dislocation that began in the early twentieth century, what some Salvadoran intellectuals call "the American Century" (*ECA* 2008), and escalated during the Cold War and El Salvador's civil war, when the nation became a stage for U.S. imperial ambitions. What this story makes clear is that the intimate relationship between El Salvador and the United States preceded and transcends the current wave of migration, and that the experience of Salvadoran youth today, in the United States and El Salvador, must be understood in the context of this historical, asymmetrical relationship. Much as multiple dislocations precede migration, we argue, Salvadoran youth in both poor and elite communities in El Salvador

are experiencing cultural displacement, a characteristic of diasporic subjects as residents in their home countries. Their responses to this displacement and the new affinities they form in the diaspora lend insight into a
new U.S.–Latin American borderlands as a space of belonging and citizenship formations. As Elana Zilberg writes, "The need to cross geopolitical
lines between the Americas to grasp the blurred cultural zones that people
inhabit has been a defining tenet and contribution of those working in
border regions. . . . Salvadoran transnational migration and community formation allows us to see just how much further south that contact zone
between the United States and Latin America extends" (2011b, 19).

In the pages that follow, we briefly outline this historical context and the
contemporary conditions in El Salvador to illustrate the multiple ties to
the United States. We suggest that processes and policies of securitization
and neoliberal economic development that have their roots in a long history
of U.S. hegemonic influence in the region have displaced Salvadoran youth
in their home country, severing them from their histories and from opportunities for national belonging. Drawing on Susan Coutin (2016), we see this
displacement as a form of dismemberment in which the violence of war,
emigration, and immigration laws (and neoliberal economic policies) "dis-
members" individuals and nations. As Coutin writes, "Dismembering . . .
refers to the separation of persons from history, the literal injury or
destruction of bodies, the embodied nature of structural violence
(Farmer 1996), and the denial of membership, either by forcing people to
flee their country of citizenship or by preventing them from being granted
membership in the country where they reside" (2016, 4).

Analyzing school processes at our two schools within the context of
these wider processes, we aim to show that Salvadoran youth in poor communities were socialized to imagine futures as undocumented immigrant
workers in the United States, as an expendable labor force valued primarily
for their remittances but lacking citizenship rights in both the United States
and El Salvador; or else they were targeted as potential security threats, as
gang members/deportees, and therefore as enemy-outsiders to the nation.
In the elite school, by contrast, young Salvadorans were socialized to imagine futures as neoliberal entrepreneurs, as a mobile, moneyed class of self-
sufficient individuals who pursue their economic interests in global circuits,
with clear distinctions between them and fellow Salvadorans of less privileged backgrounds. Notwithstanding real differences in the economic and
legal statuses of young people in these two communities, both groups expe-

rienced contradictory forces of cultural socialization that encouraged them to look to the United States for opportunities and at the same time communicated the inaccessibility or unattainability of full membership there.

We argue that students' experiences in the diaspora—their participation in a diasporic social imaginary, whether they had actually traveled to the United States or not—lent them critical insights into the processes of dismemberment that severed them from the Salvadoran national community and denied them full membership in the United States. When provided a forum to examine and reflect on their experiences as diasporic citizens, students demonstrated "partial penetration," in Willis's (1977) words, of the determining conditions of their existence, including the unequal position of El Salvador relative to the United States and the subjugation of Salvadoran culture, society, and identity within a transnational field. Although this awareness took different forms for students in the elite school and those in El Rio, students in both schools articulated a critique of U.S. society, noting especially the discrimination against Salvadorans and other Latinos, and a pride in El Salvador as *un país sufrido* (a long-suffering country) (Dyrness 2014). Re-examining our data in light of recent work on transnational citizenship and activism (Coutin 2016; Abu El-Haj 2015; Wiltberger 2014), we suggest that Salvadoran youths' participation in a transnational social field uniquely positions them to recognize contradictions in (North) American discourses of democracy and freedom and offers a potential resistance to processes of dismemberment that challenge democratic citizenship in El Salvador, staking out what some activists have called the "right to not migrate" (Coutin 2016; Wiltberger 2014). We are careful to emphasize that this resistance is only potential; young people may not have the skills or the support to translate their awareness into civic action. Based on our experience in these two schools, we suggest that participatory research provides one way of engaging students in examining their own transnational realities that becomes a form of civic education and produces critical, action-oriented civic identities.

Neoliberal Citizenship Regimes

The Colossus and the Flea

How did the United States come to take such an interest in a tiny Central American country that Salvadorans affectionately refer to as *el pulgarcito de centroamérica* (the little flea of Central America)? In the introduction to a special issue of *Estudios Centromericanos* (*ECA*) titled "El Salvador and the United States: A Century of Relations," the editors remark that it was not by accident that the United States refers to itself by the name of the continent, America, for "that hegemonic zeal is profoundly embedded in its geographic and political imaginary" (*ECA* 2008, 148).[4] The United States arguably had its sights on Central America since the Mexican–American War and the acquisition of Northern Mexico in 1848, but the construction of the Panama Canal in 1914 firmly established the Central American region as a strategic area for U.S. national interests. From that point a neocolonial policy unfolded, defined by the editors of *ECA* as "a new modality of relationship between metropolis and periphery that no longer requires direct occupation of the territories, but collaboration—through a combination of seduction and coercion, that only in special cases resorts to military action—of formally independent, weaker national states" (*ECA* 2008, 148). The "seduction and coercion" of the United States, "the colossus of the North" (149), in the form of economic, ideological, cultural, and military intervention imprinted Salvadoran society throughout the twentieth century but dramatically escalated during the Cold War, when El Salvador became a school where the United States "studied how to execute imperial violence through proxies" (Grandin 2006, 4). El Salvador became an iconic case of what Grandin (2006) has called "workshop of empire," a "flexible system of extraterritorial administration that allowed the United States, in the name of fighting Communism and promoting development, to structure the internal political and economic relations of allied countries in ways that allowed it to accrue more and more power and to exercise effective control over . . . resources—all free from the burden of formal colonialism" (40).

The United States' effort to keep Communism out of the Western Hemisphere targeted Central America for economic aid and military assistance to promote internal security, economic development, and a "pro-U.S. ideology" (Menjívar and Rodríguez 2005), and eventually, under the National Security Doctrine, military intervention in support of dictators who unleashed campaigns of state terror (*ECA* 2008; Menjívar and Rodríguez 2005). As Grandin (2006) details, Central America came to be considered "the most important place in the world for the United States," in the words of President Reagan's foreign policy advisor, and "colossally important to vital national interests" (71). In El Salvador, over the course of a decade, the United States provided "more than a million dollars a day to fund the lethal counterinsurgency campaign" (71). State violence and repression, including the use of death squads, were justified in order to restore order, preserve American economic dominance, and restore American military prowess in the world (Grandin 2006).

Over the course of El Salvador's civil war from 1980 to 1992, seventy-five thousand people died and over two hundred thousand were displaced, many of them fleeing to the United States. In an especially cruel twist of Cold War fate, Salvadorans who fled during the 1980s were not granted asylum by the United States, which designated them "economic migrants" (Coutin 2016). This set off cycles of illegality, precarious living in the shadows, deportation, and clandestine return migration that continue to shape Salvadoran communities today (Coutin 2016; Zilberg 2011b). In the postwar era, criminal violence replaces political violence as a driving force behind transnational migration as people flee El Salvador to avoid extortion or threats by gangs and, in turn, the U.S. immigration system deports record numbers of Salvadorans to El Salvador for gang activity or minor criminal infractions. In Zilberg's (2011b) analysis, U.S. security policies including the enforcement of national borders and the exportation of "zero-tolerance" policing strategies create "securityscapes" that "not only constrain but also fuel mobility—legal and illegal, licit and illicit" (4). Zilberg's study of these transnational securityscapes reveals "the ongoing participation of the United States in the production and reproduction of violence in El Salvador" (2).

For our purposes here, the political violence of the war and the postwar security state are continuous in that both rely on public discourses that criminalize certain segments of the population, rendering them outside the bounds of state protection and justifying violence against them. During the civil war, state terror depended on the making of an "internal enemy," which initially targeted anyone suspected of sympathizing with the guerrillas but eventually included intellectuals, teachers, students, nuns and priests, and anyone opposed to the established social order (Chávez 2017; Menjívar and Rodríguez 2005). Joaquín Chávez (2017) shows how state agencies, paramilitary groups, and business associations articulated symbiotic public discourses that depicted unionized teachers and peasant activists as incarnations of the "internal enemy" or the foot soldiers of an international Communist conspiracy that sought to undermine "democratic" institutions in El Salvador. In the postwar security state, the new internal enemy are gang members and criminal deportees, who become conflated with terrorists.

As Zilberg (2011b) shows, the War on Terror after 9/11 was actually a continuation of the Cold War, and it helped seal the interconnections between gangs, immigrants, and terrorists in the public mind. She writes, "Just as cold war technologies of war and policing were animated by a substrate of fantasies about communists, more contemporary shared fantasies were triggered by the menace of criminals and then, or yet again, terrorists" (16). From the National Security Doctrine to transnational security agreements, the Salvadoran state "repackage[d] their internal enemies in terms of the governing security paradigm of the United States" (17–18).

Along with security discourses, modalities of citizenship in El Salvador are shaped by the spread of neoliberal reforms, which intensified after 1980 as part of the United States' effort to promote "free-market absolutism" (Grandin 2006). With deregulation and the shrinking of public investment in social services, emigration became a fundamental survival strategy for ordinary Salvadorans and was increasingly promoted as economic development policy by the Salvadoran government (*ECA* 2007; Wiltberger 2014). Ironically, as Salvadorans responded to the denial of citizenship rights at home by emigrating, emigrants were heralded by the Salvadoran government as a new kind of ideal citizen, whose remittances would put El Salvador on a path to progress and modernity (Wiltberger 2014). As Wiltberger details, the developmentalist logic behind "the political project advanced by the state to send away people and secure their financial remittances" was viewed as conducive to El Salvador's neoliberal economy (42). Immigrant remittances became El Salvador's largest source of revenue. The editors of a special issue of *Estudios Centroamericanos* devoted to migration wrote, "El Salvador is able to maintain its current model of economic growth due to the fact that it massively expels a significant proportion of its population, which not only relieves social pressure internally, but also contributes in a determining manner through the sending of billions of dollars each year [in remittances]" (*ECA* 2007, 8). In these analyses, economic displacement is not an unintended consequence of neoliberalism but a deliberate strategy of the neoliberal state.

Along with economic displacement, neoliberalism brings new modes of governmentality, or ways of regulating and disciplining citizens' behavior to align with the free market (Ong 1996, 2006). As Aihwa Ong (2006) observes,

> Neoliberal policies of "shrinking" the state are accompanied by a proliferation of techniques to remake the social and citizen-subjects.

Thus, neoliberal logic requires populations to be free, self-managing, and self-enterprising individuals in different spheres of everyday life—health, education, bureaucracy, the professions, and so on. The neoliberal subject is therefore not a citizen with claims on the state but a self-enterprising citizen-subject who is obligated to become an "entrepreneur of himself or herself." (14)

As the values associated with the market become the ideals of citizenship—talent, self-enterprise, self-discipline, and productivity—those citizens who are "judged not to have such tradable competence or potential become devalued and thus vulnerable to exclusionary practices" (6–7). This exacerbates existing social inequalities (Ong 2006; Wiltberger 2014), placing those who are unable to "do for themselves" outside the protections of citizenship.

Thus, in El Salvador, neoliberal reforms intersected with security discourses to channel poor youth into informal and criminal economies and into the migration circuit (Zilberg 2011b). As Zilberg documents, immigrant remittances and extortion are fundamental means of survival in El Salvador's neoliberal economy: "In this sense, migrants, gangs, and criminals are mimetic of the normative ideological figures of the neoliberal era, the entrepreneur and the consumer" (6). At the same time, neoliberalism's emphasis on personal responsibility over social welfare promotes zero-tolerance policing strategies, which "fast-track" youth into the criminal justice system and immigrant youth into the deportation pipeline—thereby supporting lucrative private prison and detention industries (7–8).

Young people in San Salvador's urban marginal communities encounter neoliberalism and U.S. imperial influence not only in harsh zero-tolerance policing but also in the well-circulated greasy dollar bills that are their currency (El Salvador adopted the U.S. dollar as its sole currency in 2001) and in the proliferation of U.S. fast-food restaurant chains on every thoroughfare in the city, at which they likely cannot afford to eat because the food is sold at U.S. prices. Since dollarization, the prices for basic goods and services have risen, while wages remain low.[5] McDonald's and Burger King, with their glossy clean interiors and private playscapes, are popular birthday party destinations for the middle class and closed to youth from poor neighborhoods. Other corporate retail chains that line La Gran Vía, a high-end shopping promenade in San Salvador, pay security guards to patrol their premises to ensure that undesirable citizens do not enter (we were once stopped by an armed guard who asked us not to take pictures of a store's sign). These are the visible displays of a neoliberal citizenship regime in which belonging is conferred based on one's ability to consume and the boundaries of belonging are strictly policed.

Salvadoran intellectuals have long criticized the effects of U.S. imperialism on Salvadoran society and national identity. In the lead-up to the civil war, the Salvadoran teachers' union organized two major national strikes to oppose the 1968 education reform, which they saw as an effort to consolidate U.S. cultural hegemony in El Salvador (Chávez 2017). The strikes were met with brutal repression and the teachers' union became part of the "internal enemy" targeted by the military. In the aftermath of the war, the right-wing Alianza Republicana Nacionalista (ARENA) government's education reforms attempting to instill "civic and social values" were criticized for following neoliberal models of individual advancement that emphasize personal responsibility (or blame) without taking into account El Salvador's history of repression and structural inequalities, and for failing to acknowledge El Salvador's indigenous ancestry (DeLugan 2012; Huff 2007).

In November 2008, a few months before the historic election that for the first time brought to the presidency a candidate from the Farabundo Martí National Liberation Front (FMLN), the leftist political party formed from the former guerrilla forces, we attended a forum organized by a group of Salvadoran intellectuals on the topic of "national identity and Salvadoran culture" at the Francisco Gavidia University. There, various speakers raised concerns about the impact of globalization and neoliberalism on national culture and identity, and the "large percentage of Salvadoran youth [whose] dream is to emigrate to the United States without staying to build a common country" (field notes 11/15/08). In a panel on Salvadoran education and national identity, the writer Benjamín Palomo lamented that "education has become an instrument of capitalist manipulation and domestication," lacking the cultivation of critical consciousness and "knowledge of self." He noted that the country had adopted English as a second official language for obligatory study in school, "which prevents us from connecting with our own vernacular languages and cultures, [but] allows us to be better consumers," and that schoolchildren read foreign literature instead of "our own stories" (field notes 11/15/08).[6] Such criticisms directly connect the U.S. influence on Salvadoran education, including the teaching of English, with neoliberal capitalist domination. In an interview published in the *Periódico Nuevo Enfoque* about the forum, the Salvadoran journalist and poet Néstor Martínez argued:

Both national identity and Salvadoran culture were influenced by the earthquake of neoliberalism, which hit the country with all its force. It's under this attack that the Right in power has introduced a change in values, starting with dollarization, considering that a currency reflects a culture; the reinforcement of United States influence; the educational curricula that tend toward these influences . . . in the end we are configured into a state that has little by little decomposed [its] national identity and Salvadoran culture, creating a cultural dependency that brings us closer to a conquest of one country by another, supported in that conquest by Salvadoran politicians, especially those on the Right. (*Periódico Nuevo Enfoque* 2008; our translation)

These concerns highlight the multiple forms of neocolonial relationship between the United States and El Salvador and the complicity of the Salvadoran ruling elite—represented by the right-wing ARENA government that held the presidency from 1989 to 2009—in maintaining this relationship.[7] In raising these concerns, Salvadoran intellectuals posed the subordination of Salvadoran identity to U.S. interests as a problem separate from migration.

A final example of the clientelistic relationship that has characterized United States–El Salvador relations and the complex ways this intersects with the Salvadoran diaspora can be seen in the most recent presidential elections. Even before El Salvador passed legislation in 2013 granting citizens living abroad the right to vote in presidential elections—the result of years of activism of the diaspora (Hallett and Baker-Cristales 2010)—the diaspora figured prominently in presidential campaigns. During the 2008 to 2009 election season, the year of our fieldwork, the incumbent ARENA party called on historical clientelistic relations to stoke fears that an FMLN victory would mean an end to positive relations with the United States and an end to remittances. Statements made by two U.S. Republican congressional representatives that an FMLN victory would endanger the Temporary Protected Status (TPS) of Salvadoran immigrants in the United States and the flow of remittances were splashed across the front pages of the major (ARENA-controlled) newspapers in the days before the elections.[8] The language of the statements suggested that TPS was a "favor" the U.S. government bestowed on El Salvador as long as El Salvador was friendly to its interests. By portraying the FMLN as a Communist party with links to terrorist groups such as the Revolutionary Armed Forces in Colombia (FARC), U.S. state officials and ARENA leaders reproduced Cold War rhetoric of the Communist internal enemy. Representative Connie Mack, Republican of Florida, was quoted in the newspapers saying, "Should the FMLN win this Sunday, El Salvador likely would quickly become a satellite and proxy of Venezuela, Russia, and perhaps Iran."[9]

The same tactic had been employed in the 2004 elections, when ARENA ran ads warning that Communist Cuba was El Salvador's future if the FMLN should win. In those elections ARENA ads also claimed that an FMLN victory would jeopardize the flow of remittances from Salvadorans in the United States, strategically invoking Cold War geopolitical relations; some observers believed this swayed the election in their favor. In 2009, as the leftist FMLN party was poised to win the presidency for the first time with a moderate candidate who was the first FMLN leader not to have fought in the civil war, the ARENA campaign sought to yoke the FMLN to its wartime past. Ads and reporting in the mainstream ARENA-controlled media emphasized the wartime atrocities committed by the FMLN and, in the words of one local analyst, "the long trajectory of violence and Communist ideology that the FMLN has always had."[10] With campaign slogans including "Yo voto por mi libertad" (I vote for my freedom) and "¡Patria sí! ¡Comunismo no!" (Homeland yes! Communism no!), the ARENA campaign pitted the values of "freedom" and "patriotism" against "Communism" and suggested that continued alliance with the United States and the ideals of democracy and freedom depended on ARENA rule and its neoliberal agenda. But in 2009 the strategy was not successful. The Obama State Department and the U.S. Embassy in El Salvador, largely under pressure from activists in the diaspora, issued statements of neutrality and willingness to work with whichever candidate was elected. For its part, the FMLN party, in the wake of President Obama's victory in the United States, mobilized the diaspora to support "change" using U.S. Spanish-language media. In an interview with Univision's Jorge Ramos for a transnational Salvadoran audience, FMLN candidate Mauricio Funes used the hard realities of migration to expose weaknesses in ARENA's economic policy. In El Salvador, the FMLN ran a television ad comparing Funes to Obama, and the attacks against Funes to the attacks against Obama during the U.S. presidential campaign. In the ad, a Salvadoran in the United States tells viewers in El Salvador that Americans didn't surrender to the politics of fear, and neither should they: "Don't be afraid of change."

What this story tells us is that the role of the diaspora in national politics in El Salvador, and its relationship to U.S. imperialism, is complex and paradoxical. As the authors of the editorial "Un 'siglo americano' " write, "The diaspora represents a great promise for the country" (*ECA* 2008, 151). While neoliberal reforms brought greater precarity and inequality to El Salvador, and emigrants have suffered innumerable hardships in their journeys for a better life, Salvadorans in the United States have also achieved important gains in access to education and democratic participation that can benefit their homeland. The story of the relationship between El Salvador and the United States may have begun in the twentieth century, "with the movement of capital and merchandise that accentuates our dependency and weakens our opportunities to become a more just and democratic society. But it ends with a movement in the opposite direction of people, who open up new horizons, goals and hopes for our country in particularly difficult times. It's a history, in short, where we glimpse the possibility that human creativity might prevail over the power of money" (*ECA*, 151).

A Tale of Two Schools

The Lincoln School, an elite private school with a U.S. curriculum, sprawls across a lush, landscaped thirty-five-acre campus in one of San Salvador's poshest neighborhoods.[11] One of several prestigious international schools in the city, the Lincoln School serves a student body that is 95 percent Salvadoran and only 5 percent international. It has a local reputation as the emblem of and gateway to the Salvadoran elite. Among its alumni are several former presidents and vice presidents whose framed photographs are prominently displayed on the lobby's "wall of fame"; the school prides itself on raising the future leaders of the country and was often referred to informally as *la cuna de ARENA* (the cradle of ARENA). A majority of the students have dual or triple citizenship and travel to the United States frequently (according to our survey of the senior class, roughly 60 percent had two or more passports). The school follows a U.S. curriculum and a U.S. high school structure with tracking and the corresponding features of hierarchy and choice: students may choose from twenty Advanced Placement (AP) courses and over one hundred total courses in the upper school, as well as thirty-two different sports. Seventy-five percent of graduating seniors go on to college in other countries, the vast majority in the United

States. At the school's graduation ceremony, the graduating seniors' names are called out along with the name of the college they plan to attend and the state or country in which it is located. These features allow administrators to call the school "an American prep school in El Salvador."

On the opposite side of the city, in a densely packed settlement of brick and scrap metal homes along a polluted river, sits Centro Educativo Católico La Esperanza, a public school operated by a Jesuit NGO, serving students in one of the poorest and most violent neighborhoods of San Salvador.[12] The residents of El Rio experience a much different side of migration to the United States: they are family members of undocumented emigrants— loved ones left behind, waiting to go themselves—or friends, neighbors, and family members of deportees. The neighborhood is controlled by gangs that demand payments from residents and businesses as a condition of avoiding harassment and death. Such extortion is a frequent cause of both internal and external migration, as families move to avoid retribution when they cannot pay the demanded sum (UNHCR 2015). Students and school staff described gang shootings, violence, and intimidation that affected their lives daily. The majority of families financially sustain themselves in the informal economy, where work is transient, irregular, and often illicit; parents are itinerant vendors of food or pirated CDs and DVDs or are undocumented immigrant workers in the United States sending remittances home to their families. La Esperanza is part of an international federation of popular education organizations in Latin America that calls itself a *movimiento de educación popular y promoción social* (movement for popular education and social advocacy). Its founder in El Salvador was one of the six Jesuit priests killed by the military in 1989, who along with Archbishop Óscar Romero have become "martyrs" of the leftist social movement in El Salvador. These two schools were in many ways emblematic of the ideological poles in El Salvador—the Left and Right—and the distinct socioeconomic realities that differentially condition the construction of citizenship in El Salvador. Both La Esperanza and the Lincoln School served grades K–12, but our research focused on students in high school, or *bachillerato* in the Salvadoran system.

Most of the data in this chapter is drawn from ten months of fieldwork in 2008 to 2009 in which we conducted participant-observation and interviews at both schools. We observed classrooms, staff meetings, staff development sessions, and school assemblies, and attended school celebrations, field trips, and service-learning projects. We conducted over sixty in-depth interviews with students, teachers, and administrators. At El Rio, we had the opportunity to develop a participatory research "course" with ten *bachillerato* students in which the students conducted interviews and observations in their communities, wrote reflections, and met regularly with us to analyze our collective data. Through our intensive interactions with these youth researchers and our access to their data and reflections, we were given a privileged perspective on youth civic identity in El Rio. We did not have this opportunity at the Lincoln School due to the rigidity of the school's schedule and the lack of time or flexibility to engage in activities not already programmed, but we were allowed to conduct a focus group with the students enrolled in AP English, which provided a forum for collective discussion and reflection. Below, we describe each school's formal attempts at civic education, along with the informal and implicit mechanisms of identity formation through which students in each community were socialized to imagine themselves as particular kinds of citizens. We then describe students' emerging critical perspectives on these processes, elicited through participatory and collective inquiry, in which students demonstrated an eagerness to discuss their multiple identities and a partial awareness or "penetration" (Willis 1977) of the determining conditions of their lives.

Civic and Social Identity at the Lincoln School

At a Lincoln School assembly celebrating national Independence Day in September 2008, elite Salvadoran students listened quietly to a speech given by the national minister of tourism. The minister, the parent of a ninth grader at the school, talked about his new propaganda campaign exhorting Salvadorans to beautify and invest in their country. One ad in the campaign was titled "Sé un turista, mantén limpio tu país" (Be a tourist, keep your country clean). In the speech the minister called on Salvadorans to be like the foreigners who come to their country to pay homage to their natural and cultural patrimony; they know how to appreciate what we have, he told them. Throughout the city the ads could be seen on billboards, bus stops, and street signs: "Sé un turista en tu propio país" (Be a tourist in your own country). The message was clear: be like them and not like us. The school's choice of speaker on this symbolic occasion of national identity and pride and the content of his message reveal a "pro–North American" conception of citizenship in which the most important models for improving the country come from abroad. The assembly revealed several aspects of the neoliberal agenda of the ruling ARENA party, including the importance of the tourist industry for the country's economic development and image abroad (and the elevation of international image above local concerns of poverty and inequality); the commodification of natural resources, positioning El Salvador as a country for the use, enjoyment, and appropriation of a moneyed class of foreigners; and the promotion of this desirable class of travelers, a global elite to which students were encouraged to aspire.

The Lincoln School had a two-pronged mission: to prepare bilingual, bicultural students to be successful in a global context, and to contribute to the development of El Salvador, or "national uplift," in the words of the school superintendent. The latter goal was frequently expressed by teachers and students as "educating the future leaders of the country." This two-pronged mission reflected the two sides of the U.S. neocolonial mission in El Salvador: on the one hand, to be a civilizing force for an "underdeveloped" local culture, and on the other, to cultivate a neoliberal elite that would defend the interests of the market. The president of the school's board of directors, a Salvadoran mother of three students who had graduated, explained, "[This school] was founded precisely to give, I mean this country was, we were very primitive, to be able to give a different culture." She continued, "The vision of the board of directors is . . . to prepare these kids to develop in a globalized world. . . . Nobody can be only a localist now, these are kids of the world, but we have to give them the tools . . . to make it possible for these kids to go out into the world and develop like my own children have developed in universities of the First World" (interview 6/16/09; our translation). Her reference to "the First World" and to the success stories of her own children who had attended elite U.S. colleges reflects a pro–North American model of citizenship rooted in neocolonialist visions of El Salvador.

The school's superintendent, an American from the U.S. South who had no previous experience in Latin America before assuming leadership of the Lincoln School, likewise expressed disparaging views of Salvadoran culture as something the school hoped to change by "modeling American values and virtues." In his view, American values that were "counterculture" in El Salvador included "critical and creative thinking" and the "act of reading as a way to expand your horizon," because Salvadoran culture is "a very nonreading culture" (interview 5/13/09). He repeatedly described Salvadoran culture as "traditional" ("this is a very much more traditional culture"), in opposition to the values the school hoped to instill, which he associated with what "the United States represents and stands for or an American education stands for" (interview 5/13/09). Such dichotomies, according to Mignolo (2011), reflect the "making and remaking of colonial differences" within global linear imperial thinking that underpins Westernization and coloniality (78). As the school's leaders associated the United States with modernity and progress and El Salvador with tradition, it is not surprising that students absorbed this message.

In the minds of many students and teachers, the school's U.S. curriculum contributed to a pro–North American conception of citizenship in which students imagined their futures in the United States or Canada. Students did not study Salvadoran history or politics until their senior year, in a required course called "Salvadoran studies." All classes except Salvadoran studies and Spanish literature were taught in English, and even the Spanish language and literature textbooks were compiled by North American scholars and published by North American textbook companies.

We chose to regularly observe classes where we thought rich discussions of citizenship would take place: Salvadoran studies, sociology, history, and language classes. However, in our extended observations of these and other classes, we heard no teachers refer to national citizenship or civic duty. Even more striking was that although our research took place during a historic election year, the presidential campaign was rarely, if ever, discussed in classrooms. Considering the enthusiasm with which students and teachers were discussing the elections *outside* of class, its absence from classrooms was marked. In a conspicuous example of this, Andrea attended a sociology class the week after the elections and the historic FMLN victory, curious to hear the students' discussion of the election results, only to find the class watching *Snow White* for the start of a unit on "the media." They watched the film in its entirety. When she later asked the teacher whether he had already discussed the election results with his students, he said "Oh, no!" He wanted to wait until more time had passed "and feelings have died down" before bringing it up. As surreal as it seemed at the time, we argue that this reflected the school's practice of *nonengagement,* in which teachers regularly avoided discussing local issues with students for fear of touching a political nerve. This practice of nonengagement, together with a student body that was socioeconomically homogeneous and a pro–North American conception of citizenship that did not encourage students' identification with El Salvador, constructed the local context as dangerous and something to be avoided.

Interviews with teachers revealed that many were critical of what they saw as a failure of the Lincoln School to prepare "citizens of El Salvador." A Salvadoran teacher who was herself a graduate of the Lincoln School said, "I don't think anybody knows what it really means to be a citizen of El Salvador. . . . I don't see that kids or anybody is very proud of being a Salvadoran, except maybe on football [soccer] games . . . I don't see that the school is doing anything in that respect." Another teacher, also a graduate of the school, said, "We don't emphasize [Salvadoran citizenship]. Most of our kids just want to get out of here." Teachers often spoke of students' family ties to the United States as negatively affecting their identity and commitment to El Salvador. As one American teacher said, "I think students that have family in the States that are sort of doing really well, that they look up to the States as kind of an escape from here completely. I think it undermines their ties to El Salvador completely." In our survey of the senior class (n = 76), 93 percent said they had family members living in the United States, and 99 percent had been to the United States to visit. Of those who had been to the United States, 70 percent said they went at least once a year. Fifty-eight percent said they planned to attend college in the United States next year, and another 24 percent were going to another country outside El Salvador. The Salvadoran studies teacher told us his students were developing a "pro–North American identity."

One program that aimed to involve students in the local context, and also presented the greatest opportunity for discussions about citizenship, was the service-learning program. In order to graduate, seniors were required to complete thirty hours in one of several community-service projects that the school arranged for them, from teaching English to students in a rural town to participating in environmental clean-up projects, building homes with Habitat for Humanity, or working in a home for orphaned boys. The goals of the service-learning program, according to the service-learning coordinator, were to teach students leadership skills (communication, public speaking, organization, etc.), to help poor communities, and to promote interaction with and exposure to different social groups. This last goal was considered most important to school leaders. As the service-learning coordinator explained, "The biggest part is for our kids to see these different lifestyles, to see people that come from different backgrounds than their own, and hopefully that's going to instill in them a sense of responsibility." The president of the board said that Lincoln students needed "to see how the other half lives," because "our kids live in a little bubble." Many teachers believed the service-learning program played an important role in developing students' civic identities and commitment to El Salvador.

As we followed two service-learning projects over the course of the year, from the first orientation meetings to the culminating projects, we observed several factors that seemed to undermine the goals of the program. First, on all trips off campus, including for service-learning projects, students were accompanied by an armed escort. Usually, a pickup truck carrying two, three, or more uniformed guards with rifles or machine guns followed the school van. With this practice the school sent a message to students that identifying with poor communities was neither possible nor desirable. The school administration also cancelled service-learning trips frequently, at the slightest threat of bad weather or "security risk." Even trips within the San Salvador metropolitan area were cancelled for heavy rain or because an armed robbery had recently taken place somewhere in the vicinity. During the month before the elections all service-learning trips were cancelled because it was considered unsafe. With each cancelled trip, the opportunities for developing relationships in the service communities were diminished, and students were taught that these communities mattered little to the school, after all.

Some teachers who chaperoned the service-learning trips also communicated this message, demonstrating disregard for the goals of the program. During one Saturday trip to teach English in a rural community, as soon as the group arrived at the site the two accompanying teachers settled themselves on a bench in an adjoining courtyard, not bothering to oversee the students' activities. They remained there for the whole day. On another after-school trip, although the session was late getting started, the teacher chaperone was adamant that the group leave immediately at the scheduled departure time of 4:45 because, she said, "this is a dangerous neighborhood." The students' lesson time was cut short to twenty minutes. In light of these messages from teachers and administrators, it is no surprise that students did not demonstrate enthusiasm for their projects and completed them only after intense coaxing and prodding by the service-learning coordinator.

The service-learning coordinator, a former Peace Corps volunteer, expressed frustration at her inability to hold the students accountable.

Although service learning was a graduation requirement, she told us, "Nobody is going to back me up if I try to hold a kid from graduating because they didn't do their service learning." The fact that she had no class time to work with the students meant that there were few opportunities for debriefing and reflection, so service learning for most students remained a fleeting, surface-level experience. "To be honest, I think a lot of it is propaganda," she confessed. "Because thirty hours, there's only so much English you can teach. . . . I don't know to what extent we're really helping these people and to what extent we're doing it just for show." In suggesting that the school's outreach programs were "propaganda," the coordinator pointed to the school's public role in Salvadoran society as winning support for U.S. interests in the region and promoting a "pro–U.S. ideology," a key part of the U.S. neocolonial mission going back to President Kennedy's Alliance for Progress in the 1960s (Menjívar and Rodríguez 2005).

Not surprisingly, students testified that the impact of service learning on their civic identities was limited. "It's not going to make anyone more socially responsible if you weren't already," one senior told us. Several students said that the most common response of their classmates to service learning was "laziness." As one said, "It's really hard to be touched by three Saturdays." The coordinator suspected that many students resented the requirement. One boy evinced an ambivalence about the program's goals: "I don't think we owe it to society to do it, you know. Like service learning . . . I think, we don't owe it to them, but I think we can do good in our society, [so] why not."

Even students who said they enjoyed the service learning and felt they learned a lot from it revealed complacent attitudes toward civic participation. When asked what they had learned, the most common response was "to appreciate what I have" or "to appreciate my bed!" One student said that she learned from her experience that "they [people in the rural town] have more problems." When asked how that knowledge affected her or changed her attitude, she replied, "Well, I can say that I'm really fortunate because I don't have those problems, right?" None of the students expressed feeling a responsibility to work for change; in fact, the experience may have solidified their sense of entitlement to the privileges they enjoy. Seeing how little the students in the rural town had, one student said it made him feel "lucky, and not just lucky, but thankful . . . thankful for my Dad's hard work, and my grandfather's hard work, all my family's hard work, that gave me the opportunity to come here, having this education." In his thinking, his place at the Lincoln School was the result of his family's hard work; by extension, the students in the rural town who did not have his opportunities presumably came from families who did not work hard. Nothing encouraged the Lincoln students to question why students in such different social circumstances had so much less, or why those students who were otherwise "just like us" had so many "more problems."

The Lincoln School's approach to service learning resembles Westheimer and Kahne's (2004) personal responsibility citizenship, and what some have called a "thin" service model (Koliba 2004), in its deliberate avoidance of politics, discussion, and reflection. Koliba argues that "thin" approaches, common to U.S. practitioners who fear inserting politics in their teaching, reproduce privatized notions of citizenship and contribute to the "downsizing of democracy." At the Lincoln School, the exposure to difference through service learning without serious opportunities for reflection or dialogue with the "Other" seemed to reinforce students' class privilege and entitlement. The invitation to "see how the other half lives" without an interrogation of their own relationship to that reality seemed to promote apathy.

The service-learning program became one of many factors that reinforced the separation of Lincoln School students from fellow Salvadorans of different social backgrounds. The program positioned members of the poor communities Lincoln students visited as objects of their benevolence, deserving pity, or as potential security threats whom they should fear, but not as equals or peers. The superintendent described the school's service role as stemming from "noblesse oblige," suggesting a reinscription of a colonial hierarchy in which inequality was an inevitable part of the social order, and elite Salvadoran youths were encouraged to think of themselves as apart from and superior to the majority of Salvadorans.

Other social processes and practices at the school contributed to the reproduction of distinct class-based and political identities in El Salvador (Dyrness 2014). While many aspects of the Lincoln School oriented students toward the United States and other countries in search of "opportunities," the Lincoln School was also a community of insiders with rigidly policed boundaries. At the graduation ceremony, graduating seniors were recognized not only by identifying the U.S. or international college they planned to attend but also, for the vast majority, for having attended the school *desde Kinder* (since kindergarten), signaling the marking of status based on their ability to pursue higher education abroad *and* their long-term membership in the community. While students were encouraged to look abroad, they were protected from encounters with difference and inequality at home, reinforcing their collective identity as members of a privileged class.

Students and teachers alike often said that the Lincoln School was a "bubble," a private, exclusive, protected enclave where students could live their lives without ever having to learn about "reality," which was "out there." Students were driven to school in private chauffeured vehicles, usually SUVs with tinted-glass windows. Their drivers often doubled as armed bodyguards. The ubiquitous presence of armed escorts on all school trips was the most visible reminder of students' privileged class status. Concerns about student security were paramount and sharply limited students' exposure to people of different social class backgrounds, who were seen as a security threat. By design, the school had no students from lower- or working-class backgrounds; there was no financial aid program in admissions.[13] Students spent their free time at exclusive country clubs and popular nightclubs in the Zona Rosa and at their families' beach houses or lake houses. These were spaces where they would not interact with people unlike them; in fact, they were closed to those people. The membership of Club Campestre, one of the primary country clubs, was restricted to persons over a certain income, and it did not admit black or Arab residents. For most Lincoln students, their only interactions with working-class Salvadorans were with their household service staff—maids, drivers, gardeners, and guards.

Along with the exclusive and homogeneous social climate, the selective omission of political issues from class discussions contributed to a culture of political intolerance in which the acceptable boundaries of political identity were strictly policed. As mentioned, we rarely saw the elections discussed in the classroom. Students and teachers told us that to do so would be too dangerous, given the strong passions and the students' family ties to ARENA. The officially nonpartisan stance translated into a silence that worked to protect the privileged status of the ARENA political identity. Discussions of events in history became platforms for displaying and maintaining this dominant identity. One morning, the Salvadoran history teacher announced he was going to show a movie on Óscar Romero, the archbishop whose assassination in 1980 marked the beginning of El Salvador's civil war. When he began to provide some background on Romero he was interrupted by a chorus of comments from students, both derisive and hostile.

One female student blurted out loudly, "Why did he insert politics into religion? That's what rubs me the wrong way." Later, when the same student asked, "And it was never found out who killed him?," the teacher said no. After class I asked the teacher privately, wasn't it recognized that the one who ordered Romero's assassination was Roberto D'Aubuisson, the founder of ARENA? (This had been the finding of the United Nations–sponsored Truth Commission.) The teacher replied, "I would not dare to sustain that here." A key piece of El Salvador's history was withheld for fear of challenging students' political identities.

Civic and Social Identity at La Esperanza

The responses of young people in the urban marginal community of El Rio to the iconic figure of Archbishop Romero offer a case in contrasts and lend insight into their group identity as members of *la clase baja* (the lower class). La Esperanza School commemorated the anniversary of Romero's assassination in March with a schoolwide assembly celebrating his life. To prepare for this celebration, the *bachillerato* watched a documentary on Romero's life. Before it began, the teacher asked students what they already knew about Romero. They immediately called out, "He was a good person, and he helped the people who most needed it," "He helped the poor," "The political parties threatened him," "He believed in human rights," "He was one of the people who most denounced injustice and struggled for the people," "They killed him for being just." For students at La Esperanza, knowledge of who Monseñor Romero was, and who killed him and why, was integral to their social identities. In another exchange we observed, the social studies teacher and two students were discussing a recent ARENA campaign ad that listed all the people FMLN vice presidential candidate Sánchez Cerén had killed during the war. The teacher remarked in disgust, "And on their side they have [Roberto] D'Aubuisson who created the death squads!" A female student added, "And ordered the killing of Monseñor Romero!" Informal exchanges such as this, as well as the formal ceremony honoring Monseñor Romero, solidified young people's identity as part of *el pueblo sufrido* (the long-suffering people) and as *gente luchadora* (fighters).

On that hot Tuesday morning in March, smoke from a nearby trash fire filled the air as students crowded onto the courtyard for the school's celebration of Romero. From the stage, a series of skits, songs, prayers, and poems performed by students paid homage to "the suffering of the Salvadoran people" and Romero's vision of justice and solidarity. The ceremony was replete with calls to denounce injustice and inequality, demand rights from the government, and work for social change. The implications for students were made clear in staff members' exhortations such as "Romero said change is necessary. And who starts [it]? Me." And "It's our challenge: we have to love all those who defend the poor. Let there be justice!"

Public ceremonies like the Romero celebration reinforced the civic identity of *el pueblo sufrido,* positioning students as victims of injustice and agents of social change. These events foregrounded inequality and injustice as problems to be addressed by students' own work for change. But in everyday classroom pedagogy and in numerous *actividades de convivencia,* or community-building activities integrated into the curriculum, educators reflected a citizenship of personal responsibility (Westheimer and Kahne 2004), emphasizing values of responsibility, honesty, and respect and the need for individual behavioral change, echoing the neoliberal ideology of the ARENA government's postwar reform (DeLugan 2012). In a seeming contradiction of the message of the Romero ceremonies, El Rio educators frequently blamed students' or their parents' "lack of values" for the problems the students faced.

In Latin America, education for democratic citizenship has often been linked with the formation of "values" and the prevention of undesirable attitudes and behaviors in youth (Levinson 2005; Levinson and Berumen 2007). In El Salvador, the Ministry of Education (MinEd) adopted a values-formation program in the mid-1990s that, as James Huff (2007) notes, "clearly placed the blame for young Salvadorans' social problems on their own shoulders" (84). While the values associated with the personally responsible citizen are not necessarily in conflict with a justice-oriented conception of citizenship, in the context of El Salvador, where youth gangs are the target of zero-tolerance policies, the adoption of a values-formation discourse lends itself to the criminalization of youth and to social exclusion. As Huff (2007) writes, the values rhetoric has been invoked by MinEd officials to advocate "the view that Salvadoran youth are largely the victims of their own alleged pathological habits and philosophies" (84).

Other social processes worked to position youth in El Rio as objects of law enforcement, surveillance, and control, reproducing the social identity of *el pandillero* (gangster). Many students we came to know worked hard to resist the identity of *el pandillero,* which would otherwise be the default identity for youth in their community. One female student told Andrea that she had transferred to La Esperanza School from the local *instituto* (public high school) to avoid being recruited into a gang. She explained that youth gangs in the public high schools were connected to the larger street gangs 18th Street (Mara 18) and Mara Salvatrucha (MS-13) and served as avenues of recruitment; the national institutes were affiliated with Mara 18 and the technical institutes with MS-13. Students who refused to join were threatened. She explained, "If I go to the national [institute], if I graduate from there, I'm obligated to join the 18th [Street gang]." Her transfer to La Esperanza was an act of resistance to gang identity. Several students described the constant negotiation of gang turf and identities in their daily lives. Adolfo explained, "I live in the nest of MS-13 and I study in El Rio, which belongs to the 18th. Some claim the 18th here, that's why I don't identify with anyone. I don't tell them where I live."

Although La Esperanza School was intended to provide an alternative to gang life, everyday practices of discipline and pedagogy in the school reinforced larger social processes that constructed students as security threats and objects of law enforcement. Students in our discussion groups complained of criminalizing discipline practices that "treat us like delinquents." Students described and we observed frequent demoralizing disciplinary lectures by teachers and administrators who berated students for their behavior and/or grades. These routine lectures constructed students as objects of remediation rather than agents of change. On two occasions, our focus group discussions were interrupted when a teacher came in to search students' backpacks for missing objects, a book and a calculator, that were presumed to have been stolen. In instances such as these, the expectations of teachers and administrators for these students appeared to mirror those of the wider society for *la clase baja.*

In our group discussions, students expressed their awareness of class discrimination and described the differential treatment they received and the rights they were denied because they lived in a *zona de riesgo* (slum or ghetto). When we asked the students what images the wider society has of youth in their community, they immediately answered *asesinos, ladrones, pandilleros, delincuentes, drogadictas, incapaces, haraganes* (murderers, thieves, gangsters, delinquents, drug addicts, incompetents, lazy). Students were clearly aware of the ways that poor youths from neighborhoods like theirs were constructed by others. They discussed the unequal application of the law for *la clase baja,* arguing that government officials who embezzle thousands get off without punishment, while if "we get caught with petty theft, they send us to Mariona," a notorious high-security prison. One student shared a local saying that illustrates this inequality: "tanto tiene, tanto vale" (you are valued as much as you have).

One of our student coresearchers, Elmer, described El Rio this way: "It is considered a hole. A forgotten place, where you can throw trash." He added that it is a place where the threat of violence always exists, where many have left for the United States or are looking to go north, even as far as Canada. Finally, "Es un lugar donde hay muchos homeboys por todas partes" (It is a place with many homeboys everywhere). As Elmer's words suggest, identity formation in El Rio was mediated by students' experiences in the diaspora. In our survey of El Rio *bachillerato* students (n = 54), 76 percent had family members in the United States; 19 percent had immediate family members there (father, mother, or sibling). Only one student (2 percent) had ever been to the United States. However, because of students' contact with deportees and migrants, they had a high level of familiarity with the life of undocumented immigrants in the United States.

According to Zilberg (2011a), "deported Salvadoran immigrant gang youth oscillate between 'home' and 'abroad,' where both home and abroad are themselves unstable locations. At the same time, Salvadoran gang youth who have never been to the United States construct their identities around imagined urban geographies of cities like Los Angeles" (498). Deported Salvadoran gang youth and nongang youth who occupy their social space exemplify a new space of identity formation that diaspora scholars, citing Bhabha (1990), call a "third space" (Hall 2002; Lukose 2007; Siu 2005). Lukose writes, "Diasporic identities are produced through difference, a difference situated between the 'here' of the host country and the 'there' of origin, between the 'us' of a dominant community and the 'them' of multiple forms of racialized identification" (2007, 410). In the case of San Salvador's youth, we might switch the "here" and "there" to say that they are situated between the "here" of the home country and the "there" of the neocolonizing power, the United States.

The young people we worked with in the impoverished urban community of El Rio in metropolitan San Salvador were residing in their country of birth with full legal citizenship. Yet, evidence of their citizenship rights was hard to find in communities like theirs, which lacked decent jobs, housing, safety, public services, and access to free quality education. Pursued by both gangs and the police, these youth constitute "a new class of refugee" (Zilberg 2011a, 497). Due to the presence of organized gangs and the lack of police protection, El Rio was considered a "no-go" zone for many government workers and private companies. In a neighborhood abandoned by the state, a transnational social imaginary flourishes, linked to the pervasiveness of transnational gangs that control the area and nourished by U.S. media and the continuous deportations of migrants from the United States since the 1990s.

Although the youth in our research took pains to avoid and distance themselves from the violence of gang members, homeboy expressive culture performed by both gang and nongang members attracted and interpolated El Rio young people as much as it repelled most of the older generation (Dyrness and Sepúlveda 2015). El Rio youth embodied and performed homeboy expressive culture in their daily interactions, language, dress, and gestures. Some male youths who sympathized with but were not officially members of the La 18 gang openly displayed "La 18" tattoos in old English lettering, similar to those seen in urban Chicano/Latino barrios in the United States. Others kept their tattoos hidden for fear of retaliation and showed them to Enrique only in private. Homeboy expressions were also evident in the way they stood against the wall hanging out with their friends, or "homies," during recess, in hand gestures and movements at key moments when talking and sharing stories, and the subtle, non-contact greeting of a head nod upward, sometimes accompanied by an "órale" or "q-vole" (short for "que hubole," which roughly translates as "what's happening").

We regularly heard U.S. mainstream English and vernacular English from Los Angeles Latino barrios spoken in the streets, around the school, in taxicabs, and on TV. Words such as *cora* and *dólar* (quarter and dollar), *fulear* (to fill a gas tank), *homeboy, homie, clika* (clique), and *hood* (neighborhood) were common in the lexicon of El Rio's youth. When Enrique came upon a group of boys in the schoolyard discussing Obama and U.S. presidential politics, they greeted him with a familiar handshake from a California urban barrio context before continuing their discussion. Zilberg (2004) writes, "Youth deported from Los Angeles walking the streets of San Salvador calling themselves 'homies' are the shock effects of globalization.... They are the embodiment of a forced transnationality" (762). In El Rio, deportees and nondeportees alike, both socialized in the diaspora, embody this forced transnationality.

The performance of diaspora identities was especially apparent in the school's English classes. *Bachillerato* students in El Rio had three forty-five-minute periods of English each week. When we first met the English teacher, Mr. Campos, a cheerful and affable man in his forties, and told him of our interest in the effects of migration, he immediately understood why we were there. "The dream of every teenager is to go to the United States," he said. Then he added that we should also ask the teachers how many of them want to go. He said he and his wife would love to move to the United States if they could both find jobs. Even though he knew they would probably face discrimination, the economic opportunity would be so much greater. He told us that his sister lives in San Francisco and that he had spent six months there improving his English skills. With this unprompted revelation we were introduced to two central features of Salvadorans' imaginaries of the United States: the awareness and acceptance of discrimination they would face as Salvadorans there, and the certainty that there were superior economic opportunities that made moving there desirable (or perhaps necessary).

In spite of Mr. Campos's confidence in his students' desire to go to the United States, he struggled with engaging them in English class and believed they were not motivated to learn. Indeed, students' behavior in English class was a far cry from what we witnessed in their animated exchanges in homeboy language in the schoolyard. Mr. Campos's classroom instruction focused on teaching isolated grammatical skills through repetition, with the vast majority of time spent on individual, written exercises rather than interactive and conversational activities. Mr. Campos would explain an example on the board—for example, the use of "have to" and "want to"—and then direct students to apply the rule in forming sentences on their own. Much of his class time was spent checking students' notebooks for both class and homework exercises, during which time some students copied the exercises from others while other students enjoyed free time, conversing with their friends. Occasionally students asked us for help in completing an assignment, confessing that they did not understand the grammatical principle involved. These conversations allowed us to see how little the students understood the English Mr. Campos was teaching them. In fact, not only was comprehension absent from many of the teaching-learning exchanges in the English classroom, but neither the students nor the teacher seemed to expect these exercises to be meaningful.

In reflecting on the significance of English instruction in which so little English was taught and learned, we are led to the question posed by Hurtig (2008) in her ethnography of coming of age in Venezuela: "Just what were [these students] learning when, while, and perhaps because, they were not learning English?" (140). In Hurtig's analysis, Venezuelan students were learning to be neocolonized subjects of the United States; the nonlearning of English amounted to "the constant establishment of an expectation and the deferral of its fulfillment," which relegated students to a "subordinate position of material and cultural longing in relation to the United States" (150). This analysis, which refers to the expectation that students will become upwardly mobile English-speaking world travelers, is useful for understanding the role of English lessons in El Rio, where Salvadoran youth were also socialized into unequal relations between El Salvador and the United States. But from a transnational social field perspective, recognizing that "San Salvador is now deeply linked to spaces inside Los Angeles" (Zilberg 2011a, 495), we suggest that English instruction reinforced not a longing for the United States but a *belonging* in the diaspora. It is not that El Rio youth longed to go to the United States—many of them did and many of them did not—but rather, as exemplified by the expressions of homeboy culture, they were already living in its margins. In this context, English lessons were one of many forces that socialized El Rio youth into double marginality—the simultaneous exclusions from their home country and from full participation in the United States—and into a diasporic third space (Sui 2005). English classes in El Rio prepared students for future lives as undocumented immigrant workers in the United States, where their labor would be exploited but their right to belong would always be questioned.

Nowhere was this more apparent than in an English class Andrea observed one Tuesday morning in February, when Mr. Campos departed from his usual format to engage students in a series of role-playing activities. He announced that the topic of the day's lesson would be "A Day in the United States: Applying for the TPS." (TPS, or Temporary Protected Status, is a temporary immigration status that allows recipients to avoid deportation and obtain work authorization.) He told students they would be enacting the interview between a U.S. immigration official and a Salvadoran immigrant applying for TPS. In previous classes students had learned the structure for basic questions and answers, and Mr. Campos wanted them to practice this. He started by calling on two students who had high grades in the class to enact the first dialogue. He appointed Alicia, a light-skinned female, to be the U.S. agent and Juan Miguel, a dark-skinned male, to be the Salvadoran immigrant—to much whistling and hooting from the class. For the first thirty seconds of Alicia and Juan Miguel's dialogue the students were exceptionally attentive and engaged, but as the pair continued reading basic questions and answers from their script in barely audible English, the class soon dissolved into side conversations. This continued for the next several dialogues, as the student actors mumbled and fumbled with "What is your name?" and "Where are you from?" By the end, it seemed that only the teacher was paying attention to them.

However, after four or five of these role-playing dialogues, the students asked Mr. Campos and me (Andrea) to come forward to enact the interview. They wanted me to play the immigration official and Mr. Campos the Salvadoran applicant. Mr. Campos readily agreed. Now the whole class was paying attention. We spoke more loudly and clearly than the student pairs had, and we departed from the script of questions and answers. I found myself feigning the suspicion I imagined a U.S. immigration agent might have. When Mr. Campos said it wasn't safe for him in El Salvador because of the gang situation, I asked him, "Are you in a gang?" When he said no, I asked, "Are you sure?" At the end, he asked me if he got the TPS. I said no. The class roared and howled with laughter. I realized I had given them the performance they wanted and expected. I had been recruited into their script of Salvadoran exclusion at the hands of U.S. immigration officials. After class, several students wanted to talk to me about life in the United States. At last, that day's lesson had captured their attention.

The TPS immigration status has been described as a "condition of 'permanent temporariness,'" a legal limbo that amounts to an experience of continuous displacement and confinement for Salvadoran immigrants in the United States (Rodríguez 2005). Yet, for youth in this marginal community in San Salvador TPS was a household word, the ticket to a life of economic opportunity in the United States. Local newspapers covered the vicissitudes of TPS for Salvadoran immigrants almost daily. Its use by the English teacher in this example was a key educational moment in the cultural production of diasporic subjects, in which "diasporic un/belonging is articulated most clearly, crystallized, and made lucid for a short while" (Siu 2005, 28). The TPS role playing, occurring in the context of English instruction that denied students conversational fluency, simultaneously encouraged students to construct identities as future migrants in the United

States—for whom English would be essential in interactions with key gatekeepers—while still reinforcing their subordinate status as limited English speakers and persons with limited legal rights.

Critical Democratic Yearnings in Transnational Social Fields

The preceding discussion described school and social practices that reflected dominant neoliberal citizenship regimes in El Salvador that socialize students for roles as future migrants in the United States, either as undocumented immigrant workers or gang members (if they are from El Río) or as members of a U.S.-educated neoliberal elite (if they are from the Lincoln School). However, at the same time that these students' education severed them from belonging in El Salvador, making future trajectories toward the United States all but inevitable, it also promised a belonging in the United States that they recognized might be elusive. When provided a forum to examine and reflect on their experiences as diasporic citizens, students demonstrated a consciousness of the contradictory and contingent status of those identities. We argue that this *consciousness of contradiction,* a characteristic of the diaspora and the third space, holds the potential to interrupt processes of neoliberal citizenship formation, offering a critical awareness or "partial penetration" (Willis 1977) of the determining conditions of students' lives. Tapping into this consciousness as critical pedagogues and participatory researchers, we open a space to reimagine national identity and belonging in the service of democratic inclusion.

English Lessons in Neoliberal Space: "This Type of Education Also Closes Doors!"

At the Lincoln School, interviews with students and a focus group with eleven seniors enrolled in the AP English class offered students an opportunity to reflect on what it meant to them to be educated in English in El Salvador. They were often surprisingly candid and thoughtful in recognizing the privileges and the trade-offs that this entailed. From their responses it became clear that the ability to speak English (and speak it well, "without an accent," as many said) was a key identity marker that separated them from their non-English-speaking (and less privileged) Salvadoran peers. Fluency in English was a form of cultural capital that cemented their privilege and, as it did so, made it more difficult for them to identify with and as Salvadoran citizens.

Lincoln students described the importance of English in terms that reflected the neoliberal ideology of competition and individual advancement in a global economy. Speaking English was a competitive advantage, and the words *advantage* and *privilege* recurred again and again in their talk about English; tellingly, in the words of one young man, "We have a step up when we're compared to other schools." Another said, "I think it puts me ahead of a lot of people." Another common trope was that "English opens doors," as students described a whole host of prospects available to them as English speakers—opportunities for study, travel, and jobs. Certainly, these students had already used English in their travels. Our survey of seniors at the Lincoln School (n = 76) showed that 93 percent had family members living in the United States and 99 percent had visited the United States; 70 percent of them went at least once a year. In interviews many also spoke of using English on trips to Europe. With English, the world was their oyster.

Some saw English as part of globalization and as an index of the development and "Westernization" of El Salvador. One student, when asked how English affected her identity, reflected,

El Salvador in itself is so [intertwined] with the States because of all the illegal immigrants and everything, so . . . our culture nowadays isn't eating *pupusas* for breakfast because we have to, or stuff like that. . . . It's more Western, it's more American, our everyday life. But that's just a global thing. The more developed we are the more Western we're going to be.

She explained that all Salvadoran teenagers consumed "American" movies and music, adding, "It's a mix, I think, for all of us Salvadorans. I don't think we can only call ourselves Salvadorans anymore because we're not." Interestingly, this student referenced both U.S. popular culture and "all the illegal immigrants" as trends that were changing cultural identity for all Salvadorans. English was important not only for economic opportunities but also for keeping up with these cultural changes.

These students mostly took for granted that speaking English was an unqualified good. However, when we engaged them in deeper discussions of national identity and citizenship, some students became reflective about the implications of this privilege for their civic identities and, in particular, the implications of their separation from non-English-speaking Salvadorans. One female student, when asked if she was like other Salvadorans, said, "I think I'm alike in the fact that I feel—I love the country . . . but at the same time, being an English speaker, a traveler, that kind of makes you—it makes you different."

Many students at the Lincoln School were very aware of how sheltered they were from the lives and realities of ordinary, non-English-speaking Salvadorans, and they were critical of the role their education played in this separation. In the AP English focus group, students were discussing the importance of English and all the doors it opens when a female student, Cristina, blurted out, "But this type of education also closes doors!" She went on to say, "You don't learn the other side. We don't learn the Spanish. We live in El Salvador. We don't know what other Salvadoran children who are going to public schools know. So it closes doors." In the discussion that followed the students debated the pros and cons of their American education. While two students vociferously defended their education and the opportunities it gave them, several others listed all the things that were closed to them because of their education in English. They pointed out that they did not know how to do science or math in Spanish, which made it difficult or impossible for them to pursue higher education in El Salvador or another Latin American country. Cristina, the only student in the group not planning to attend college in the United States, explained her decision to attend university in Mexico. She knew it would be a challenge for her academically because she had received all of her instruction in English, but she felt that the setting would be more comfortable for her culturally. She said she believed many students at the Lincoln School would be happier at (and better served by) universities in Latin America, but the school did not guide them toward that option.

There were two elements to Cristina's critique. One was that the school was failing to educate students about their own cultural heritage and thereby separating them from their fellow citizens. Second, the school was channeling students toward a future in the United States that might not be for them and thus might be setting them up for failure. Cristina lamented the lack of Salvadoran authors in their Spanish literature class: "I've been telling Mr. Cortes since the beginning of the year that we should study Salvadoran literature, that it's really important, that it's really good! And he told me, like, 'We can't, we can't, because we have to learn from other

countries.' And we have, like, one week of Salvadoran literature, one week."
Such longings offered a corrective to the view of the superintendent that
Salvadoran culture was a "nonreading culture." Cristina's classmate, Maribel, lambasted the school's emphasis on American history at the expense
of Salvadoran history.

> Here we get taught about Abraham Lincoln and George Washing-
> ton since kindergarten, every grade . . . then [not] until senior year,
> the last year, we get taught about our country's history. We should
> be getting some of our country's history since kindergarten. It's
> even more important than learning about Abraham Lincoln and
> George Washington. It's where we *come from!* No one knows
> anything about our country in this school.

While teachers often said students' ties to the United States were weak-
ening their Salvadoran identity, many students were quick to point out the
school's role in this process, critiquing the projection of a North American
identity over a Salvadoran one. Raquel shared in her interview that limiting Salvadoran studies to one year at the end of high school was "a mistake"
and contributed to "this feeling of internationals being better than Salvadorans. It's the fact that we lack learning on our country." She did not feel that
the school prepared students to be citizens of El Salvador because "the
school is mostly concerned with seeking education elsewhere. . . . The
main goal is to send you away to a school in the U.S." These students clearly
drew the connection between their education in English and their identities as people who were *removed from* other Salvadorans. As the discussion
in the focus group unfolded, it became clear that some students felt inca-
pacitated in their roles as citizens of El Salvador. In the words of one male
student, they were "blinded" from local realities, which included not only
conditions of poverty but also local opportunities and cultural wealth.
This student explained in his interview, "The first choice is always outside [abroad], and if possible to stay there and not return. . . . It creates a
great devaluing of everything that is here. [The school] fails in the area of
social conscience, and without conscience, the academic preparation
fails, too."

At the same time that their education closed doors in El Salvador, making future trajectories toward the United States all but inevitable, it also
promised a belonging in the United States that the students recognized

might be elusive. While most students believed their education had prepared them academically for higher education in the United States, many
did not believe that they or their peers were prepared socially and culturally for life in the United States, particularly for the experience of being a
racial minority. They recognized that the class privilege they enjoyed in El
Salvador would not carry over to a racially diverse society and that they
might not be ready for, in the words of one young man, "the segregation
and maybe the racism that we may [experience] when we get there." Ger-
ald, a graduating senior, planned to pursue a career in the theater industry
in the United States but had mixed feelings about the discrimination he
would face there. Code-switching between English and Spanish, he said,
"I like being Salvadoran, pero al mismo tiempo siento que [but at the same
time I feel that] once I go to the States, I don't know. . . . Van a tener un
estereotipo no muy inteligente de mi porque soy salvadoreño, entonces
siento que [They are going to have a not very intelligent stereotype about
me because I'm Salvadoran, so I feel that] being a Salvadoran will become
a liability."

Some of these students had firsthand experience with discrimination in
the United States, having spent summers there. Many others knew Lincoln
School students who had started college in the United States and then
returned after one or two years of struggling to adjust to life there. College
dropouts and returnees were the subject of much discussion in our private
conversations with students and some teachers who were critical of the
school, but they were never openly acknowledged by school administrators.
Instead, school administrators liked to cite the high admissions statistics
and the amount of fellowship and grant money offered to their graduates
by U.S. universities. What happened to the students once they got to these
institutions was seemingly beyond the purview of the school.

The figure of the Lincoln School college dropout, a closely guarded
secret, served as a stand-in for the school's false promises of membership
in the global elite, measured by a successful life in the United States with a
U.S. college degree and a high-paying job. Of course, many graduates of the
Lincoln School did go on to assume positions in the global elite, and we
do not mean to suggest that Lincoln School graduates were disadvantaged
in any material sense. However, the students in the AP English focus group,
in their critique of the school's vision for them and its implications for their
citizenship, showed a consciousness of contradiction that we argue is characteristic of the diasporic subject position. As Siu (2005) writes, diasporic

citizenship involves a "tension between one's affinity and affiliation with these sites and one's acknowledgement of only partial belonging and acceptance by them" (11). While everything in their schooling purported to prepare them for and ensure them full membership in the United States, these students demonstrated "partial penetration" (Willis 1977, 3) of the determining conditions of their existence. In spite of their privilege, they experienced a form of double marginality that prevented them from fully identifying with citizens in either El Salvador or the United States. Students at the Lincoln School recognized the cultural politics that positioned them as *better than* their non-English-speaking Salvadoran peers but *less than* white U.S. citizens, and they were hesitant to embrace the identities the school offered them.

Participatory Research in El Rio: "They'll See That We're Not All Gangsters"

Several weeks into our observations at El Rio, we obtained permission to work with a group of first-year *bachillerato* students ranging in age from fifteen to nineteen in a participatory research class focused on migration and citizenship. We initially recruited eighteen students, nine from each of the two curricular strands in the school, *bachillerato técnico contador* and *general* (accounting and general), based on our interactions with them and their demonstrated willingness to engage in reflective discussion. Just ten students stayed with the group all the way to its conclusion. Several students dropped out when they realized the project would require work outside of class and that we would sometimes meet more than once a week. We emphasized that the project was voluntary but required a commitment, and we worked with the ten students who chose to stay.

In keeping with the goals of participatory research, our purpose in involving the youth was to build on and enhance their own capacities for critical analysis and social action while generating a richer knowledge base about the experience of migration.[14] Because this method aligned well with La Esperanza School's social justice mission, our proposal was enthusiastically received by school administrators, who gave us classroom space and time during the school day.[15] We met with the youth weekly or twice weekly over a four-month period in a series of focused sessions in which we presented them with our research questions, engaged them in discussion about these topics, and invited them to participate as coresearchers of their communities. Our group meetings served a dual purpose of generating insights into how the students thought about these questions and training the students in qualitative research methods. Students conducted observations in the school and community, wrote reports and reflections, and conducted at least one formal interview each; in our group meetings we discussed findings and analyzed our data collectively. Our collective inquiry and reflection proved to be a stimulus for powerful discussions on citizenship, and we learned that students were eager for the opportunity to talk about their experiences of migration and identity in school.

To structure our research process, we used the Freirean technique of "generative themes" (Freire [1970] 1999), selecting from their responses key themes for further discussion and exploration. The four questions we explored were: What does it mean to be an educated person? What does it mean to be a citizen? How does education prepare young people here to be citizens? and How is migration affecting this community? For each question, we solicited their individual reflections and written responses, then discussed their responses in pairs, small groups, and as a whole group. At the next meeting, we reflected back to them a theme that had emerged from their responses, posing it as a question for further probing. Inevitably, the generation of themes led to a spontaneous exchange of different opinions and reflections as students responded to each other's points, offered examples, and sometimes argued with each other. From these discussions we selected homework questions to guide their own research activities in exploring the topic in the wider community. When students returned with their observations and reflections, we engaged in a deeper level of discussion.

One of the first themes that emerged in our discussions of citizenship was inequality—in particular, the violation of citizenship rights of the poor. Students' initial responses to the question "What does it mean to be a citizen?" were full of the language of "rights and responsibilities." So we asked them, "What are the basic rights of citizens?" The group immediately generated a list: education, decent housing (*vivienda digna*), nutrition, clothing, health care, security (safety), decent work, and a living wage. Before we could ask them about citizens' responsibilities, one student immediately protested, "estos derechos no se cumplen!" (but these rights are not granted!). There ensued a heated discussion about how each right is denied in El Rio. After one student described the different kinds of substandard houses that exist in El Rio and others discussed the barriers to getting an education, Karina, a soft-spoken, thoughtful girl, said it was because they live in a *zona de riesgo*. This indicated an awareness, apparent throughout our discussions, of the unequal distribution of rights based on where you live, and a shared identity as members of an oppressed community. As they were invited to describe the conditions in their community, they connected these to larger structural forces. For example, as they discussed the minimum wage, which at $184 per month barely covered the cost of the *canasta básica* (basic basket, minimum nutritional needs), they brought up dollarization and inflation.[16] One student, Yanira, said the government had promised that when they switched to the dollar the people would be paid U.S.-level wages, but in reality they make the same or less than what they made in *colones,* while the prices of everything have gone up. Students connected issues of economic justice to political justice, observing that the poor who committed petty theft would get much harsher punishments than did rich government officials who embezzled ("They send us to Mariona").

Having established students' shared experience and identity as members of a group that was denied citizenship rights, we asked them about the options for citizens when their rights are denied. How do people respond? Students answered this question based on their own experiences, then conducted observations and interviews in the community. The research question became "¿Que hace la gente para salir adelante cuando se les niega sus derechos?" (What do people do to get ahead when their rights are denied?). The answers they generated included: protest (a subject that spurred a long discussion about the inefficacy of protest in El Salvador); violence and delinquency (from murder and extortion to drug dealing and petty theft); emigrate; sell goods in the informal economy; get trained in a trade; use remittances to start a business;[17] combine remittances with other earnings; prostitute; send your children to work; and work in the *maquilas* (factories with notoriously poor working conditions and wages). Together we classified these actions as destructive actions, actions for survival/subsistence, and actions for social change, acknowledging some overlap. For example, students pointed out that gangsters' killings, the most obviously destructive actions, are also acts of survival because the law of the streets is "kill or be killed."

Two of the students chose to interview gang members (*pandilleros*) and a third interviewed a deportee, offering intimate glimpses into illicit means of survival. These interviews and our group discussions about them allowed the youth to humanize people vilified as security threats by state discourses, reconnecting them to the social conditions that shaped their behaviors. Karina returned excited after her interview with a *pandillero*, which had gone very well. With emotion, she said, "One has a very negative image of them, but they are human" (field notes 6/16/09). Through these interviews and our discussions, students developed an analysis of destructive and/or stigmatized behavior as evidence of a broken social contract; in a situation where the government does not bestow citizenship rights, citizens do not submit to its laws.

Migration emerged as a pressing theme before we asked about it. It was seen as a creative response to the denial of citizenship rights at home, but one that results in further fragmentation and social disintegration. We quickly learned that our students associated migration with social disintegration. They used the phrase "victims of migration" to refer to the children left behind by migrants, including themselves. Of our ten students, two had a parent living in the United States and a third had seen her father deported back to El Salvador after five years in the United States. All ten students had some family member(s) in the United States and all of them knew personally someone who had been deported.

Students were quick to bring up migration's harmful effects on those left behind. As Alicia put it, "For every migrant who leaves, there are two new *pandilleros*." She was referring to the migrants' children left behind who turn to gangs for social support. In their written reflections, all students highlighted family separation and its associated problems as the primary consequence of migration on their community. After listing all the things that can go wrong when a parent migrates, Edgar concluded his reflection with this: "Young people in the absence of a parent fall into the wrong path, and that stalls the progress not only of the community but also of the country." The problems we discussed included increased crime and gang activity among unsupervised youth, neglect and abuse of children left behind, school desertion and other schooling problems, dependence on remittances, and identity conflicts for those who migrate. Students shared examples of each of these from their own experiences and from the testimonies of the people they interviewed (three had chosen to interview a "victim of migration"—the left-behind child of a migrant or a deportee). Jenny, the student whose father had been deported after five years in the United States, questioned whether the expanded opportunities in the United States were worth the suffering. In her written reflection responding to the question "How has migration affected this community?," she wrote:

> It's true that in this country there are not many job opportunities, but the fact of emigrating to another country causes much suffering for the migrant and his family. For example, a migrant arrives in the United States and what he gets is to sleep in the streets, to run around fleeing so that they can't deport him, washing dishes, working in supermarkets. And this is no good because you arrive to suffer more than what you suffer in our country.

Jenny's portrait of the undocumented immigrant ("run[ning] around fleeing so that they can't deport him") revealed her awareness of migrants' lack of legal and social rights in the United States, challenging discourses about the United States as a land of freedom, opportunity, and progress.

Our interviews with students in which they reflected on what the United States meant to them and the connections, if any, they felt to the United States revealed their intimate knowledge of the hardships faced by undocumented Latino migrants gleaned from U.S. movies, local news media, and personal contact with migrants and deportees. Seventeen-year-old Eduardo shared, "I've heard about how hard the journey of the wetback is, the butchers on the trains. They pushed a migrant friend of mine and he fell off the train and now he has no legs." Discussing the American Dream, Eduardo said, "La imagen es chivo pero la realidad es aguantar desprecio y discriminación" (The image is cool, but the reality is to endure contempt and discrimination). This awareness of the reality of hardship for immigrants like them was a common theme in our discussions with students (Dyrness 2014). Yanira, a sixteen-year-old student in El Rio whose father was in Washington, D.C., explained:

> For me, the United States is a generator of opportunities, but at the same time like I see that they also live some of our reality that we live here . . . more than anything the Latinos, the question of racism and all of that that I have seen so much in movies, that they have told me. So, I feel that if it is true that are many opportunities, they [opportunities] are also denied.

By noticing that "some of our reality that we live here [in El Rio]" also exists *over there* in the United States, Yanira revealed her awareness of the shared plight of poor Salvadorans ("Latinos") in both places. She also questioned the discourse of opportunity in the United States from the personal experience of her father: "If it is true that there are many opportunities, [opportunities] are also denied." A kinship (literal and figurative) with Salvadoran migrants in the United States shaped these students' understandings of the American Dream and their identities as members of a transnational marginal class. As we discuss below, this critical perspective on the American Dream nurtured what we call "democratic yearnings," in which students longed for the ability to stay in El Salvador and work for the conditions that would make a dignified life there possible (Wiltberger 2014).

For the students in El Rio, the opportunity to examine their reality and their place in relation to structural inequality was a key step in the transformation of their identities from "victims of migration" to agents of change. At the end of our project, we compiled our findings and prepared a presentation titled "Education, Migration, and Citizenship: A View from El Rio" for Universidad Centroamericana (UCA).[18] The presentation at the university assumed symbolic importance for the youth as a forum to publicly present on their own terms their identities and their aspirations for social change. Initially, many of them doubted their ability to present in a university setting, but they committed to preparing for it and embraced the opportunity to share their knowledge. When one student, Jaime, expressed reservations, saying, "We can't be compared to university students, because we're not at that level," a fellow student, Yanira, assured him, "They [university students] are going to have a more advanced vocabulary, but we bring knowledge of our reality." The students also noted that by going to present at the university they would be breaking the stereotypes about young people from their community, because "they'll see that we're not all gangsters." Their success in projecting their new identities at their presentation prompted the school principal, who was in the audience, to exclaim, "I didn't know we had students like these!"

A New Way of Being Salvadoran?

While the effects of transnational migration in both communities clearly had the potential to reinforce national divisions—deepening marginalization in the poor community and further separating the advantaged from the realities of the poor—what is significant in our findings is that students in both schools advanced a *critique* of these processes, which contained the seeds for critically aware civic identities and a pride in El Salvador as *un país sufrido.* They rejected the identity of a U.S.-bound migrant who was expected to leave behind or look down on El Salvador; the awareness of *desprecio* (contempt or devaluing) of Salvadorans and El Salvador by North Americans figured strongly in their identity formations. Students in both schools articulated that the United States offered more opportunities for them, but not necessarily the kind of life or cultural values that they wanted. As we show below, they expressed tremendous pride in El Salvador in ways that surprisingly crossed the class and political divides of their communities. Significantly, in spite of their many connections to the United States, both groups of students demonstrated similar degrees of ambivalence about whether they would want to live in the United States themselves. Responding to the survey question "Do you see yourself living in the United States at some point in the future?," 43 percent of Lincoln students and 47 percent of El Rio students answered "don't know," while 40 percent of Lincoln students and 43 percent of El Rio students answered "yes" and 17 percent of Lincoln Students and 10 percent of El Rio students answered "no." The similarity in the degree of uncertainty in both groups is striking considering that so many Lincoln School students had dual citizenship and other privileges that should have made their transition to the United States seamless. Evidence from interviews in which they described their perceptions of the United States and their relationship to it lends insight into this surprising parallel. In their critique of U.S. society and corresponding defense of Salvadoran values, both groups of students articulated a belonging in El Salvador that ran against narratives of neoliberal citizenship.

Roberto, a nineteen-year-old senior at the Lincoln School who was born in the United States, explained that those who leave El Salvador to live abroad "pegan contra una pared que quizás no se esperaba" (hit a wall that that they didn't expect). Having spent a previous summer in California and another in Europe, Roberto felt that there was an "absence of values" in those places. He explained: "The developed world, I feel, has lost something that we still have here. Moral education, like to say please, thank you. That human warmth." He gave an example of being mistreated while going out to eat in restaurants in the United States. Such experiences gave him a critical perspective on the American Dream. As he put it, "You're here on the other side of the coin thinking, oh there is the freedom, there is the place, [and] when you get there and you realize it's so different from what you're used to and it's also hard." Roberto's experiences made him critical of discourses that painted the United States as the land of freedom and progress.

Across town in El Rio, Alicia, when asked what the United States means to her, said, "I don't like the part that is racist, that they discriminate against people for a skin color, or for a nationality. That does not appeal to me." When we asked what being Salvadoran meant to her, Alicia had this to say:

> I am very proud of being Salvadoran, and if I could be born again, I would be born Salvadoran. I love El Salvador so much . . . maybe because of the fact that we have faced a war and we have reached, we have known how to reach an agreement . . . and maybe also because the Salvadoran has always stood out as a hard worker. Whatever part of the world you go to there is always a Salvadoran who stands out for his work. Maybe for being such a small country they discriminate against us, but they don't know that in El Salvador there is a lot of mental wealth. Somebody who can persevere and get ahead, somebody who is well prepared, because there is a lot of intelligence in El Salvador.

Here Alicia expresses both an awareness of discrimination and pride in Salvadorans' ability to continue no matter what. She also suggests that discrimination is due to El Salvador's subordinate status in the global economy ("for being such a small country") and implicitly makes a distinction between the economic wealth that gives nations power and the "mental wealth" that El Salvador has, which goes unrecognized by those who discriminate.

The ability to face hardship and emerge stronger was a quality that students in both schools associated with being Salvadoran. In spite of their distinct social experiences in El Salvador, their shared history of the war, natural disasters such as earthquakes and hurricanes, and discrimination as Latinos in the United States created a unified imaginary of "being Salvadoran" for students from both communities. Marcos at the Lincoln School, echoing Alicia in El Rio, reflected: "To be Salvadoran is to be a strong person with very strong character who has gone through natural disasters, earthquakes, wars. Even though I didn't live the war, but I have felt the weight of the war. Wars, things like that. No matter what happens. . . . They throw us down to the ground but we manage to get up." Karina in El Rio, explaining why she considered it an "honor" to be Salvadoran, said, "El Salvador is a long-suffering country . . . and with all that, it has tried to come out ahead . . . everyone tries to get ahead. And that's important, we try to struggle, little by little."

It may seem odd that privileged students from the Lincoln School expressed a sense of their people as an unjustly disparaged group who persevere and overcome adversity. Significantly, for many students at the Lincoln School, their participation in transnational social fields gave them their first personal experiences of discrimination, albeit on a different level from that experienced daily by students in El Rio. Trips abroad at summer camps or summer programs with American teenagers who expressed ignorant and disparaging views of Salvadorans occasioned their first critical awareness of inequality. Lucia, one of the few Lincoln students who did not have family in the United States, encountered stereotypes about Salvadorans among American teenagers at a summer camp in Paris. The Americans, surprised that she spoke English, peppered her with questions suggesting they thought she "lived in the jungle." Lucia recalled this experience when explaining that being Salvadoran for her meant challenging these assumptions: "The responsibility as a Salvadoran [is] making people understand that there's educated people here, that it's not as bad as they make you seem. Yeah, we have violence and everything, but it's not just that, we're much more than that and that's a huge part for me being Salvadoran, just proving that we can make something out of our lives, out of our country." Lucia's words recalled those of Alicia in El Rio, that "they [people in the United States] don't know that in El Salvador there is a lot of mental wealth."

In comparing these students' awareness of discrimination in the United States we are not suggesting that the actual experiences of discrimination suffered by members of these groups—privileged, bilingual students and undocumented immigrants—are the same or even similar. Diasporic experiences and identities are always conditioned by differing social locations based on race/ethnicity, class, gender, and legal status. What is significant is the awareness, on the part of students in both social groups in El Salvador, of the experience of inequality of Salvadorans in the United States and the way this awareness figures in their civic imaginaries.[19] Students' experiences in the diaspora offered a new shared framework for citizenship because the shared experience of subordination is a powerful force shaping collective identity (Gilroy 1987). For many students in both schools, the sense of being unfairly stereotyped was a powerful motivator for constructing an alternative identity, a source of civic pride.

As these students contended with dominant U.S. stereotypes about Latino immigrants including perceptions of outsiderness and criminality, they shared many of the same experiences of Salvadoran youth who grew up in the United States and expressed many of the same responsibilities and desires of young Dreamers in the United States (Coutin 2016; González 2016). For both groups, their relationships to the United States and their collective identity were shaped by how others perceived them and by their desire to counter unjust depictions of immigrants. However, while Dreamers' activism has centered on their right to belong in the United States, the Salvadoran youth in our study narrated identities that claimed the right to belong in El Salvador. Using Coutin's framework, we see their narratives as giving voice to the "dismemberment" that has fragmented their communities. In critiquing narratives of migration as the path to upward mobility and progress, the students in our study challenged processes of neoliberalism that encouraged them to seek individual economic gain above the well-being of their (and other) communities in El Salvador. Most importantly, they expressed a yearning to identify with and to more fully know El Salvador.

In her study of Salvadoran transnational youth, Coutin (2016) writes, "Exclusion disconnects individuals from national histories such that accounts of the processes that led to and followed their migration or displacement can be submerged, denied, or ignored" (207). This is the essence of dismemberment. Coutin argues that this can be countered by "re/membering," by "recuperating and recognizing submerged histories," making it possible to reconnect the historical conditions that provoke migration to the outward effects of these conditions (e.g., joblessness, illegality), which otherwise might appear to be intrinsic characteristics of migrants. As Coutin describes it, in the lives of 1.5-generation Salvadoran immigrant activists in the United States, re/membering is a "quest for self-knowledge, historical memory, and legal recognition" (215). Through re/membering, Salvadoran migrant youth seek to reconfigure their relationship to the United States and El Salvador in ways that account for the contradictions between their lived experience and national narratives, and to push for more inclusive futures.

As we have seen, the young people in our two school communities in El Salvador were being disconnected from their histories even before migrating. We see their insights into this process in their critique of their schools' failure to engage their history and reality and in their longing to connect to this history. At the Lincoln School, students lamented the lack of attention to El Salvador's history and culture, connecting it to "this feeling of internationals being better than Salvadorans," as one put it. Another student there exclaimed, "We're supposed to be the future of this country, and we don't know anything about this country!" At La Esperanza School in El Rio, in spite of the school's social justice–oriented vision, teachers enacted a personal responsibility citizenship that decontextualized students' problems from the realities of their everyday lives. The students in our participatory research group were sensitive to these contradictions and to the lack of attention to what they called "our reality." They expressed a longing for a socially engaged citizenship in their articulations of what constitutes a good citizen and in their critique of educational processes that discourage this. In their words, a good citizen should "benefit their society," should "be concerned about their country," should "be concerned about their social history," and should "know and recognize their national history." Even before we began our discussion of what it means to be an educated person, students pointed out that schooling did not make a person a good citizen. Alicia said, "An educated person can become selfish. They forget where they come from and the problems that might be there." This resonated with the group and provoked much discussion. Elias shared the saying "The champion never forgets where he was born."

Both education and migration might contribute to "forgetting" where you came from. In addition to discussing the negative effects of migration on family members left behind, students in El Rio also noted the effects of migration on those who leave, using the language of forgetting. Yanira said that many times migrants develop disdain for El Salvador and only "want to be gringo. They forget their roots." On another occasion, Elmer said people change when they moved to the United States: "They forget about us." These comments reveal deep concerns about trajectories of upward mobility that separate Salvadorans from their communities.

In El Rio, our participatory research project became a venue for students to explore these concerns, to critically examine the processes that dis/member their communities and articulate their yearnings for alternative futures. An analysis of students' reflections at the end of the project in group discussions and recorded interviews shows evidence of active, critical civic identities rooted in an intimate knowledge of and commitment to their community. Early in our research students had said that being "successful" would surely mean leaving El Rio, but by the end of the project they expressed pride in being from El Rio because, as Yanira put it, "We are in touch with society's problems, because we live them every day." Students testified that they appreciated the opportunity that the research provided to explore their "reality." Yanira said that the research "made me realize more what we live, that maybe I had not stopped to think about or analyze before." The experience made her rethink her plans for the future: "Before, when I attended [national institute], I started to study hospitality and tourism, because I really like tourism. . . . But I've started thinking after this research, I think I would rather change my career to something more like sociology, to get more involved in the reality in which we live. So, I would like to study that, sociology or anthropology." What is important here is her reason for choosing a new course of study—her desire to "get more involved" in her own reality.

Another student, Karina, also expressed a new vision for her future:

> I used to think that I was going to buy a house [in a nice neighborhood] and take my family and live there. Now after this research and seeing the reality people live, no, I want to help, I want to contribute. I want to be part of the change. I want to be part of the change because I do have hope now that things can be changed.

She further marked her identity as a change agent when she said she did not think she was like other Salvadorans. "There are people who couldn't care less what happens, it's all the same to them. In contrast, I try to see the reality, the injustice. There are people who couldn't care less. 'Oh, well, it can't be changed.' They don't struggle."

Similarly, Elias said he was not like other Salvadorans because he had no desire to migrate to another country. He explained, "I think the reality here is too wide, too complex, to blindfold myself and say everything is fine and go to another country and stay there with my arms crossed, and not do anything for the country. . . . I think I would do more here than in another country." Elias expressed a view common in our research group, that people who migrate may improve their own situations but not that of the community they leave behind. But it was extremely difficult to hold onto this identity—a Salvadoran who does not want to migrate—in the context of such powerful forces of displacement. As Elias so poignantly put it, "To be Salvadoran, to me, is to struggle against wind and tide."

As students in our research bore witness to the harmful effects of migration, they joined a chorus of transnational Salvadoran migrant activists who were raising concerns about the human toll of emigration and criticizing El Salvador's neoliberal migration-development strategy (Wiltberger 2014). In the wake of a transition to a leftist government in El Salvador, organizations and networks representing migrants began calling for "an option to *not* migrate" (Wiltberger 2014). Diaspora leaders pressured the new government to "address the transnational reality of hardship that Salvadoran migrants were facing" by extending services for migrants abroad, deportees, and migrants in transit in Mexico, and to provide "other options than undocumented emigration for marginalized Salvadorans" (43). This represented a shift in transnational activists' strategy, to promote not only migrant rights in places of destination but also "the collective sense of dignity and well-being of migrants' communities in places of origin" (45). In doing so, these activists contested the neoliberal ideology that valued economic growth and productivity above human rights and communal well-being. They opened a space where Salvadoran young people's desire for life in El Salvador could be taken seriously and supported. As Wiltberger argues, regardless of the feasibility challenges for policy in building "an option to not migrate," the strategy marks an important transformation in El Salvador's civic imaginary in which undocumented migration is framed as "a problem capable of being addressed, rather than a naturalized, unwavering trajectory into the future" (58).

The young people in El Rio were not activists, nor were they connected to the transnational activist campaigns of their compatriots in the diaspora. However, when offered a venue to explore and narrate their identities, they expressed incipient critiques of their realities and imaginings of different futures, which we call "democratic yearnings." They are democratic in that they aspire to more just, equal, and inclusive futures and want to contribute to democratic social change in El Salvador. The students in our research expressed their aspirations for social change in the context of defining themselves as citizens, assuming the responsibility to work for change as a core aspect of their identities. Even in the context of extreme hardship, they suggested, it is not enough to survive and get out. As Yanira put it, "So many refuse to see beyond their noses. If they do have ambition to succeed, it is to succeed only for themselves, and not perhaps to change where they live, to help the rest. So no, I wouldn't be the same as them." These students yearn for the opportunity to connect their education to their community, to engage in re/membering and restoration of their fractured lives.

We call these "yearnings," however, because we do not presuppose that young people have the skills or the support to translate their awareness into democratic civic action. As we have seen, their schooling socialized them to take individual responsibility for their own behavior but not to understand or collectively confront the larger forces of displacement that threatened their communities. In this respect, we argue that the yearnings represent a *potential* that must be cultivated by critical educators to bear fruit, a resource for democratic citizenship that must be harvested (Dyrness and Sepúlveda 2017; Dyrness and Abu El-Haj 2019). Processes of popular education and participatory research inspired by Paulo Freire, one version of which we employed here, offer a framework for cultivating these yearnings and young people's critical consciousness and beginning the process of re/membering. These processes have been shown to be healing and "wholing" the fragmentation experienced by Latinx communities in the diaspora (Ayala et al. 2018). According to Coutin (2016), some transnational Salvadoran youth activists in the United States cited Paulo Freire as inspiring their efforts to learn and record their own histories. She quotes one interviewee who told her, "I'll give you the—hueso duro de mi filosofía, de donde sale. De Paulo Freire, *Pedagogy of the Oppressed*. Very simple. In order for someone to advance in society, in *any* society, they need to know where they come from. Where they're at. Politically, economically, and culturally" (119).

The students in both communities in our research, like the activist quoted here, emphasized the need to "know where they come from" as a key part of citizenship. This was a need that was largely denied them by their schooling in El Salvador, as they were socialized to become "entrepreneurs of themselves" (Ong 2006; Zilberg 2011b). In voicing their desire to maintain their Salvadoran identity and culture, to find value "at home" (Wiltberger 2014), youth in both communities expressed resistance to neoliberal processes of dismemberment that severed them from their communities. They also made an important distinction between, on the one hand, the economic opportunities promised by neoliberal ideologies of development, and on the other, the social and cultural belonging they felt in El Salvador. Like the transnational Palestinian youth in Abu El-Haj's (2015) study, Salvadoran youth recognized that the United States offered them important opportunities but not social or cultural belonging. Not only would they face racism and discrimination in "the land of opportunity" (and also, in the case of El Rio youth, the painful exclusion of undocumented status and "illegality"), but they also would be disconnected from the family and networks of neighbors and friends that sustained them. Explaining why she would not want to live permanently in the United States, Martina from the Lincoln School said, "I feel that me and my family are very close—I mean, my cousins, my aunts and everyone. We are very close, all of us, and we are many. Just the fact that when I was there [in the United States], *púchica* I miss my cousins!" Another student said, "No, no, because I like the idea that here in El Salvador everyone knows everyone. You have connections to everyone. And everyone helps out everyone." These students spoke to what would be lost if they pursued the path to success offered by their schooling; they gave voice to the hidden and erased histories of migration (Coutin 2016).

Notwithstanding real differences in the economic and legal statuses of the young people in these two communities, both groups experienced contradictory forces of cultural socialization that encouraged them to look to the United States for opportunities but also communicated the inaccessibility or unattainability of full membership there. As Salvadoran youths recounted the experiences of their friends and loved ones in the United States and those that had returned, they punctured the illusion of the American Dream and the discourse that framed " 'the exterior' as a place of 'progress' " (Wiltberger 2014, 48).

So where does that leave these youths, who did not feel they were citizens of either El Salvador or the United States? Diaspora studies highlight the in-between spaces, produced through multiple exclusions, as spaces of possibility. In this third space, in Salvadoran students' consciousness of their in-between status, the possibilities for new forms of belonging and becoming arise. As Siu (2005) writes, "Diasporic citizenship . . . suggests marginality, difference, and lack of full belonging to any one nation-state, yet it also holds out the possibility of creativity, innovation, and perseverance that come with occupying this intersection" (6). We see creativity and resistance in the critique by students at the Lincoln School, who first recognized the cultural politics that positioned them as *better than* their non-English-speaking Salvadoran peers but *less than* white U.S. citizens and then rejected these terms for their own identities. We also see resistance and creative hybridity in the students in El Rio, who embraced homeboy expressive culture and discussed U.S. politics while insisting on their right to stay and contribute to the advancement of their community.

Without suggesting what policy changes might be necessary to make possible the alternative futures for which they long, we argue for increased attention to these new subjectivities in the diaspora as a space for new citizen formations. Citizenship education in El Salvador and for migrant youth in the United States might engage students' diasporic subjectivities as sources of critical insight, imaginative possibility, and civic responsibility. Students in both places are longing for ways to make sense of the position of their homes against a backdrop of global inequality. At a time when neoliberal narratives of progress and upward mobility call for migration abroad, it may be that educators have a more urgent responsibility to engage students in exploring their local environment. The eagerness with which students in both schools talked to us about the meaning of Salvadoran citizenship in the context of migration underscores the importance of this topic to them and the need to incorporate it into the formal educational process. Likewise, Susan Coutin's (2016) research documents the hunger of Salvadoran youth in the United States to connect to their Salvadoran histories. Placing our findings together with hers, our research suggests that students' transnational experiences provide a unique educative context that could be used to counter the dismemberment wrought by migration, neoliberal economic development, and U.S. immigration policies. Students' knowledge of and experience in the diaspora offers educators a unique opportunity to discuss Salvadorans' experiences with inequality at home and abroad and to excavate a shared civic imaginary.

But the responsibility for new citizenship formations must not be shouldered by Salvadoran youth alone. U.S. media discourse has become increasingly violent with regard to Central American migrant youth, with the U.S. president publicly calling unauthorized immigrants "animals."[20] It is our responsibility as researchers to forward humanizing, multidimensional portraits of Salvadoran youth, connected to the historical, economic, and political contexts that shape them (Fine 2018). The experiences of youth in these two Salvadoran communities contest the omissions and distortions of media discourses around unaccompanied Central American minors, officially designated by U.S. law as "unaccompanied alien children." Mainstream media accounts of gang violence and crushing poverty behind the "surge" in child migrants from Central America do not account for how the United States contributed to those conditions, for the extreme hardships faced by immigrants in the United States, or for their yearning to stay in their home countries. Obscured in this coverage are the multiple forms of displacement Salvadoran youth experience in their home communities and the multiple ways they are already inextricably connected to the United States, for better and worse, due to the history of empire. Most importantly, the young people in our research ask us to consider their desire for a life where economic opportunity would not mean giving up El Salvador or a Salvadoran identity. They ask us to listen to their stories, and for the chance to make their own histories and be Salvadoran in a new way.

CHAPTER 3

Negotiating Race and the Politics of Integration

Latinx and Caribbean Youth in Madrid

I N THE 2000S SPAIN became the second most important destination country for immigrants from Latin America after the United States and the first ever European Union country whose immigration is predominantly Latino. By 2012 immigrants made up 14 percent of Spain's population. As a new receiving country for the Latino diaspora, Spain is a stark contrast to the United States. Latino immigration began only in the late 1980s, with the most rapid growth occurring between 2000 and 2008, bringing a significant Latin American presence to Spanish society almost overnight. Spain offers a much more favorable legal and political framework for Latin American immigrants than the United States, privileging Latin American nationals over other groups in its immigration and citizenship laws. However, expectations of smooth integration based on friendly citizenship laws and official rhetoric of cultural, linguistic, and historical similarity between Spaniards and Latin Americans belie complicated and conflicting realities for Latino immigrants in Spain.

In this chapter, we analyze the ways immigrants, race, and cultural difference are treated in popular and policy discourses in Madrid and trace these to transnational racial and cultural constructs stemming from Spain's colonization of Latin America and the Spanish-speaking Caribbean. We draw on fieldwork at two neighborhood-based family service agencies in Malasaña, a central city neighborhood with a high concentration of Latino immigrants where Spanish "social educators" provided after-school programs and services to immigrant youth. A framework of coloniality helps us understand how race was both denied and made salient in everyday interactions with and discourse about immigrant youth. Culturalist explanations for the poor school performance of Latino immigrant youth, along with a discourse that racism in Madrid was diminishing, masked the persistence of racism and reproduced Latino immigrant youth as racialized colonial subjects. In the last section, we explore the role of race and cultural difference through the voices of Latino and Caribbean youths in our study. Drawing on role play, video, identity diagrams, and group dialogues, we illuminate how immigrant young people's lived experiences as racialized minorities conditioned their sense of belonging in Spain, even as discourses of integration rendered them less able to identify, understand, and confront their experiences of racism.

The Context of Latin American Immigration in Spain

Before the economic crisis hit in 2008, Latin American immigrants to Spain encountered a growing economy and comparatively friendly immigration policies, especially after the election of the Socialist Party in 2004.[1] In 2005 the Socialist government under President Zapatero initiated the largest legalization campaign ever in Europe, legalizing nearly six hundred thousand unauthorized immigrants, and designated a large fund for integration programs, emphasizing education (Kleiner-Liebau 2009). Latin Americans have been favored in Spain's immigration laws due to the historical relationship between the regions and presumed cultural and linguistic similarities that facilitate integration; they are eligible to apply for citizenship after only two years of legal stay in the country, compared to ten years for other immigrant groups. Spanish political discourse about migration and foreign policy reflects a commitment to Latin America and a sense of cultural kinship that stems from Spain's colonial past on the continent. For example, in a speech given in January 2005 to the Spanish community in Argentina, President Zapatero defined Spain as being both European and Ibero-American (Kleiner-Liebau 2009, 151). Conservative Popular Party politicians also referenced Latin Americans' cultural proximity to Spain as a reason why they were more easily integrated compared to other immigrant groups such as Moroccans (176). One member of Congress predicted in 2005 that "within one generation . . . they [Latin Americans] will be indistinguishable [from Spaniards]" (176). This can also be read as a normative statement that immigrants *should* become indistinguishable, that successful integration requires the erasure of difference.

However, the economic crisis in 2008, which brought Spain one of the highest unemployment rates in the Eurozone, abruptly ended the era of government spending on immigrant integration and dramatically changed the socioeconomic context for integration. Immigrants were the hardest hit by the crisis because they were concentrated in the most vulnerable positions in the economy—domestic service, hotel and restaurant service, and construction. By 2013 the unemployment rate was 24.8 percent for native Spaniards and 36.4 percent for immigrants (Actis 2013). In 16 percent of immigrant households all of the breadwinners (economically active people) were unemployed. In 2010, 43.5 percent of foreign-born adults in Spain were living in poverty (Actis 2013).

The crisis ushered in an era of austerity and government cutbacks that eliminated many public services just when they were most needed. The integration fund for immigrants that had been lavishly funded from 2005 to 2008 was steadily cut until it finally disappeared in 2012 (González-Enríquez 2014). The staff in the agencies we worked with directly felt the impact of these cuts, finding themselves with more work and fewer resources. The family service agency that was our primary research site depended heavily on public funds from the municipal government of Madrid that had been channeled from the government's integration fund. Since the advent of the crisis, its annual budget had been reduced sevenfold. In 2012 one of the first moves of the new Popular Party government was to eliminate health care for unauthorized immigrants, a social right they had enjoyed since 2000. The move reflected a growing public hostility toward immigrants. In fact, the crisis accelerated what had already been a steady trend since 2000 of deteriorating public attitudes toward immigrants (Actis 2013; González-Enríquez 2014).

After the intense immigration growth in the early 2000s, the years after the crisis saw a leveling off, and by 2013 the talk in Madrid was of return migration—that is, Latin American families returning to their countries of origin after failing to find (or regain) work. However, data from the municipal registers in 2013 showed that there was not a generalized or massive exodus and that not all groups were leaving (Actis 2013). For example, Dominicans, Peruvians, and Venezuelans maintained their numbers, while Ecuadorians, Argentineans, and Bolivians saw significant drops from 2008 to 2013. In a further twist, as the crisis deepened, many native Spaniards began emigrating to Latin America. In 2012 the number of people who left Spain for Latin America exceeded the number of Latin Americans who migrated to the European Union, according to the International Organization for Migration, and this trend continued through 2014.[2] It remains to be seen how renewed Spanish emigration to Latin America will affect views of Latin American immigrants in Spain or the experience of the Spanish Latino diaspora.

Latinx Students in Spanish Schools

In the wake of the crisis, growing concern has focused on the second generation—immigrants' children born in Spain or brought there as young children—who are coming of age in a time of poor economic prospects. How these children fare in schools has been a chief preoccupation of policymakers and researchers because it is seen as an indicator of the state's ability to integrate them. Much like in the United States, researchers in Spain have documented a significant educational achievement gap between immigrant and nonimmigrant students (Aguado 2009; Gibson and Carrasco 2009; Lucko 2011). The children of Latin American immigrants are among the worst performing.[3] Recent qualitative research has pointed to the institutional contexts that produce these patterns of failure, highlighting factors such as tracking and segregation of immigrant students, unchallenging classes, poorly trained teachers, and enduring ethnic stereotypes (Gibson and Carrasco 2009; Aguado 2009; del Olmo 2010; Franzé 2008; Poveda et al. 2012; Lucko 2011). Latino students in Spain are overrepresented in compensatory and vocational education programs and underrepresented in academic tracks that lead to university and they are far more likely to drop out of school (Poveda, Jociles, and Franzé 2009, 2014; Franzé et al. 2011; Gibson and Carrasco 2009). Such research challenges the supposedly integrative role of educational policies and programs (Franzé et al. 2011; Ríos-Rojas 2014).

Also challenging assumptions about the smooth integration of Latino immigrant students, a growing body of ethnographic research highlights the role of Spanish educators' discourses about Latin Americans and deficit views of Latin American cultures in shaping Latino students' poor school trajectories (Poveda, Jociles, and Franzé 2009, 2014; Franzé et al. 2011; Lucko 2011; Ríos-Rojas 2014). According to a multiyear ethnographic study of a majority-Latino high school in Madrid, teachers held a series of beliefs about Latin American students in which their "cultural origin" played a central explanatory role in their school performance. Latin American students were described as culturally and cognitively deprived. Educational placement decisions were rationalized based on perceptions of linguistic deficiencies (due to the different forms of Spanish they spoke), assumptions about inferior schooling in Latin American countries, and speculations that students' families and their values did not support educational achievement (Poveda, Jociles, and Franzé 2009, 2014; Franzé et al. 2011). These views persist in spite of the fact that research on Ecuadorian immigrant parents in Spain shows that they highly value their children's education and that they immigrated in order to give their children better educational opportunities (Moscoso 2009). Another ethnographic study in Madrid showed that stereotypes circulating in schools portrayed Latino immigrants as poor and uneducated; culturally inferior and socially backward; and illegal, dangerous, and a threat to social cohesion in the country (Lucko 2011).

In her ethnographic study of Ecuadorian immigrant teens and Spanish education professionals in Madrid, Jennifer Lucko (2014) describes the ways a pervasive discourse of integration was interpreted by teachers and internalized by immigrant students. In their understanding of integration, Spanish teachers and professionals viewed Latin American immigrant students' cultural differences as deficits that needed to be overcome in order to integrate into Spanish culture and society. Responsibility for integration thus fell on the immigrant students, who had to show themselves willing to change their behaviors and leave their parents' ways behind. Lucko refers to a Spanish social worker who told her in an interview that "the Latino culture is not as 'evolucionado' [evolved] as the Spanish culture. She elaborated that Latinos are very religious, sexist, and have many children—unlike Spanish people" (149). Such examples of "cultural racism" reveal the enduring influence of colonial hierarchies on the incorporation of migrants from former colonies who are "colonial/racialized subjects of empire" (Grosfoguel, Cervantes-Rodríguez, and Mielants 2008, 10).

Another ethnographic study at a Barcelona institute similarly found that educators used "culture-based" explanations for the underachievement of South American students, feared that Latin American students would join gangs, and associated Latin American students' self-segregation in the school with "ghettoes" (Ríos-Rojas 2014). In these studies, expressions of Latin American solidarity or ethnic identity were perceived by educators as threats to both school achievement and social cohesion. Latino students are thus given the message that their "cultures" and ethnic identities are obstacles to their school success and integration, even as they are exposed to official discourses that portray Spain as an open and tolerant society that welcomes immigrants. As Ríos-Rojas (2014) writes, the lives of immigrant youths in Spain are shaped by "this fundamental tension between the welcoming of difference and a more tacit nationalist impulse to discipline difference in the interest of preserving the nation" (3). We can make sense of this tension within a framework of coloniality, which reminds us that "migrants arrive in metropolitan spaces that are always 'polluted' by colonial history—that is, a colonial imaginary, colonial knowledges, a racial/ethnic hierarchy linked to a history of dominance, and subordination in the interstate system that can be traced to empire building and colonial relations" (Grosfoguel, Cervantes-Rodríguez, and Mielants 2008, 8).

This colonial imaginary undergirds concerns for national integration that require cultural assimilation—for the good of the immigrant and the greater good of Spanish society. Walter Mignolo (2011) explains the logic of coloniality: "The rhetoric of modernity is a rhetoric of salvation . . . but in order to implement what the rhetoric preaches, it is necessary to marginalize or destroy whatever gets in the way of modernity" (xxiv–xxv). Colonial subjects were produced by an epistemic system that classified them as deficient (*anthropos,* who are at once barbarian and traditional), and "Two choices are given to the anthropos: to assimilate or to be cast out" (82). "Epistemically disavowed colonial subjects" are now migrants in Western Europe and the United States. The children of these migrants occupy a special place in discourses of integration. As we will show, the children of immigrants are simultaneously objects of hope and fear: hope for their potential to integrate, which is seen as greater than their parents' due to their exposure to "European" society and values from a young age; and fear where they continue to segregate and remain visible in their difference. In both cases, they are objects of remediation and intervention by education professionals who seek to transform them into acceptable subjects of the nation-state.

In her ethnography of Muslim immigrant youth in Denmark, Reva Jaffe-Walter (2016) argues that Danish integration policies enact "technologies of concern" that target immigrant communities and families as sites of state discipline and intervention. These technologies, "everyday practices of coercive assimilation," are aimed at separating immigrant youths from their communities, values, and cultures, which are seen as intolerant and oppressive, and transforming them into "enlightened liberal subjects" (64). According to Danish integration policies and discourse, Muslim immigrant enclaves and immigrants who insist on maintaining visible differences (e.g., by wearing the hijab, speaking languages other than Danish, refusing to eat pork) are examples of integration failures and pose a serious threat to Danish society. Like the Spanish teachers in the ethnographies cited above, teachers in Jaffe-Walter's study attributed the challenges of immigrant students to their families' traditions and cultural values and their residential segregation. Schooling was a key mechanism of integration that provided Muslim students with "proximity" to Danish students. In this context there could be no Muslim student clubs or organizations, and "any attempts by Muslim students to gather were treated as a threat. . . . At Engby School it was understood to be a problem when Muslim students were together in groups without ethnic Danish students" (129).

These discourses of integration hold immigrant communities and their cultures accountable for their own integration or failure to integrate, obscuring the role of social and structural barriers including racial discrimination, socioeconomic inequality, and narrow notions of national belonging for immigrant youth (Jaffe-Walter 2016; Lucko 2014). According to Grosfoguel, Cervantes-Rodríguez, and Mielants (2008), culturalist explanations for migrants' failure or success are central to "new forms of 'antiracist racisms' in the core of the capitalist world economy that . . . justify the supremacy of certain groups and states vis-à-vis the majority of the world's population" (10). Because of their ability to reinforce and justify the former colonizer's domination, we should pay careful attention to these discourses.

In Madrid in 2013, in the wake of a dramatic rise in the immigrant population and an economic crisis that left one out of every four adults unemployed, the public discourse about immigrants reflected broad social anxieties about immigrant integration and cultural diversity. The prospect of a disaffected immigrant underclass instilled fear of unrest, constructing immigrant youth who had failed to assimilate as a threat to peaceful democratic society. Media reports of high rates of school failure, Latino youth gangs, and immigrant crime stoked fears of immigrant youth as dangerous cultural Others. A typical headline from February 2013 read, "33 Members of Two Latino Gangs Detained in Madrid."[4] Another, more alarmist headline announced, "Gang Members Getting Younger" with subheads reading "The police detect two violent Latin gangs behind frenzied brawls" and "The groups are recruiting minors as young as 14 years old."[5] Headlines like these reinforced the association of Latino youth with criminality in the public mind. A national opinion poll in 2010 found that 79 percent of interviewees considered the number of immigrants in the country to be high or excessive and 75 percent believed that provisions regulating immigration were more liberal than they should be (González-Enríquez 2014, 348).

Alongside these indicators of public hostility toward immigrants, another discourse circulated among educators, social workers, and scholars who were sympathetic to immigrants. This discourse expressed the optimistic view that Madrid had successfully weathered the challenges of immigration and that immigrants were successfully assimilating. In this narrative the children of immigrants were objects of hope who were leaving their parents' cultures behind and leading the way to a more tolerant and peaceful society. In the following section we analyze examples of this discourse we collected from scholars, policymakers, educators, and social workers during our ethnographic work in Madrid. Our participatory research with teenagers at the two neighborhood agencies, which will be described in detail below, was supplemented by ethnographic interviews and observations in multiple contexts in order to understand the larger public and policy discourses surrounding immigrant youth. We conducted interviews with educators and social workers, attended staff trainings and conferences for educators and social workers on the subject of immigrant youth, and accompanied the youths on field trips and excursions whenever invited. Through the examples presented here, we show that the discourse of positive integration, while self-consciously an effort to counter the discourse of fear and intolerance, ultimately preserved the logic that immigrant youth, in their difference, posed a threat to the nation-state.

Scholarly and Policy Discourses on Integration in Spain

Spaniards anxious about immigrant integration found positive news in the work of sociologist Alejandro Portes and his Spanish colleagues, who conducted the first longitudinal study of immigrant self-identity in Spain, focusing on the second generation.[6] The assumed perspective of the nation-state frames their study: "This second generation poses a series of challenges for receiving societies and governments that must seek to integrate and educate its members to become law-abiding and productive citizens" (Portes, Vickstrom, and Aparicio 2011, 409). To determine the Spanish state's success at meeting this challenge, their quantitative study, based on a survey of roughly seven thousand immigrant teens, inquired whether or not these youths self-identified as Spanish. The study poses a rigid binary between "resilient foreign identities," which they associate with resistance, protest mobilizations, and revolts, and "identification with the host society," which represents, for them, a "definite sign of integration and establishes the psychological basis for pursuing upward mobility within it" (409). Youth who did not self-identify as Spanish are described with negative words such as *alienated, confrontational, reactive, militant, oppositional.* In their first survey in 2008, only one-third of the youths self-identified as Spanish (i.e., answered yes to the question "Do you consider yourself Spanish?"). A follow-up survey reinterviewed 73 percent of the respondents three to four years later (2011–2012), plus a new sample in the same schools. In this follow-up survey 50 percent of the youths self-identified as Spanish and 50 percent did not.

These results made the news in Spain, appearing in *El País,* the country's largest daily newspaper, under the headline "50% of Second Generation Immigrants Feel Spanish," with two subheads: "The largest study carried out in this country confirms a steady advance toward integration" and "Experts attribute this to the absence of large ghettoes."[7] The self-congratulatory tone of the article is barely concealed. A sociologist at the Universidad Nacional de Educación a Distancia interviewed for the article (not one of the study's authors) commented: "It's a success if you consider that the majority of immigrants [their parents] have been here a very short time, barely a decade. The surprising thing is that the children feel Spanish. The second generation is primarily native, born in Spain, but its process of socialization is produced in the family, and the parents are foreigners who behave as such" (our translation). Here, it is assumed that foreign parents socialize their children in ways that would obstruct their integration, making the results of this study "surprising." This sociologist later suggests that "the dispersion" of the immigrant population has contributed to the smooth integration, citing the fact that "we don't have ghettoes or big concentrations [of immigrants] like exist in other countries." Dispersion and proximity with native Spanish people presumably counteract the negative influences of socialization by foreign parents. The authors of the study are similarly optimistic, writing in a Spanish report published online in 2013, "The data lead us to conclude that the children of immigrants have integrated into Spanish youth and the differences between them and the children of natives are diminishing over time."[8] A book published in English elaborates on the support for the assimilationist perspective, concluding that "for an important group of children of immigrants by average age 18, integration into Spanish society is an accomplished fact" (Portes, Aparicio, and Haller 2016, 229).

These scholars' assertions are explicitly aimed at quelling alarmist rhetoric about failed integration: As Portes and Aparicio write, their results "do not support negative or alarming conclusions about the integration of the second generation."[9] However, their nationalist rationale inadvertently supports the conceptual scheme on which such alarmist discourse rests. The absence of threat is predicated on national identification and the "diminishing" of differences between the children of immigrants and the children of natives over time. Immigrants who reject Spanish identification and embrace their cultural and ethnic identities are therefore to be viewed with suspicion because there is no alternative to the *either* Spanish *or* oppositional binary.

The open condemnation of immigrant concentration as "ghettoes" by scholars and policymakers negatively sanctions immigrants' cultures and ethnicities without resorting to overt racism. Significantly, in talk of ghettoes and "ghettoization" in Madrid, it is not economic isolation, disenfranchisement, or neglect—qualities usually associated with ghettoes in the United States or France—that are seen as worrisome. Rather, it is cultural and ethnic isolation that are positioned as problematic and inherent threats to social cohesion. This is reflected and codified in Madrid integration policies, as described by Spanish scholars Francisco Velasco Caballero and María de los Angeles Torres (2015). First, the authors acknowledge the close relationship between the discourse of positive integration and the discourse of fear, asserting, "Fear-driven debate about immigrants in Spain has in fact resulted in programs to bring them into the national cultural landscape" (5). In their analysis, local (municipal) governments in Spain are highly involved in integration policies that "seek to foster a high level of social coexistence and social cohesion between immigrants and citizens" by providing social assistance and preventing social exclusion. In the area of education, integration is conceived as an "adequate distribution of the immigrant population among schools," in opposition to "ghettoization," which is defined simply as "a high concentration of immigrants in certain schools" (206–7). The mere concentration of immigrant students, regardless of levels of conflict or inequality, is seen as a threat to social cohesion: "The existence of schools where, for example, the student body has more than 50% immigrants is a social issue that affects us all—if there is no integration today, there will be no social cohesion tomorrow" (197). Therefore, the major municipal task regarding integration policies through schooling is the prevention of segregation, such as through policies to decouple residence from school attendance, to avoid "the replication of urban ghettos in schools" (205).

Notably absent from this framework are policies that seek to counter hatred and intolerance, xenophobia, discrimination, and economic inequality. Dispersion is prioritized above all else: providing resources to "concentrated immigrant schools would not help future social cohesion" (207). Thus, in municipal integration policies immigrant students are positioned as threats to social cohesion by their mere presence and numbers, and above all, as a problem for the nation-state: "Immigrant minors' integration presently constitutes one of the biggest challenges of the capacities of our social state" (197). The urgency of dispersion, reflected in both educators' discourse and municipal integration policies, poses cultural diversity as something that requires management and discipline (Ríos-Rojas 2014); it must be noted that this mirrors the cultural racism undergirding Spain's colonization of the Americas and the resulting displacement and dispersion of colonized peoples.

The Conference on "Crisis"

The construction of immigrant youth as objects of fear was on full display in a two-day conference we attended early in our fieldwork, titled "The Challenge of Big Cities in the Context of Crisis: Present and Future of the Children of Immigration." Sponsored by the Madrid municipal government's Department of Public Safety and attended primarily by police and social workers who worked with immigrants, the conference aimed to provide information on the children of immigrants that would facilitate the goals of *convivencia* (living together) and *seguridad* (safety) in Madrid. As invited speakers presented various perspectives on immigrant conflict and revolt and ways to avoid it, immigrant youth were depicted as potentially violent and dangerous.

In the most direct example of this, a speaker from the research unit of the Department of Public Safety presented a study of Moroccan immigrant youth that was commissioned, she explained, because of "concern of the chief of police of Madrid that the Paris riots of 2005 could be replicated in our territory."[10] The goal was to study the "protagonists of those riots

(Moroccan youth) in the neighborhood with the highest percentage of these youth in our city." Here, immigrant youth were figured as "protagonists of riots." To our surprise, as the researcher detailed a multitude of ways Moroccan youth in this neighborhood were marginalized and discriminated against, she was heckled by the audience. A murmur of disapproval rose in the room as she spoke, and someone near us called out, "I know that neighborhood, and it is *not* a ghetto." When she finished, there was little applause, and the tension in the room was palpable. As outsiders, it was not initially clear to us what the hecklers were reacting to. Were they objecting to the presenter's sympathetic view of immigrant youth, that she described the barriers to integration as structural rather than cultural? Or that she challenged the image of Madrid as an integrated city without ghettoes? What was apparent was how emotionally charged discussions of integration were, and how close to the surface fears of conflict hovered. With the benefit of hindsight, we see it as an example of resistance to talking about race and racism in relation to immigrant youth, which became very clear in our research. During the rest of the conference a recurring theme mentioned by both speakers and audience members was that Madrid had avoided the major conflicts around immigrants that had afflicted other European cities because it did not have "ghettoes," or immigrant neighborhoods. In the discourse of integration, the condemnation of "ghettoes" achieved the effect of associating any visible display of ethnic identity or cultural expression with potential conflict. Immigrants were not a threat as long as they remained culturally indistinguishable or invisible as immigrants.

Democratic Integration as Cultural Assimilation

The two neighborhood associations in our study, both funded by the municipality of Madrid, aimed to integrate low-income, "at-risk" youth, almost all of whom were children of Latin American immigrants. In the first association and our primary research site, Asociación de Servicios Integrales (ASI), we conducted a "citizenship workshop" consisting of twelve weekly sessions with structured activities designed to provoke reflection and dialogue on issues of identity and citizenship.[11] We introduced poetry written by other migrant students, identity reflection exercises, dramatic role play, and videos to stimulate discussion on complex issues of race, culture, and identity. Several of the participants conducted interviews with immigrants in their families and communities, which we analyzed together. At the end of the workshop, we conducted individual interviews with each of the participating youths (twelve of whom were children of immigrants) and collectively planned and delivered a presentation on our research with five of the youths at the Autonomous University of Madrid. In the second association, we held a series of three focus-group sessions, incorporating some of the activities we used in the workshop. All sessions were recorded and transcribed. In these two locations, through poetry, identity reflection exercises, photography, interviews, and group discussions, we engaged in a process of collective inquiry that shed light on how immigrant young people forge a sense of belonging to multiple communities and how they contend with dominant discourses of integration.

The ASI youth center is a small, two-room space a short block away from a historic plaza that is the bustling heart of Malasaña. The space feels improvised, as if it had been temporarily repurposed to host children, with barely enough room for the tables and chairs that make up the principal furniture. When the director first showed us the center, taking us downstairs into the brick-walled "cave" that houses the program's younger children, she remarked that the space was more appropriate for a bar ("para tomar unas copas") than a children's center. The less than adequate space reflected larger conflicts around the role and place of poor immigrant youth in a bohemian neighborhood that was rapidly gentrifying. While still home to one of Madrid's largest immigrant communities, Malasaña was a popular night spot with new trendy bars opening almost weekly. As pricey bars and restaurants took over public spaces on plazas where immigrant youth had previously gathered, the neighborhood was beginning to feel less and less accessible to low-income families.

The first time we visited the youth center was for a party: a *despedida* (goodbye party) for one of the boys who was moving away. The space was crowded and festive, decorated with balloons and streamers; the walls were covered with photo collages of happy children and teenagers at activities and summer camps. There were bowls of chips set out on the table, and a staff member sat playing music from a laptop computer. Teenagers were chatting animatedly while younger children ran around shrieking. Our first impression of the staff that day was that they were very affectionate with the kids and very preoccupied with manners and behavior. This excerpt from Andrea's field notes is illustrative:

Lina called [the kids] to eat and they all sat around two long tables placed together in the center of the room. Lina and Mateo passed out cups of soda and packaged cupcakes. When Lina invited them to help themselves to chips, she directed them to be polite and not to grab too many. When a couple of boys raised their voices, they were reminded not to shout. A couple of times the staff used humor to highlight their behavior, emphasizing the need for manners and self-discipline. (field notes 9/20/13)

This emphasis could reasonably be expected at an event where young children were present. But further fieldwork revealed that a focus on habits of behavior and "social skills" was central to the programming of ASI, and the disciplining work of the staff extended to the teenagers. An emphasis on personal behavior was part of ASI's vision of promoting *convivencia* (social coexistence or life together), as explained in their annual report of 2013: "With the families and youth we continue working on their habits and skills, emotions and types of thinking that are conducive to peaceful coexistence." This focus reflects the discourse of integration in locating responsibility for "peaceful coexistence" in the behavior, "emotions and types of thinking" of immigrant families. When we first obtained permission to conduct a twelve-week citizenship workshop with the teenagers at ASI, the director and adolescent educator told us that our objectives fit very well with theirs under the area of "social skills."

The slogan of ASI, printed on its organizational materials, is "Construyendo la democracia más pequeña en el corazón de la sociedad" (Building the smallest democracy in the heart of society). Staff at the NGO believed that their organization and other NGOs were playing a vital role in preparing immigrants for citizenship and for a healthy democratic life together. In their view, this required overcoming deficits in students' cultural and family backgrounds and countering the isolation of immigrant communities by facilitating their connection to mainstream institutions, cultural resources, and public space. These beliefs and strategies essentialized immigrant cultures and censored cultural expression, and at the same time obscured the role of racial discrimination and socioeconomic hardship in immigrant young people's lives. Negative views of students' languages, cultures, ties to home countries, and ethnic identities, along with the hopeful insistence that immigrant youth were assimilating, reproduced immigrant youth as objects of intervention and discipline.

Overcoming Cultural Deficits

Students' families and cultures were explicitly targeted for intervention in the program materials and expressed goals of both youth-serving NGOs in our study. The program goals of Asociación para Familias, Educación y Paz (AFEPA) read: "We will develop interventions that combat social marginalization in pockets of poverty in the province of Madrid, *especially in the family environment*" (emphasis added)."[12] Both NGOs received funding from a municipal government institute under a program called Infancia en Dificultad Social (INDIS; Childhood in Social Difficulty), which staff explained was for *menores en riesgo social* (at-risk youth). When describing their clients and their families, staff members used the language of "risk factors" and described them exclusively in deficit terms. We were told that the youth faced extreme academic challenges and "delays" that were attributed to family and cultural problems. For example, when describing one Brazilian youth who had hearing impairment, the director of ASI told us, "The mother speaks terribly." Enrique asked, "You mean she speaks Spanish poorly?" The director clarified yes, the mother speaks Brazilian Portuguese. She then said that school professionals have been imploring the mother to speak Spanish at home with her children, but she won't (or can't). In this example, the Spanish language was positioned as "language," ignoring other languages; a mother's inability to speak Spanish with her children was blamed for her child's academic difficulties.

In the ASI annual work plan of 2014, students' "culture" appears several times as a "risk factor"; for example: "57% [of the youths] have difficulties at school, primarily for cultural reasons and difficulties in relating to teachers." Such explanations conflated academic, economic, and "cultural" problems. The director of AFEPA, explaining in an interview how students are referred to her program, said, "The referrals tend to come from social services or from the schools. Above all it is the school where they detect an academic problem, which is always related to a family problem."

At ASI, Latina girls in particular were seen as having culturally determined gender roles that prevented them from benefiting from ASI training. In conversations with Lina, the educator, and in the ASI program documents, students' "cultural roles" are positioned as an obstacle to the program's goal of promoting gender equality. Lina shared her frustration that activities designed to prompt the girls to think critically about gender roles had not been successful. She explained, sighing, that unequal gender roles "are so normal to them" that they don't notice them. The ASI work plan for 2014, under the heading "Protection Factors Considered," notes: "The youth know information about risky sexual practices, how to avoid them, and what resources to access if necessary through workshops carried out in [a partner association], *but, in the case of the girls, in their relations they assume cultural roles*" (emphasis added). "Cultural roles" are here set in opposition to "information" and "resources" that would keep young people safe. As scholars of liberal democratic nationalism have observed, framing minority groups as being controlled or dominated by culture and "us" (the dominant group) as *having* culture is a key strategy in the depoliticization of conflict and inequality (Brown 2006; Jaffe-Walter 2016; Abu El-Haj 2015). Jaffe-Walter writes, "The general feeling in Denmark is 'we Danes' have culture while culture has 'them' [Muslim immigrants]" (2016, 57).

Similarly, a social worker in another Madrid agency told us, "The characteristics of the Latino culture lead girls to probably have sexual relations very early, early pregnancies and . . . even the girls themselves don't understand it but they seem to be pushed by, by, by maybe family or group pressure from the culture, no?" (interview 10/22/13). While later in the interview he described the circumstances of economic desperation that lead some Latina girls to prostitution, where they could earn as much as 600 to 1,000 euros in one night, the tendency toward early sexual relations was explained as a "characteristic of Latino culture."

A concern about poor health and hygiene, central at both organizations, also showed the ease with which educators slipped from recognizing economic challenges to perceiving cultural deficits, speaking of "poor habits" and "social skills." A prime example is found in ASI's annual report from 2013. After mentioning that 60 percent of the families served suffered from unstable income or unemployment, the report went on to describe the conditions in these households as follows:

> In these spaces, we find families with unhealthy habits and behaviors of sleep, primarily, and of hygiene and nutrition. . . . Furthermore we detect that 80% of the families present deficiencies at all levels, which impedes the development of positive parenting skills, revealing . . . a lack of knowledge of the needs of the youth, unclear criteria for establishing norms and boundaries, problems of communication, lack of attention to affective needs, lack of clear criteria which causes inconsistent educational styles. (our translation)

In the work plan for 2014 the word *hygiene* appears nine times, as in the statement that 19 percent of the adolescents enrolled "still have not acquired adequate habits of hygiene." Similarly, at AFEPA, the educator explained to us the purpose of the afternoon snack: "In the afternoon we have snack, as you saw the other day, where we work a little bit on that, on habits, habits of nutrition and above all of washing your hands, picking up, being more autonomous." The preoccupation with hygiene and social skills suggests that these educators saw their job as a civilizing mission reminiscent of colonial hierarchies of civilized/primitive peoples.

In the current neoliberal context, this approach suggests "the construction of citizenship as a private practice of self-improvement" (Kwon 2013, 16) or "personal responsibility citizenship" (Westheimer and Kahne 2004). Writing about immigrant youth–serving nonprofits in the United States, Soo Ah Kwon (2013) argues that nonprofits play an important role in "civilizing" youth for neoliberal citizenship. Viewing "uncivil youth" as a social threat, nonprofits have developed a tradition of youth-management strategies to improve young people's lives and enable them to become worthy individual citizen-subjects (16). Her chapter "Civilizing Youth against Delinquency" locates youth-serving nonprofits in the United States in a long history of programs created to transform poor, marginalized, immigrant and ethnic youth into worthy American citizens. While Spain does not share this history, Kwon's analysis of nonprofits as a "technology of neoliberal citizenship" is relevant to youth-serving NGOs in Madrid. She contends that "nonprofit organizations are called upon to regulate as well as to empower 'at-risk' young people to exercise responsibility and self-government in what I call an affirmative governmentality" (9). There are two parts of this argument that are useful for understanding immigrant youth in Madrid. The first relates to the ways these programs are designed for young people to internalize the mechanisms of their own control and regulation (drawing on Foucault's concept of governmentality). The second has to do with the close relationship between intervention strategies designed to reform (and enable) young people, and programs designed to prevent (and control) them from becoming "risky," uncivil subjects (40). In Kwon's analysis, these are two sides of the same logic of social control. Likewise, the discourses that construct immigrant youth in Spain as objects of hope (successfully integrating, not displaying difference) and objects of fear (still segregating, clinging to difference) are two sides of the same logic that poses immigrant youth in their difference as threats to the nation-state.

In the next section we describe how this becomes apparent in educators' and social workers' talk about segregation, integration, and Latino immigrant youth.

Preventing Ghettoes

In the narratives of the educators and social workers we interviewed, a key criteria for successful integration and a healthy democratic life together (*convivencia*) was the absence of ethnic conflicts and the absence of "ghettoes." This meant avoiding any kind of ethnic association or emphasis on ethnic identification. The director of ASI, Alexa, was critical of previous government initiatives that had created immigrant associations. During the period of Socialist government–financed integration, the Madrid municipal government had sponsored ethnic associations for immigrants known as *centros de encuentro y participación para inmigrantes* (CEPIs) focused on national-origin groups (e.g., Centro Hispano-Colombiano, Centro Hispano-Peruano). By 2013 these were being eliminated due to budget cuts, but in Alexa's view, they had "generated their own ghettoes" (interview 12/18/13). By contrast, ASI's model aimed to mix immigrant youths with others because, as the educator Lina explained, "the last thing that was going to help those kids was a ghetto. That they had to live a normalized situation, with other kids their age and that there be diversity, because that was really what was going to help the people with most difficulty to get out of there" (interview 11/19/13). In practice, very few nonimmigrant youths came to ASI (there were only three out of fourteen in the group we worked with), but it is significant that Lina emphasized the importance of their presence. Helping immigrant youths "to get out of there," to get out of ethnic and economic isolation, was a primary goal.

Both Alexa and Lina explained in their interviews that a major part of their role in preparing citizens was helping young people access the resources of the city so they would not be confined to their *barrio* (neighborhood), by teaching them to use the metro, public libraries, parks, plazas, and museums. We observed this in practice during several field trips, activities, and excursions that took place in public spaces. These activities increased the presence and participation of immigrant youth in the city's public spaces, but it is important to note that they were not opportunities for immigrant youths to display publicly their cultural or ethnic identities or to *be visible as immigrants*. In fact, because the intention was to help immigrant youths blend into the city, their unique identities and experiences as immigrants were often silenced. The following example from early in our fieldwork is illustrative.

In early October Andrea accompanied a group of students from ASI on a field trip to the Thyssen Museum, one of Madrid's premier cultural institutions. The field trip had been arranged in coordination with a senior center in Malasaña, to bring youths and senior citizens together around art. The five youths who had volunteered to attend were all girls, all of them visibly dark-skinned next to the six light-skinned elderly ladies from the senior center. The long, dark, and frizzy hair of the young women was also a stark contrast to the cropped hair of the elderly ladies. They greeted each other cordially, if shyly, and without further conversation. Together with Lina, the group accompanied a museum educator, Tomás, on an orientation tour of selected works. As we stopped in front of paintings, Tomás engaged the group in discussion by asking what each person saw in the picture. He took their interpretations and expanded on them, juxtaposed them to each other's, probed with further questions, and got everyone involved. The following excerpt from Andrea's field notes highlights one discussion that stood out:

> During discussion of the first painting, *Grand Central Station,* which was a metaphor of the city, Tomás asked who would leave Madrid if they could (to live elsewhere). Only one of the six senior citizens raised her hands, but almost all of the five youths did. After one of the seniors spoke eloquently about how Madrid is in her blood, that she misses it and longs for it when she is away, Tomás asked her how long she has lived in Madrid, and she said 51 years (out of 65). He said that people who have many years of experience in a place carry memories of their past with them, while people who are sixteen, he indicated to Luisa (after asking how old she was), look to the future. He did not acknowledge that the youths might have memories of another place, another city in another country; that perhaps their attachment or sense of belonging to Madrid was fraught for other reasons besides their youth. It made me wonder about the silences around immigrant background. (Luisa and Mariela were born in Spain to a Dominican mother; Esther, Milena, and Isabela are all immigrants.) (field notes 10/5/13)

During this activity, which otherwise drew beautifully on life experience and clearly engaged everyone, differences in the cultural backgrounds of the senior citizens and the youths were flatly avoided, even when they were highly relevant. We did not interview Tomás to find out whether he intentionally avoided marking students' immigrant backgrounds or it simply did not occur to him, but regardless of his intention, the effect was to erase the young people's immigrant experiences.

When analyzed with educators' and social workers' narratives about positive integration in Madrid, the museum activity becomes part of a narrative about Madrid in which the fragile social peace depends on the invisibility of cultural difference. The educators and social workers we interviewed considered the absence of ethnic conflict to be key to healthy social cohesion. They believed that Madrid had made progress on this because there was a lesser level of conflict in 2013 than there had been in the late 1990s and early 2000s. In 2005 the Socialist minister of labor and social affairs said of the challenge of immigrant integration, "The Spanish society can be proud of the way it has responded to this challenge. There have been a few outbursts of rejection, but fortunately they have been overcome" (Kleiner-Liebau 2009, 174). This point of view reflects the optimistic narrative we heard in Madrid, that the problems with regard to immigrants had largely been resolved, that the worst period of conflict was over, and that Madrid was exceptional in comparison to other European cities because of its lack of ghettoes. The discourse of successful integration, we will show, was a direct reaction to the discourse of fear; it aimed to reframe immigrant youth as successfully assimilated and Spanish-identified, and in the process, it rendered cultural difference problematic.

Conflicts Were in the Past

In the narratives of educators and social workers we interviewed, the integration of immigrants in Madrid was described in the context of a recent past when conflicts around immigrants were more prominent. Alexa, the director of ASI, acknowledged that issues of cultural diversity and conflict had been dropped from their programming because "there is not the level of conflicts in this neighborhood" that there used to be. She recalled a period of serious "insults" between ethnic groups in the late 1990s when they did concentrated work on the problem, but now, she said, discussions of cultural diversity were limited to "foods of the world" and Christmas celebrations. "We have almost like accepted that the center [of Madrid] is Latino, and okay, we're all equal here, and come on, we're going to stop [talking about difference] . . . but because conflict is not assumed, and there was a time when it was assumed." These narratives painted a picture of forward progress in which the worst period of conflict and xenophobia was safely in the past. They also suggest that cultural differences are important or worth addressing only when there are conflicts.

Lina, the adolescent educator at ASI, contrasted the group of teenagers we worked with and the group that that had been at ASI when she first arrived eight years earlier. Back then, she said, immigration was new and conflicts were common. "There was a stronger racism" and "the kids had identity conflicts" as well as conflicts among themselves. The sudden presence of immigrants in the neighborhood and the city was a big change ("It was a very big shock, I remember") but now everybody is used to seeing immigrants, "There is a much greater integration today," and it is better in Malasaña than in other parts of the city (field notes 11/12/13).

A social worker at a major Madrid agency, Alberto, likewise recalled a period of intense anti-immigrant sentiment in the late 1990s as he explained his agency's current choice to avoid the word *immigrant* and instead use *neighbors*. Relegating conflict and discrimination to the past was a key strategy in the discourse of successful integration, as was the explicit attempt by interlocutors to distance *themselves* from the anti-immigrant rhetoric that was still prevalent; as Alberto said, "We want to dilute it somehow."

Countering the discourse of fear and intolerance required reframing immigrant youth as well assimilated, meaning both not discriminated against and culturally similar. Alberto insisted that Latino immigrant youth in particular were well accepted: "There is a very extensive process of integration. I mean, native kids from long-standing Spanish families, they don't look strangely at a Dominican, an Ecuadorian, a Peruvian. . . . They don't see him as strange, they don't see him as different." Such sentiments revealed a vision of integration that erased cultural differences and ethnic distinctions in the name of equality, like the colorblind discourse of educators in the United States (Pollock 2004). Alberto believed immigrant youths' experiences in the educational system had prepared them to be models of integration:

I mean, we always say the youth, adolescents, children, adolescents are an example in this sense. But because they have lived a framework that is . . . that is normally the educational, where there is a context that is very neutral, equal for everyone, where the relationship is different and where other links can be forged that aren't so burdened with stigmas.

In the educational context, he asserted, immigrant youth were losing the "stigmas" of their ethnic identities. As further evidence of forward progress toward integration, Alberto believed immigrant youths experienced discrimination not from other youths, only from adults: "So the young people maybe don't . . . among themselves they don't experience it. . . . They experience it only when they relate to adults. . . . Like for example when they are applying for a job. This discrimination for being Ecuadorian or for being Latino or for being Moroccan in regards to work, yes is starting to happen a little bit." Lina at ASI similarly expressed that the presence of immigrants had become "normalized" compared to the recent past:

I do see that [the immigration issue] has calmed down a lot, 'cause it was really hard during the arrival . . . [now] *people have gotten used to living together, they normalize it.* There are still some sites where they [immigrants] are really clustered. If you go a bit to the periphery and see, the Ecuadorians set up their thing in the park to play volleyball and their stall and such . . . then you go on a Sunday to a park and you see families and at another park you see only Latinos with their thing, their history assembled there. *So I think in some places integration has still not. . . .* [trails off] (emphasis added)

In Lina's view, while immigration was accepted, the visible presence of Latinos hanging out with their own in some areas was not compatible with integration.

Yet these educators also explicitly denied that immigrant youth could feel anything but Spanish or face any unique set of challenges as immigrants. Alberto insisted that the problems facing immigrant youth were the same as those of Spanish youth: "Now the problems that immigrant youth and specifically Latinos have are the same that the Spanish have, which are, I'm studying, do I abandon my studies or keep studying? And . . . what do I do with my life? Because there's no work." In the context of the discourse of successful integration, this denial of differences of race, cultural identity, and marginalization could be seen as an attempt to protect Latino immigrant youth from the stigma of difference. As Alberto explained, using the word *immigrant* is "a way of stigmatizing them."

"They Feel Like They're from Here"

Lina, the adolescent educator at ASI, insisted that the youths in our group identified as Spanish because they had lived in Spain since they were small: "They have lived a more European culture, they feel like they're from here." She added that they might still identify with their cultures of origin in their homes, but not outside: "Maybe in their homes their fathers might be *machista,* but they know that Spanish society is not like that." Lina's only references to Latino culture(s) were about machismo and sexism, which she found difficult to change in her young Latino/a charges: "They carry that [sexism] deep inside, even though like I told you they've grown up here and everything, that from the Latino culture."

Here Lina was struggling with the apparent contradiction that Latino youth *feel Spanish* because they grew up here (they are successfully assimilated) and yet they "carry" cultural differences that are incompatible with Spanish society (they are unassimilable). Lina reconciled this contradiction by relegating culture to the private realm of students' homes—"maybe in their homes, their fathers might be *machista*"—where it will not interfere with their successful integration in the public sphere. Presumably, if it is only their parents who are sexist, those norms will fade away with time.

Leaving aside for the moment Lina's claims that "Spanish society is not [sexist]" and that Latino youths "feel Spanish" (points to which we will return), we take note of the discursive work by which educators located problems of integration within immigrant students' cultures and in the private realm, thereby avoiding recognizing inequalities in the public realm—such as racial and economic inequality—that affected young people's ability to "integrate." It was a colonial mindset that allowed Lina to be reflective about gender inequality in the lives of her students, an area where she believed Spanish society was more advanced than Latino "culture," and seemingly unaware of racial and ethnic inequality. By locating Latino young people's challenges in their homes and cultures, educators reproduced immigrant youth as objects of Spanish benevolence while shielding themselves from claims of racism and insisting that these students were not excluded or marginalized in Spanish society. Ultimately, their focus on immigrant homes and families as sites of intervention and remediation prevented them from seeing or addressing the struggles that immigrant youths faced outside the home. This both protected Spanish society from criticism and made immigrant students more vulnerable to experiences of racialized violence.

Immigrant Youth: Experiences of Racialized Violence

Through a process of group dialogue and individual interviews with immigrant youths at the two neighborhood associations, we learned of many experiences that placed limits on their sense of belonging in Spain. Experiences of racialized violence on the street and at school were a part of daily life for immigrant youth from Morocco, South America, and the Caribbean who had dark skin and African or indigenous features. Police surveillance and harassment were the most common expressions of this violence and shaped young people's understandings of who had the right to belong.

At AFEPA the issue of police racial profiling came up in our first session during a discussion about Spanish stereotypes of immigrants. The students mentioned many negative images Spaniards have of immigrants, including the image of the delinquent, and seventeen-year-old Maritza shared the following story:

> The police stop people who aren't Spanish, and that really bothers me. Because one time I was walking with my boyfriend and he was playing with his iPad, and then they stopped him, they searched him. I said this is outrageous. Then, of course, my friends tell me, "The police gave me a fine of 600 euros for drinking in the street" and whatever, and it is all simply because, of course, normally the Ecuadorians, the Moors [Muslims] and the Moroccans are the ones who get stopped.

In this example Maritza, who was born in Spain to Moroccan immigrant parents, identifies a pattern of racial/ethnic discrimination in which immigrant youth, specifically Ecuadorians, Muslims, and Moroccans, are targeted by police simply for being visible as immigrants. Sometimes the police suspected the youth of being involved in illicit activity and used the occasion to ask them for their documentation (proof of being in the country legally), as in the following example shared by Paula, a seventeen-year-old born in Spain to parents from the Dominican Republic:

> I was in the park one night. And we were all there, Dominicans and such, and the police come and start to shine their flashlight on us. And they say, "What's going on, eh, stop smoking, I know you're smoking." And we weren't doing anything. We were talking. . . . We were talking, on a bench, and listening to music, and they started to search us and [to] the people who didn't have their DNI [national identity card] they started to say, "Next time I'm going to take you in to the station because you're an immigrant without papers." And I was like, how awful. I did not like that.

Although she had her DNI, Paula reacted negatively to a situation in which police were making immigrants feel vulnerable. In Madrid, spending time outdoors in public spaces is a cherished pastime and plazas and parks are often crowded late into the night. The presence of groups of people in the park at night was not unusual as it might be, for example, in the United States. But by asking immigrant youths for their documents, police restricted their right to belong in a public space. Sometimes police asked immigrant youth for their documents when there was no suspicion of illegal activity. Carla shared that she had been stopped two times and asked for her documentation for no other reason than "porque soy morena" (because I'm dark-skinned). Another student, Razena, said that police had come into a Burger King where she was waiting in line and taken out all the Dominicans to the plaza to search them.

It was common for police to stand outside the metro stations in immigrant neighborhoods to stop people coming out of the metro and ask them for ID. Andres, a twenty-four-year-old activist from Ecuador, clearly identified the racial overtones of these "raids": "Me, my mother, all the immigrants in working-class neighborhoods, they would stop us at night and ask us for our papers. And if someone didn't have indigenous features, they would let them pass." Elena, a thirty-year-old activist from Venezuela, explained the raids this way: "It's for racist motives. They say now that it's because of the rates of criminality, and whatever. But it is the criminalization of immigration, and it's doubly racist. . . . A police stands in front of you. Police, man, Western, white, who intimidates you. Woman, migrant, in a poor neighborhood. I mean, we are talking about multiple distinct discriminations" (interview 11/24/13). Elena said she had been stopped only twice, and felt fortunate compared to her Bolivian friends who were stopped frequently, but she remembered them as traumatic experiences. "I've experienced that myself in the flesh, a couple of times. I felt . . . horrible, like a nonhuman."

While the teenagers in the youth associations did not use the terms *racism* or *discrimination* to describe the treatment they received from police, a point we will return to later, they identified patterns of racial profiling and noted these as unjust. Encounters with the police often became physically violent, and this made a lasting impression on both victims and witnesses. Immediately after Paula shared her experience of being searched in the park, Maritza told the story of two friends who tried to sneak into the metro on one ticket:

> Then the guards caught them. . . . They didn't say anything to the girl, but to the boy, because he had Ecuadorian features, Latin American features, they said, "Documentation, show me your documentation" and such, and you know there are cameras in the metro, and they got away from the cameras and said to him, "Kneel down and get like this." He got down and they started to kick him.

In this case, when the young people were caught in fare evasion, the police took the opportunity to teach them a lesson by using physical violence. By moving away from the surveillance cameras, they stepped outside public view and the law. It was not lost on Maritza that the boy was really being punished for having "Ecuadorian features." Such experiences of police brutality were not uncommon.

Police abuses of immigrants, particularly the raids in public spaces, became the target of an activist movement in Madrid called Brigadas Vecinales (Neighborhood Brigades). Brigadas Vecinales were groups of volunteers who appeared at locations of raids to monitor police behavior and report any abuses. The group also collected data on, publicized, and denounced racially motivated police harassment. Their report of November 2012 to October 2014 (covering the period of our research) concluded that "racist raids have continued in a massive, daily, and habitual form. They are based on identifications that have no relation to the activities of the people who are asked for documentation, but are prompted by their physical features."[13] During our study we tried without success to bring a volunteer from Brigadas to speak to the youth in the associations. In general, the teenagers were not aware of any rights they had in encounters with the police; they believed they had no choice but to "keep quiet."

At ASI we showed a video excerpt about Brigadas Vecinales to the youth during one of our workshop sessions. They had never heard of the movement and were not aware of anyone who fought for the rights of immigrants. Although we had technical difficulties with the projector (the sound was not working), the images alone were powerful enough to spark lively discussion of police raids and racial profiling. Watching the police harass immigrants on the screen, Marilyn, a seventeen-year-old Ecuadorian, remarked, "That happens all the time." When we switched off the video, she shared a story of her brother going out to buy rice for their mother. As he walked home carrying the bag of rice in his arms, the police stopped him to see if there were drugs in the bag. Her mother saw the incident through the window and leaned out to shout at the police to leave her son alone, that he was doing nothing wrong. Immediately, two other girls shared similar stories of police confrontations. This was the first time the issue of police harassment had come up in this group, and it was our tenth session. Significantly, some of the youths pointed out that it was not only immigrants who were targeted by the police, but young people in general.

Yet, their own families' experiences challenged the notion that the police were targeting youth in general. Isabela was a fourteen-year-old from Venezuela who had been present at the group discussion but had not spoken. During her interview, she described an experience she had had with her mother, brothers, and uncle at a shopping mall, where they were stopped by the police and asked for their documentation. Isabela shared this story in response to the question "What would you most like to change about Spanish society?"; she answered, "Well, I guess Spanish people's way of thinking about immigrants." She said that they had their DNIs with them and were able to show them to the police, but as they walked away, "I heard the police say that they didn't trust immigrants, and that's why they stopped us" (interview 12/3/13). She also didn't like that they had asked her mother for her documents "in a bad way," which made her feel bad. Her story was not the only one we heard of families being followed in stores and asked for ID, and it showed that it was not only teenagers who were persecuted by the police. Young people were particularly sensitive to how their mothers were treated by the authorities.

Unlike the teenagers at AFEPA and the activists Andrea interviewed, who all mentioned immigrants' physical features as a factor in harassment by the police, the teenagers at ASI often downplayed the role of race and the existence of discrimination against immigrants, even when their own experiences showed otherwise. In spite of clear patterns of racial discrimination, the youths did not readily identify as members of a racialized minority or even as immigrants. As ethnographers from the United States, we initially struggled to understand this surprising finding. If we had not paid close attention to the discourse of integration in Madrid and employed multiple methods of engaging the young people's lived experience, we might have gone away concluding that these youths were successfully "assimilated." Instead, we realized that direct questioning of students at one moment in time did not reveal the complex and nuanced thinking that emerged from layers of multimodal data collection, reflection, and dialogue. A pattern of conflicted identities, denial of racism and discrimination, and painful experiences of exclusion suggests that young people had internalized the discourse of integration. The discourse that immigrants were assimilating and racism was diminishing both denied immigrant youths' lived experiences of racism and complicated their efforts to understand it, rendering their very identities precarious.

In one group session at ASI early in our research, which was memorable for how poorly it went, the students seemed not to understand or want to respond to our carefully prepared questions about how they identified themselves and how others identified them. When they did respond, their answers were short (one word) or seemed superficial or off-base. Several said they could not answer the questions; others answered in terms of individual personality traits that defined them (e.g., proud, cheerful, rowdy, serious), even when pressed to think of identity groups to which they belonged. Had that been the only data we collected, we might have agreed with the educators and social workers we interviewed that these youths did not identify as immigrants or Latinos but as *individuals*—rowdy, happy, timid, proud—just like any other Spanish teenagers.

But they *weren't* like other Spanish teenagers, as they made abundantly clear in the weeks that followed. As we scratched the surface a more complicated picture emerged. A few weeks after the session described above, a role-play activity allowed us to explore complicated understandings about race and the role of Latinos in Spanish society. Following a brainstorming of the problems facing immigrant youth, the group decided by a vote that racism was the most important problem to explore in a role play.[14] We asked for volunteers to plan a skit about racism in everyday life, and four girls immediately and eagerly volunteered. Susana and Raquel, ages thirteen and fourteen, were born in Venezuela and the Dominican Republic, respectively, and came to Madrid as children. Esther, thirteen, was born in Nigeria, and Maribel, fourteen, was Spanish with no immigrant parent. The role play they created spotlighted the dilemmas faced by Latina youth when their Spanish friends made racially insulting remarks to black immigrants.

Shivering downstairs in the "cave," which was a few degrees colder than upstairs, the girls plotted a scene in which a group of girls insult a black girl while passing her on the street. Esther volunteered and the others agreed that she should play the girl who is insulted. There was some argument about what role Raquel should play, because of her dark skin. Susana and Maribel were adamant that Raquel could not play someone who makes racist insults because a person of color wouldn't insult another person of color. Susana said, "Yo soy chocolate con leche!" (I am chocolate milk [lighter skinned than Raquel]), defending her own right to play a racist. But Raquel insisted on her role: She was to be a friend of the other two girls, but when they started picking on Esther she would drop away from them because she didn't agree with their behavior. She said this was very realistic. Asked whether she would rejoin her friends after they left Esther, Raquel said she would because she would want to make clear that they were still friends. They rehearsed the skit amid much laughter.

Upstairs, they performed their skit in front of the entire group. In the tradition of popular theater that uses drama to explore problems in everyday life, the audience was invited to comment on what they saw. We asked the students, what went on here? Mariela immediately responded, "People give in to peer pressure," seemingly focused on Raquel's role, and then added, "They don't defend [Esther, the victim]." In the ensuing discussion, the initial act of insulting Esther was not called out as the problem. Although Susana and Maribel had openly and shamelessly told Esther to "go back where you came from!," the discussion centered on Raquel's role as the bystander and her responsibility to the victim. Mariela angrily insisted that Raquel should have called out her friends, and said that she would not be friends with someone who insults black people. Raquel, clearly upset, tried to explain that she had distanced herself from the aggressors, but Mariela did not accept this and chided Raquel for insulting

Esther just like the others: "If you insult someone of your same color because your friends have done so, that is not being a friend."

The racism skit and the heated discussion that followed offer insight into the complicated balancing act Latino youth engage in as they try to belong in Madrid. Raquel's decision to play someone who wished to be friends with both white (Spanish) people who insult black people and black people who are insulted, as well as the group's focus on this role as problematic, highlights the emotional burdens of Latino youth who are positioned in between Spanish and immigrant communities. As we will explore further in the next chapter, Latino immigrant youth are often called to mediate between competing worldviews, often with themselves as the subject. As she distanced herself from Susana and Maribel without renouncing them, Raquel aimed to preserve her right to belong and maintain friendships with white Spanish youth while maintaining solidarity with targeted immigrants. Mariela's heated accusations suggest the impossibility of this in-between position. Left unexplored and undisturbed in this scenario were the roles of Susana and Maribel, and Spanish racism itself.

While directly questioning the young people about how they identified themselves and how others identified them did not yield rich information about their group identities, activities such as the role play and identity diagrams offered multiple insights into their experiences as members of racialized groups. In both youth associations we led an activity using the "identity molecule," which asks students to map the different parts of their identity by listing the social groups with which they identify.[15] The first time around, not a single student listed a group identifier based on ethnicity, race, national origin, immigrant status, social class, or gender. Instead, they listed groups such as their neighborhood association, soccer teams, their school or class, their family, a samba band (organized by ASI), the neighborhood, friends, and "friends from the internet." In the second round of the exercise we prompted them to fill in each circle of the molecule according to these five categories: ethnicity or national origin, immigrant or native, gender, social class, and age group. This second version of the molecule, filled out with coaching from us, turned up the following group identifiers: Caribbean, Dominican, Venezuelan, Latino/a, Ecuadorian Spanish, Spanish Arab, Nigerian, immigrant, youth, middle-class, and working-class/poor.[16] On the surface, the initial difficulty students had in identifying themselves as immigrants or members of ethnic groups would seem to support the views of the Spanish educators cited above—that they were no different from Spanish youth. However, students' reflections based on this activity revealed their deep attachments to their ethnic groups.

Students were asked to choose one group that would be a primary identity for them and circle it, and then to "think of an occasion when you felt very proud to be a member of that group" and "think of a painful experience resulting from membership in that group." They were asked to reflect and write quietly in their notebooks, and then to share with the group if they felt comfortable doing so.

Raquel finished quickly and wanted to share. In her ethnicity circle she had written "Dominicana/RD" (Dominican/DR), and she said, beaming, that she had been proud of being Dominican "my whole life." We asked her if she remembered a specific occasion when she felt proud. She said, "Cuando estás con tu gente" (When you're with your people). When we asked her if she had any painful experiences, she answered, "It feels bad when they discriminate against someone for being different or from another place." She gave an example of walking down the street and being passed by an older woman who gave her a dirty look. Andrea asked the group if anyone else had had this experience. Everyone raised their hands. At AFEPA, too, students told us that "la gente mayor nos mira con desprecio" (older people look at us with contempt) (focus group 12/4/13). Anna Ríos-Rojas (2011), writing about the "stares" and "gazes" that immigrant youth in Barcelona receive from others, notes that whether or not they have racist intent, such looks "illuminate the daily sense of surveillance that youth such as [these] experienced in their day-to-day lives" in Spain (79). Though we can't know for sure what caused the woman to look askance at Raquel that day, what matters is that Raquel associated this treatment with her Dominican group membership.

For Raquel, a group identity that was both a source of tremendous pride and the cause of painful discrimination was one with which she was not allowed to identify in the larger Spanish society. That her Dominican identity did not appear at all on the first version of her identity molecule should not surprise us when we consider the discourse of integration that expected immigrants to be assimilated and condemned ethnic communities and visible expressions of ethnic identity. If educators and social workers considered the word *immigrant* stigmatizing, why should we expect young people to embrace it? But for Raquel, it was being with "my people," other Dominicans, that made her feel proud. By banning ethnic identity, the discourse of integration cut immigrant youth off from an important source of pride as well as a way of making sense of discriminatory treatment they experienced.

At AFEPA, in their reflections on a painful experience resulting from group membership in their chosen identity, all three Dominican-origin young women in the group wrote about being disparaged for their skin color. In this group, the identity molecule exercise came on the heels of a rich and lively discussion about belonging and the ways Spanish society communicates to immigrants that they don't belong, in which the young people centered racism without ever using the word *racism*. Carla had begun by saying, "They [Spanish people] despise you because you are another color, from another culture." Others agreed with her, and the following exchange took place:

> PAULA: Don't laugh, one time a boy told me "Negra, there comes the negra" [using a disparaging term for a black person]. And I didn't like it, I didn't like it at all. That, that there's a lot of contempt. There's a lot of contempt from people who believe they are better than people of color or because they think differently from you. . . . I think there continue to be differences, even though they say there aren't, there *are*. . . . And I say, we are so advanced and there are still people who keep thinking like that! I don't like it, I don't think it's right.
>
> SARA: Me neither, in the full-on twenty-first century that there are kids our age thinking that! (focus group 12/4/13)

Juxtaposed with the views of educators and social workers cited above, these can be read as a sharp critique of the discourse of integration. Based on her own experience, Paula challenges a number of aspects of the Spanish collective self-imaginary: the idea that differences between immigrants and nonimmigrants are negligible or disappearing ("there continue to be differences, *even though they say there aren't*"); the idea that racism is also negligible or diminishing; and the idea that Spanish society is a more evolved or "advanced" and civilized society compared to other cultures. In her view, the persistence of racism ("contempt from people who believe they are better than people of color") proves that Spanish society is not as advanced as it claims to be. Sara supports this by pointing out that it is "kids our age" who have these views, thereby disputing the commonly expressed view that discrimination against immigrants only exists among the older generation, not among the youth.

In the ensuing animated discussion, the students discussed various forms of racism from their experiences, including their families being followed in stores by security officers, never seeing any black or brown people on TV, or seeing only negative representations of their groups in the media. Paula and Carla shared, laughingly, that when they were younger they used to wish they were white and blonde. As members of the most stigmatized groups in Spain—Afro-Caribbean, Ecuadorians, and Moroccans—the youths at AFEPA were well aware that race was a defining feature of their experience in Spain.

The role play and the identity molecule exercise (both versions) provided openings for a silenced dialogue that unearthed students' lived experiences of racial discrimination, as well as their emergent critique of it. Paula, who identified as Caribbean/Latina and wrote about being judged for her skin color, articulated on a deeper level what it meant to be part of a stigmatized group:

> I saw on the news a survey about education in Spain, and they said that the races that perform the best [are] the Chinese and the Germans, and those who [performed] the worst were the Muslims, Dominicans, and I don't remember the other one. And I said *qué fuerte,* I mean, I think there they have made it look like all Dominicans perform badly and no. I think it is very, very bad that they have done this.

Paula's critique of the media's portrayal of racial groups that lumped all Dominicans together showed her awareness of racial stereotypes and the power of media representation, as well as her sense of the injustice of these portrayals. These examples, along with the critique of police racial profiling, defied the discourse that race or ethnicity was no longer meaningful to young people in Madrid. Making sense of young people's reluctance to name racism or identify racially, alongside their lived experiences and critiques of racism, requires placing this apparent contradiction in the context of the discourse of integration, in which powerful Spanish allies expressed their hope in immigrant youth based on their ability to assimilate. The following examples show students wrestling with contradiction, struggling to reconcile their experiences of discrimination and exclusion with their desire to believe in the discourse of integration.

Junot, a sixteen-year-old from the Dominican Republic who had come to Spain at the age of eight, expressed a conflicted relationship with Spain that was typical of many of the youths. He said he felt connected to Spain because "I have my life here and all my friends," but he insisted that he did not feel Spanish "porque yo soy dominicano y eso lo llevo grabado" (because I am Dominican and I have that engraved in me). When asked if he thought he might one day come to feel Spanish, he answered ambiguously, "I don't know. It might be that I change my mind one day and feel Spanish, or I might not." But when asked what would have to happen for an immigrant like him to feel Spanish, he said, "In my view, for the simple fact that they give him new opportunities, to have the same as the Spaniards, that in fact is Spanish. For them to give you the same opportunities." Being Spanish, then, would necessitate an equality of opportunities that he did not experience. Enrique continued:

> ES: Would people here looking at you say that you are Spanish?
> J: Eh, no.
> ES: Why not?
> J: Because of the color of my skin.

For Junot, membership in the Spanish polity was racially bound. As an Afro-descended Caribbean youth with dark skin, he could never fit the Spanish profile. But that was not, for him, the same as racism. A little later in the interview, when specifically asked about intergroup relations in Spain, he admitted that there were sometimes conflicts. Asked to elaborate, he said, "For example, you're talking with a Spaniard and they insult you. And you say, 'Why have you insulted me for no reason?'" Enrique asked, "Do they insult you for being Dominican or for being another color?" And Junot responded, "No, you never receive an insult like that." Junot's insistence that equal treatment was barred from him on racial grounds was matched by his denial of racially motivated behavior. This denial that discrimination was racially based could reflect the internalization of the discourse of integration, as other ethnographers have suggested (Lucko 2014), or it could simply reflect young people's determination to overcome it. The case of Junot's sister is insightful.

Junot's younger sister Raquel, who also identified as Dominican, described experiencing racism from a teacher at school but not letting it affect her. Asked to describe the teachers at school, she said, "I have a teacher who is a little bit racist." On further questioning it emerged that this was the same language teacher who had been discussed by the group the week before, whom several students had described as humiliating. Raquel described what she did:

> Well she looks at you with a look of disgust, I just started third year [of secondary school], I get really nervous when she makes me read out loud when there are people I don't know, so I started to read all nervous like that, and she scolded me and kicked me out of class and said, "Here, start reading a book and learn how to read."

In Raquel's story, she identifies a pattern of racial discrimination in which she and other immigrant youths are singled out and explains that all of their mothers approached the school principal to complain, but the principal did nothing and the teacher continues as before. Then Raquel instinctively insists that it doesn't matter: "Yes, she looks at you with disgust and everything but I don't care anymore, I don't give it any importance, because why am I going to give it importance?"

Raquel was not the only student who told of school staff being unresponsive to claims of discrimination. Fourteen-year-old Isabela, from Venezuela, had transferred schools because of this. In her interview, when asked why she had transferred schools, she initially said she didn't like the teachers at her old school and the students there acted superior. Later on, when questioned specifically about the relations between immigrant students and Spanish students, she revealed that in her old school there were only a few Latinos and there was a "racist" girl who taunted her simply for being from another country. When asked how teachers responded to such incidents, she said she had approached the teachers but "they said it was a problem from outside, that it wasn't a school problem . . . [and that] problems from outside of school were not their responsibility."

It is clear that the youths in our study experienced significant racism and discrimination as immigrants in Spain but got little or no support for addressing it from the educators or adults in their lives. They told us that they did not discuss issues of diversity, migration, race, or racism in their schools or neighborhood associations, and until our workshop, had never had the opportunity to discuss their experiences as immigrant youth. Without this opportunity, without the space to build community around their shared experiences, they had no support for developing a critical consciousness of inequality or taking action to challenge it (Dyrness 2012; Rubin 2007; Abu El-Haj 2009). Furthermore, the national discourse of integration—which imagined Latino immigrants to be integrating smoothly, and required national identification and cultural assimilation as the basis for integration—erased immigrant youths' experiences of exclusion and, as we will see in the next chapter, the complexity of their transnational identities. The persistent discourse that immigrants were assimilating and racism was diminishing both denied immigrant youths' lived experiences of racism and complicated their efforts to understand it, rendering their very identities precarious. The violence experienced every day by immigrants in the form of racial harassment and discrimination was rendered invisible, absorbed by the immigrants themselves.

Our multilayered methodology uncovered students' experiences with racism and their critiques of it, but also their complex, nuanced identities, which did not conform to either assimilated or alienated identity options in the discourse of integration. This chapter has shown the disciplining effects of nationalism on immigrant youth identities—that is, the ways the discourse of integration limited students' options for discussing their lived experiences and drew on colonial histories to construct students' cultures of origin as obstacles to integration. Immigrant students, as objects of remediation by educators hoping to integrate them, were the Spanish state's "epistemically disavowed colonial subjects" (Mignolo 2011, 82). By blaming immigrants' cultural difference for conflict or failure of integration, proponents of integration denied and left intact the formative role of racism, reproducing racist neocolonial discourses of national belonging. Such discourses also obscured from public view the sustaining role of students' attachments to culture and transnational communities. In the next chapter we examine students' transnational belongings: how multiple connections to both their countries of origin and their home communities in Madrid, as well as multiple forms of separation and exclusion, nurtured the development of a critical consciousness and *pensamiento fronterizo* (border thinking).

CHAPTER 4

Transnational Belongings

The Cultural Knowledge of Lives In Between

¿Y entonces? Después de pasar tanto tiempo aquí, ¿Cuál es mi país?

[And so? After spending so much time here, which is my country?]

—Razena, fourteen years old

¿Española? ¿Marroquí? Nacida en tierras españolas, juzgada en todas partes.

[Spanish? Moroccan? Born in Spanish lands, judged everywhere.]

—Maritza, seventeen years old

COUNTERING THE CERTAINTY EXPRESSED by educators and social workers that immigrant youth raised in Spain felt Spanish, for Razena, Maritza, and the other young people in our study, becoming Spanish was a question mark. While Spanish adults repeatedly expressed the view that conflicts were in the past and that immigrant youth were accepted, were assimilating, and identified with Spanish ways, our exploration uncovered a more complex reality. Immigrant youth navigate multiple forms of belonging in Spain and their countries of origin, as well as multiple forms of exclusion. Their reflections and expressions in response to poetry, video, and the interviews they conducted gave voice to the experiences of loss, belonging, separation, and connection that shaped their relationships to both their home countries and Spain. To understand the ways they narrated their selves and their sense of belonging to multiple communities, it is helpful to consider the concept of diasporic citizenship. Lok Siu (2005) defines diasporic citizenship as "the processes by which diasporic subjects experience and practice cultural and social belonging amid shifting geopolitical circumstances and webs of transnational relations" (5). Central to diasporic citizenship is an awareness of contradiction, stemming from the "tension

between one's affinity and affiliation with these sites and one's acknowledgement of only partial belonging and acceptance by them" (11). As immigrant youth in Madrid articulated the ways they belonged and did not
belong in Spain and their countries of origin, their renderings gave voice
to a "third space": a place in between national, political, and cultural communities and recognized social identities. And along with the lack of full
belonging to any nation-state, diasporic citizenship also "holds out the possibility of creativity, innovation, and perseverance that come with occupying this intersection" (6).

In this chapter we call attention to the youths' complex, transnational,
and hybrid identity formations, highlighting the ways these defy and disrupt the neat categories in popular and policy discourses of immigrant
integration. Yet, we also seek to uncover the democratic yearnings latent in
these disruptions, the possibilities for "creativity, innovation, and perseverance," as well as the longings for a more inclusive, just, and humane
social order. As diaspora youth wrestle against national communities
that exclude distinct parts of themselves, they create openings or imaginings of new collectivities that embrace the fullness and multiplicity of
their varied experiences, knowledge, and ways of being.

Fourteen-year-old Raquel, introduced in chapter 3, moved to Spain from
the Dominican Republic when she was six years old, traveling with her two
older brothers to join their mother, who had been living in Santander for
two years. Asked why her mother had come to Spain, Raquel responds,
"para superarse" (to overcome, to better herself). Did her mother have family or friends in Spain already? "No," Raquel says, "She didn't know anyone;
she came alone."[1] "Your mom is brave!" Andrea offers. "Yes," Raquel nods
emphatically, and breaks into a smile that lights up her face, her eyes twin-
kling like stars. Raquel's story captures the themes of loss, struggle, and
pride that are hallmarks of the Dominican diaspora. The Dominican experience in Spain has been a story of women pioneers, family separation, and
family reunification. One of the oldest and most established Latin American immigrant communities in Spain, the Dominican population grew rapidly in the 1990s and continued to grow through the economic crisis in
2008 to 2013, when many other immigrant communities were losing numbers. Dominican immigration has been led by women, largely due to the
demand for domestic service workers, and fed by family reunification as
women have brought their families to join them (Oso Casas 2008).

But it was not until we read some poetry written by Mexican migrant youths in the United States that Raquel began to talk about her relationship with her mother and the country she had left behind. We introduced poems written by the undocumented Mexican migrant youths in Enrique's study in California, described in chapter 1. Following the process he had used with them, we asked the students to read the poems silently and reflect individually before discussing them as a group. After the discussion, we invited them to write their own poetic responses. In the group discussion Raquel was impassioned as she shared that she identified with one of the poems because she had also had to leave her country behind and she wished she could go back. People come to Spain because there are more opportunities here, she said, but that doesn't mean they want to be here. She told us that she could never belong in Spain because "here I am not even with half of my family." Although Raquel had migrated to Spain to be reunited with her mother, the move had separated her from her extended family, replacing one loss with another. This was the paradox of diasporic citizenship: belonging was always fragmented, qualified by something missing.

In our discussions it was common for the youths to talk about *mi país* (my country) when referring to their parents' country of origin, even if they had been born and raised in Spain. The students referenced strong ties to family back home and cultural differences between themselves and Spanish youth as reasons why they could not fully belong in Spain. As Mariela put it, "No eres igual aquí que cuando estás en tu país" (You're not the same here as when you are in your country).

Mariela and her sister Luisa were born in Spain to a Dominican mother and a Spanish father and had Spanish citizenship. But in spite of these ties to Spain and the great distance in time and space that separated them from the Dominican Republic (their mother had moved to Spain over thirty years ago), both sisters still referred to the Dominican Republic as *mi país* and proudly identified as Dominican and Spanish. They knew well their mother's hometown, a small town outside Santo Domingo where they had traveled on summer vacations to spend time with their family, including grandparents, a slew of uncles, aunts, and cousins, and two older siblings who still lived there. "Madre mía!" Luisa exclaims. "Every time I go there's more and more cousins!" Like other Latino and Caribbean youths in our study, family ties and memories of time spent there connected the girls to the Dominican Republic and separated them from "other Spanish youth."

As Mariela reflected, "When they tell me I'm Spanish it really bothers me because it's like yes, I am Spanish, but part of me is from somewhere else, and it doesn't recognize my whole self." Dominican youths in both neighborhood associations often spoke longingly of the Dominican Republic and the time they spent there—of trips to the beach and birthday celebrations with cousins and extended family. In interviews and group discussions they described a communal life where they belonged and where neighbors helped each other out. Seventeen-year-old Paula, born in Madrid to Dominican parents, explained, "I miss the environment and people's way of being. I mean, they help each other out and everyone knows each other and is in touch with each other. They all know each other, and the doors are always open, with music." Caribbean youths described a cultural life that revolved around extended family, being close to the land, music, and parties. Luisa described her time in her mother's hometown as follows:

> We always played a lot, for me, from the time you woke up until
> you went to bed you were doing something, always out and about.
> For example, I would help my grandmother peel the vegetables, my
> uncle would always go to the *conuco* [plot of land] as they call it
> there, like a jungle, where you plant your fruit and you go there with
> your donkey and bring it back, you go to the neighbor's house. . . .

Sixteen-year-old Junot commented that "los dominicanos son muy fiesteros, usan mucho la fiesta" (Dominicans are big partiers, they throw parties a lot). But the parties were different from parties in Spain, he said, because of the different food, the music, the dancing, and it wasn't all about alcohol. "They are very noisy, Dominican parties," he explained. "They do drink alcohol, like everywhere, but not in such quantities. Alcohol is not essential for a party in Santo Domingo. . . . They serve a lot of food, sweets, there are a ton of children, they bring music, and they dance." In his description, parties were intergenerational and integrated into the life of the community, not exclusively a place for youths to get drunk. Ana Sylvia, from Brazil, shared similar sentiments: "In my country I find many friends, more family, I feel more at home. There you have more freedom. We go out a lot to parties, we go from one place to another."

But in spite of these often idealized representations of life in their home countries, they were also aware of the ways they did not fit in there, the ways that was no longer "home." Paula shared that when she visited the Dominican Republic, "they always tell me there, 'You talk like a little Spanish girl!' [Hablas como una españolita!], and I say no, no, I speak like a Dominican in Spain!" Students discussed how their different ways of speaking, dressing, and acting separated them from friends and family who had not migrated, making it impossible for them to belong. Girls in particular remarked on the rigid gender roles in their parents' hometowns and the scoldings they received for not fulfilling gendered duties. Razena shared, "They call me useless!" Despite the ease with which they moved between two worlds, or perhaps because of it, they were made to feel their difference each time they returned or visited with family members.

We explored students' relationships to their home countries through poetry and in group discussions and individual interviews in which we asked the following questions: Do you feel a connection with [country of origin]? Why or why not? What does it mean to you to be [Dominican, Ecuadorian, or other national-origin identity]? How do you value it? How do you express it? Would you consider going back to [country of origin] to live? Why or why not? These questions generated rich, reflective answers that revealed the multidimensional, shifting, and context-dependent nature of students' identities in the diaspora. Students' awareness of disparities and inequalities between their home countries and Spain, and within Spain between themselves and nonimmigrant Spanish youth, as well as their privileged position vis-à-vis their extended families in their home countries, made it impossible for them to identify with any single place or nationality.

As students described the ways they no longer belonged in their countries of origin, an awareness of difficult material conditions, violence and insecurity, and lack of educational opportunity there was central to their narratives. When asked if she would ever want to live in the Dominican Republic, Luisa answered, "Me, for vacation, perfect, but to live, I wouldn't last." She explained, "In my mother's town there is scarcity of everything. My mother sent money so they could build a better bathroom." Her sister Mariela put it this way: "If I were living in the Dominican Republic, I would surely be barefoot and pregnant, with no schooling." Their awareness of poverty and insecurity in the Dominican Republic and the material advantages, opportunities, and safety of their life in Spain made it impossible for them to "belong" in their mother's home country.

Fourteen-year-old Isabela, describing her relationship to Venezuela, said it was complicated because of the high rate of criminal violence. She explained:

> For example, if you go to the supermarket they only let you buy like one kilo or two kilos of rice, because there's no food, there's nothing, and an aunt of mine who came told us that one day as she came out of the supermarket some kids threatened her with guns so that she would give them the food, because there isn't any.

Although she missed her family and friends in Brazil, seventeen-year-old Ana Sylvia said she couldn't see a future there because of the insecurity. She explained that they had to be inside after 8:00 p.m. because if you were out on the street late at night you could be "raped, robbed, or killed." For all these reasons, in spite of their strong attachments to their home countries, most said they could not go back to live there, that it was no longer home.

That left these youths in an in-between space, what diaspora scholars have called a "third space," or the space "between the 'here' of the host country and the 'there' of origin, between the 'us' of a dominant community and the 'them' of multiple forms of racialized identification" (Lukose 2007, 410). The youths in our study were often poignantly reflective about their in-between identities.

On Not Belonging: Lives In Between

Camilo, a fifteen-year-old Brazilian youth who came to Spain at age seven, expressed complex forms of attachment and belonging to his native country and his current country, Spain. When asked in an interview whether he felt he belonged in Spain, his response was straightforward—*yo no* (not me). This response seemed to contradict his preference for living in Spain over Brazil. When asked where he would prefer to be, he said, "Spain . . . of course, because there is a better quality of life here . . . but I will always remember where I have come from." He says that at home his family still maintains Brazilian traditions and that some of his classmates are also Brazilian and they gather to converse in Portuguese. He adds that there is a connection to Spain because he has lived there for the past eight years. But for Camilo, this connection isn't the same as belonging.

Camilo lived alone during the week while his mother worked in another house as a live-in nanny and maid. During a group discussion he surprised us by arguing, against several students in the group, that there was no discrimination against immigrants in Spain. Raquel shared the experience of her mother who works as a maid, cleaning houses "from dawn to dusk, Sunday to Sunday" for only a pittance. Students pointed out indignantly that immigrants filled the lowest-paid jobs that no one else wanted, but were still accused of "stealing" Spaniards' jobs. While some students said this made them feel rejected, Camilo said, "That doesn't affect me."

Taken by itself, Camilo's denial of discrimination might be seen as evidence of assimilation, but when analyzed together with his reflections in multiple contexts, it reveals the contradictions that are characteristic of the third space. In his interview Camilo spoke openly about continued racism in Spain and then poignantly described his partial belonging: "We live here, we know the language well, we know their customs, but deep inside we are still from our country. I mean, we get used to them, but we don't forget our customs. *We try to combine everything together, the past with the present and the future*" (emphasis added). A little while later he added, "It doesn't occur to me how I can be Brazilian and Spanish at the same time."

Camilo was wrestling with a discourse of integration that left no room for his hybrid identity. His daily life required juggling contradictions between official narratives about immigrants, based on dichotomous categories of Spanish or Other, and his own lived experience. Such complex realities underscore the need for careful analysis of the discourses that construct immigrant subjects, as well as for multiple methods of engaging young people's lived experience. Often students seemed to be speaking back to the discourse that expected them to be wholly Spanish, struggling against the erasure of parts of themselves they couldn't deny. Isabela, from Venezuela, when asked whether she considered herself Spanish, said: "Me, not entirely because well, when I got here I was Latina, I mean, I didn't speak the language, and I don't know what, I spoke with an accent, and now, no, I've been here my whole life, but I don't know, there's like a little hole in my body that I'm Latina and that you know, *I can't renounce even if I wanted to*" (emphasis added). Here Isabela describes going from not speaking the language (i.e., speaking with an accent) to speaking like a Spaniard, and yet still feeling different because a part of her was Latina. In other words, having a deep belonging to another country or culture (Venezuela, Brazil, Peru, etc.) meant having a different set of cultural and relational experiences that transcended national lines, but also being positioned as different in Spain. Being Latina, for Isabela, meant "having my roots in another place, [and] being different from everyone else."

For Latinos, the cultural differences that separated them from Spanish youth included transnational relations and experiences and having a set of family and expectations that were rooted outside of the nation-state as well as within. Their efforts to define themselves and their identities were a complicated balancing act of trying, as Camilo had put it, to "combine everything together, the past and the present, and the future." Carolina, a fifteen-year-old born in Spain to parents from the Dominican Republic, captured the pull of "here" and "there" in a poem. When asked to read, reflect on, and discuss a poem written by an undocumented Mexican youth in the United States, Carolina said she identified with him and the contradictions of migration. She wrote:

Me siento lejos de la gente que quiero,
Pero siento que para mí es necesario
estar aquí en un país que no siento mio.
. . . es una nueva oportunidad para mí
que me hace bien para tener un futuro diferente con más
oportunidades y esperanzas.
Pero siempre acordándome de las personas que quiero y
esperan mucho de mí.

[I feel far away from the people I love,
But I feel that for me it's necessary
to be here in a country that I don't feel is mine.
It's a new opportunity for me
that does me good in order to have a different future with more
opportunities and hopes.
But always remembering the people I love and who expect a lot
from me.]

Carolina's poem reveals her intimate understanding of the painful trade-offs of life in the diaspora—the "yes, but" attachment to multiple communities and the ruptured family relationships that are necessary for a future of opportunities and hope. Yet she strives to hold on to what she has left behind by "always remembering the people I love." In the group discussion after she read her poem out loud, she explained that her family in the Dominican Republic expected so much of her: "Because they see that this is a developed country, they think that you have to aspire to something no matter what, to something more, that you can't just stay there stuck. That you have to access university education and a job. And in reality I think that that's why we're here, we're not here to waste time." Carolina's comment underscores the deep sense of social responsibility that comes with having family left behind in a less prosperous country, "people who I love and who expect a lot from me." These transnational relationships both defined students' identities—in ways that were often invisible to their Spanish peers and teachers—and gave them a strong sense of obligation to take advantage of the opportunities they had in Spain.

For scholars in the tradition of anthropologist John Ogbu, this "dual frame of reference" between their parents' country of origin and their current country of residence helps immigrant students perform better in school than their "involuntary minority" counterparts (e.g., African Americans, Mexican Americans, and Native Americans). According to this theory, immigrant students' awareness of their parents' sacrifices and of the hardships in their home countries leads them to view their current situation more favorably and to develop cultural models of schooling that are conducive to school success (Ogbu 1987, 1991; Suarez-Orozco 1987). However, the narratives of the youths in our study defy an easy comparison between two places (the Dominican Republic and Spain) that would put one on top. Rather, diaspora youth form their identities at the margins and interstices of both societies, belonging to both and neither, and this work of juggling and combining is an active, never complete process fraught with loss and longing.

A poem by fourteen-year-old Razena, who moved to Spain from the Dominican Republic when she was five, is illustrative:

Intentar encajar
conseguir nuevos amigos
cambiar tu forma de hablar
Ya nada es igual.
Esos días que pasabas con toda la familia
ya no pasarán
Unos aquí, otros allá
Extrañar a tu gente, extrañar tu país

Pasar días llorando, sola en tu habitación
Extrañando cosas que ya no están allí.

[Trying to fit in
to make new friends
to change your way of speaking
Nothing is the same anymore.
Those days that you spent with all of your family
won't happen anymore
Some here, others over there
Missing your people, missing your country.
Spending days crying alone in your room
Missing things that are no longer there.]

Razena's poem captures both the rupture with an established, seemingly cohesive past and a present marked by family separation, where the emotional toll of migration is found in quotidian challenges: trying to fit in, learning new ways of speaking, and searching for new friends. Her last line, "Missing things that are no longer there," hints at the uncertainty and change of life in the diaspora. The things she misses could be actual things she left behind in the Dominican Republic, which may or may not still be there, or more broadly her life before she migrated.

After Razena read her poem aloud, the students commented on the "melancholy for her family" that she expressed and the fact that she was "incomplete." As they continued to reflect on her poem, they probed the in-between space of not belonging, highlighting Razena's term *encajar* (fitting in). Paula commented, "If you don't fit in, it's okay, I think." We asked her to explain what she meant, and she said:

It could be that people think you don't fit in, but you have a personality, from going to a world that's different from only Spain, well, you have some different concepts. And it might be that you don't fit in with people in Spain or the people in [your country] but you have more knowledge than they do. And even if you wanted to, you're not going to fit in. And that's not bad.

Paula's observation emphasized the benefits of not fitting in and the unique cultural knowledge that comes from experiencing more than one world.

In discussions like this, the students embraced *la conciencia de la mestiza* that Gloria Anzaldúa and other borderlands feminist theorists described as "the consciousness of the 'mixed blood' . . . born of life lived in the 'crossroads' between races, nations, languages, genders, sexualities, and cultures" (Sandoval 2000, 60). As Anzaldúa wrote, "The new mestiza . . . learns to juggle cultures. . . . Not only does she sustain contradictions, she turns the ambivalence into something else" (1999, 101). Paula herself had shared in the first group session at AFEPA that when she went back to the Dominican Republic her family teased her, saying, "hablas como una españolita," while in Spain her Spanish was marked as different for being Dominican. Her own experience of being in between helped her understand Razena's poem, and she pointed out that "it could be that people think you don't fit in"—noting the role of other people in policing the boundaries of belonging—but "you have more knowledge than they do." With this assessment, Paula expressed her awareness that the in-between space they occupied was born of multiple exclusions, and/but it was a rich space. National boundaries could not contain the knowledge of their experience in multiple worlds—"even if you wanted to, you're not going to fit in"—and in that case, not belonging was "not bad."

In our discussion we probed the students' awareness of the advantages of this location, asking them, "What are the advantages of one who has lived through the experience of migration?" They mentioned knowing "how to value things that others don't value," learning "to have an open mind," speaking multiple languages (and types of language), and in the words of one student, "You can adapt more easily to situations that you face in life." They discussed how Spanish youth did not know to value things like potable water running from the tap ("We can bathe in drinking water!") and having all of one's family nearby. The ability to value scarce natural resources and to adapt to different cultural contexts—to speak multiple languages or language varieties, to have an open mind and an awareness of different points of view, they emphasized—are aspects of global citizenship that are essential for our twenty-first-century globalized world, and they emerged uniquely from their experiences of migration. As Paula wrote in her reflection after the group discussion:

> For some people this [process of migration] might be a difficult process and they might be left with the worst of each experience, but for me it has helped me to learn about the difference in feelings

that can be had for the same thing, and *for me to have an intermediate point between the good and the bad.* I think that everyone could get to know two worlds or different concepts, but to emigrate and have the feelings, experiences, and a thousand other things is unique. [emphasis added]

Paula's reflection acknowledges that she is able to recognize different perspectives and feelings people have about the same thing, and she claims the space in between (*un punto intermedio*) as an advantage. She also acknowledges that while anyone could acquire experience in another culture—presumably through travel or interacting with people from other places—the experience of emigration, and all that it entails, is unique.

In our conversations students articulated the linguistic and cultural flexibility they had and how their speech shifted based on context. As Junot, from the Dominican Republic, remarked: "When I get together with Dominicans, with my friends, and they're constantly talking, I suddenly start to speak Dominican. Just like that. But here [in Spain] I normally speak like this, Spanish." However, he remarked that if he returned to the Dominican Republic "they would make fun of me . . . because I speak Spanish." For Dominican youth, switching between Spanish (Castilian) and Caribbean Spanish depending on who they were talking to was a part of daily life. As Carolina explained, "We're not going to talk at school the way we talk with each other or the way we talk at home with our family."

The fluidity that characterized their back-and-forth movement between cultural communities stood in sharp contrast to the binaries of national discourses of integration that posed immigrant youth as either assimilated or oppositional, alienated, and militant. As the students made clear, they were both readily adapted to and partially excluded from both societies. Their transnational identities, based on cultural hybridity, could also not easily be captured by traditional surveys of transnationalism that seek to measure attachment to the home nation-state. For example, in a study of the immigrant second generation in the United States, Rumbaut and colleagues assessed whether attachment to the "parental homeland" was diminished or sustained into early adulthood among children of immigrants. To measure young people's knowledge of their parents' countries of origin they asked them to state the capital of the country, the approximate size of the population, and the name of one of its political leaders. According to their survey, "virtually no one . . . answered all three questions correctly"

(Rumbaut 2002, 74). The researchers also assessed levels of transnationality using measures that were both subjective (which place feels more like home) and objective (frequency of visits and remittances). Immigrant youths were asked to state which country felt more like home and to agree or disagree with the statement "The United States is the best country in the world to live in." Based on these measures, the researchers concluded that among 1.5- and second-generation young adults, the levels of transnational attachments, both subjective and objective, were "quite small—always under 10%" (89).

Much has changed since this study was conducted in the 1990s, most notably the dramatic rise in social media and internet technology that allows immigrant young people to communicate regularly with friends and family back home. Young people, especially if they are not wage earners, may not send remittances to family in their home countries (even if their parents do) and may not travel back frequently or at all, especially if they are undocumented. "Objective measures" of attachment today would have to include frequency of contact through Skype, Facebook, Instagram, WhatsApp, and other global communication apps (Tuenti was the app of choice for the youths in our study), as well as email. By these measures, the youths in our study had extremely high levels of transnational attachment. Global communications media has dramatically changed the nature of transnational experience, facilitating cultural mixing and transnational relationships at unprecedented levels. This reality makes measures of transnational attachment based on nationalist, textbook knowledge of the parents' homeland practically irrelevant. Young people's ability or failure to name a political leader in their parents' country or tell you the size of its population cannot capture how their identities are shaped by cultural influences in transnational social fields. It cannot capture the affective dimension of their relationships to family and friends in other countries. As Patricia Sánchez (2007) defines transnationalism, it embodies "various systems or relationships that span two or more nations, including sustained and meaningful flows of people, money, labor, goods, information, advice, care and love" (493).

New research from Spain shows how these relationships of "care and love" are sustained through WhatsApp between undocumented, unaccompanied minors in Spain and their families in Morocco (Mendoza Pérez and Morgade Salgado 2018). The authors show that digital media crosses all social relations for this group and is an essential tool for studying their daily lives. In spite of their juridical designation as unaccompanied foreign minors, these young people's families continue to play a very important role in their lives through their mobile phones, unbeknownst to the Spanish social workers overseeing their cases. Pictures of newborn nieces and nephews or cousins celebrating weddings and words of advice from mothers, all sent via WhatsApp, become lifelines for teenagers in limbo awaiting asylum hearings in Spanish social care institutions. Through WhatsApp, unaccompanied migrant youth and their families create networks of solidarity that help them survive. Mendoza Pérez and Morgade Salgado's research is a fascinating study of how the daily lives of migrant youth defy the categories of the Spanish nation-state—in this case, the category "unaccompanied minor."

Instant messaging and video chat apps both allow diaspora youth to remain emotionally connected to friends and relatives in their home countries and, paradoxically, exacerbate the sense of not belonging either here or there. Video calls that collapse the time and space between faraway family members are profoundly affirming to migrant youth and dislocating at the same time. For the span of a few minutes or an hour, they allow a migrant youth to be warmed by the familiar language and affection of a loved one. But once the camera is shut off, the pain of being far away is all the more acute. Raquel expressed this when Andrea remarked on how wonderful it was that Raquel communicates so often with her family back home. "Yes," Raquel said, "but it's not the same thing to be talking though Facebook or Skype as to be there, giving them a hug. And the time is going to come when I get tired of seeing them only through a camera."

For some youths in our study, extended periods in their parents' country of origin, whether for summer vacations or for months or years at a time, reinforced their sense of not belonging to any single nation or national identity. For Rolando, a fifteen-year-old born in Madrid to an Ecuadorian mother and Dominican father, adjusting to life in Madrid was initially very difficult. He had been taken back to Ecuador at age one and spent the next four years there with his maternal grandmother and the rest of their vast clan in what he says was "a whole country village of cousins and relatives." Because Rolando hadn't known his mother for the first years of his conscious life, he didn't have an emotional connection to her (or to his country of birth). When Rolando was five his mother returned to Ecuador to take him back to Spain with her. He recalled that period of transition as full of endless tears and deep loss. He described going from a known and secure environment to disorienting, unfamiliar surroundings; from a small village to a big metropolis; from nature to concrete; from being surrounded by a big family (where everyone seemed to be related) to living with only his mother, a woman he didn't know, and having no one to play with. At his Spanish school, Rolando eventually befriended two other students who were also marked as different from the other children: an autistic Spanish boy and a Colombian immigrant girl.

Returning to Ecuador has always been a real possibility for Rolando, especially in times of economic precarity. So when asked if he would like to return to Ecuador, he responded quickly, with a seemingly contradictory answer. He said he wasn't sure because he was plagued by divided sentiments: "Cuando estoy allí quiero quedarme, pero cuando estoy aquí no quiero irme. Es así, un poco . . ." (When I'm there I want to stay, but when I'm here I don't want to leave. It's like that, a little . . .). His voice trailed off, but it was clear that his desire to remain in either place was contextual and depended on whom he was with at the time. He added, "Truthfully, I couldn't tell you because here I have my friends and my mom."

Rolando did not see himself as Spanish, despite having been born in Madrid and having lived there most of his life. "Perhaps because I have a stronger, more vivid memory of where I lived my early childhood as opposed to where I live now that I don't consider myself so Spanish . . . knowing that I was raised in a certain place in a particular way, and here, I live another way." When asked if he thought he could ever become a Spaniard, he said he wasn't sure. And yet, he also said that while he identified with each of his cultural backgrounds (Ecuadorian, Dominican, and Spanish) at different moments and in different contexts, he didn't "side" with any particular one: "No me decanto por ningún lado. O sea, ni por español, ni por ecuatoriano, ni nada." For Rolando, becoming Spanish was a question mark. Many of his answers revealed uncertainty, nuance, and a yet-to-be-determined quality. They defied easy categorization because his experiences and belongings are transnational—different from his Spanish contemporaries, with different histories that fall outside of the normative national narrative.

Razena: Navigating Multiplicity

A closer look at the transnational experiences of another student in our study, Razena, lends insight into the formative role of this border crossing on her sense of self and the invisibility of her transnational experiences to her Spanish teachers. Razena was fourteen years old when we first met her, the youngest in the AFEPA group. She had come to Madrid from the Dominican Republic when she was five. Her first poetic reflection (cited above) was about the challenges of trying to fit in. In our third focus group session she wrote about what it would mean to return to her country of origin:

> A pesar de todo, venir aquí me ha servido para mejorar en todos los sentidos: cada día me esfuerzo más y más para poder alcanzar todos los objetivos que tenía, cada día descubro cosas nuevas que no sabía, cada día extraño más y más a mi familia, cada día, cada día, cada día, ahora tengo dos puntos de vista, ahora tengo maneras de hablar diferente, ahora tengo amigos maravillosos que me gustaría que siempre esten a mi lado ... ¿y entonces? Depués de pasar tanto tiempo aquí ¿Cuál es mi país? Ahora pienso que si vuelvo a mi país de origen no me adaptaría, ahora creo que mi vida está aquí ¿y si tuviera que volver ¿Qué haría?

> [In spite of everything, coming here has helped me to improve in every way: every day I work harder and harder to be able to reach the goals that I had, every day I discover new things that I didn't know, every day I miss my family more and more, every day, every day, every day, now I have two points of view, now I have different ways of talking, now I have wonderful friends who I would like to always have at my side ... and so? After spending so much time here, which is my country? Now I think that if I go back to my country of origin I would not adapt, now I think that my life is here and if I had to go back, what would I do?]

We didn't realize at the time how prescient her last line was: "If I had to go back, what would I do?" She would find out sooner than we thought. The next time we saw the group, three months later for a farewell meal at McDonald's (their choice), the big news of the evening was that Razena was moving back to the Dominican Republic in less than two weeks. We asked her how she felt about it and she shrugged, smiling. Her father had gone back to the Dominican Republic two years earlier and they had been living apart. Now her mother and the rest of the family were joining him in a small town south of Santo Domingo. Razena was a few weeks shy of her fifteenth birthday. She had been in the Dominican Republic the previous summer, and she confirmed that she had friends there. We made her promise to stay in touch with us by Facebook and let us know how things went.

The three Dominican girls slipped into banter about life in the Dominican Republic: how their Dominican relatives don't dress as well and make fun of the girls for their clothes from Spain, how they get scrutinized more, how girls are expected to do all the household chores, how hurricane season is starting and how hard it rains there ("la lluvia pica"[the rain stings], they all agree), how there is a new mosquito that brings dengue ("It bit my grandmother," one of them said). The ease with which their lives straddled two worlds belied the pain of goodbyes that mark their transitions, a pain laid bare two weeks later when a friend of Razena's posted on her Facebook page: "There is no place more sorrowful in the world than an airport terminal."

On that evening at McDonald's, however, there was no sorrow. In the cheerful and easy banter about their experiences in the Dominican Republic, Razena's friends accompanied her in the transition, normalizing the move as a part of everyday life and affirming the cultural knowledge they gained from this movement in ways that only transnational youth could. Through their conversation they evoked the visceral experience of being in the Dominican Republic—the feel of the rain, the mosquitos—and found camaraderie and solidarity in shared experiences of being judged by family members who didn't understand their ways. Their tone was jovial and light. Far from lamenting Razena's need to leave Spain, their conversation was a celebration of their lives in between.

As it turned out, Razena's sojourn in the Dominican Republic was short—only three months. When we caught up with her in Madrid two years later on a follow-up research visit, she filled us in on her experiences. She seemed taller and more self-assured when we met her outside a café on a main thoroughfare in Malasaña. She was wearing long extension braids, a change from the short, straightened hair pulled back into a ponytail that had been her usual style before. The change in her hair, it turned out, was symbolic of other changes in herself, including growing confidence and pride in her Dominican identity. Razena told us her family is from the town of Vicente Noble in Barahona, south of Santo Domingo, which sent the first Dominican immigrants to Spain.[2] She arrived there in mid-June and started school in late August. She was then fifteen in what would have been the last year of ESO (compulsory secondary education) in Spain but was the second year of *bachillerato* in the Dominican Republic. She attended a private school run by nuns, which had the best reputation in the area, but the level of teaching and learning was so poor that it was immediately clear she could not stay. She begged her father to let her go back to Madrid. She said her classmates' reading levels were far below hers and that she had had to correct a teacher who made a mistake in his lesson. There weren't enough textbooks for all the students, so they spent most class time copying. Adding to the picture of dismal prospects in Vicente Noble was an attempted burglary of her family's home, which also housed her father's repair workshop and equipment. That convinced her parents that Vicente Noble wasn't the best place for Razena. By mid-September Razena was back in Madrid living with her uncle (her dad's brother), aunt, and cousin. Her parents and little sister stayed behind in Vicente Noble.

Razena returned to her former high school, a *concertado* (publicly subsidized parochial school), where she was welcomed back by her former teachers and the director. But when Andrea asked if her teachers had enquired about her experiences in the Dominican Republic, she replied, "¡Qué va!" (Are you kidding me?). "No, they didn't ask me anything." Razena was accepted back with no questions asked, as if the time she spent in the Dominican Republic was no more than a dream, or an embarrassment not worth mentioning. Although she continued to live a transnational life different from her Spanish peers, separated from her immediate family in the Dominican Republic and living with an uncle and aunt, at school she appeared to be a "normal teenager" like anyone else—except for her new hairstyles, which were nothing like what Spanish girls wore. As she explained,

> I've worn a lot of different hairstyles to school. They always, [here in Spain] the girls always have the same hairstyle. So, I would wear an afro, then I would wear it straight, sometimes I would put on extensions, then I'd take them off, I'd wear braids, then another kind of braid, whatever. And they would say, "Razena, but how many things can you do with your hair?" I mean, they would touch it and say, how cool! I don't know. . . . I cause them curiosity.

Razena's time in the Dominican Republic gave her respite from being a curiosity in Spain and support for the diverse expressions of African hair that were normal in the Caribbean. As she said, in the Dominican Republic "they change their hair a lot too." But she was quick to point out that she aroused curiosity there, too, because of the time she had spent in Spain. "On finding out that I've been in Spain a long time, over there this country also causes curiosity. To the people who haven't come." When asked how it felt to be a curiosity in both places, Razena replied that it wasn't bad: "I think it's good because that way they learn more about what I know, what I can offer to them, and they also offer me things from here [Spain]. . . . Then from here to Santo Domingo I also offer things to them. Or those myths that they have about Spain, I clarify them a bit." Far from being a problem for the Spanish nation-state, Razena was an asset who was able to educate nonmobile people in both countries, challenging misconceptions they had about other people and places. Razena lamented that people in Spain get their information about "people from other countries" from television, and when they see something bad about an immigrant they "put everyone from that country in the same box." She was often in a position of explaining that her country was "like every place— there are people who do good things, and people who do bad things. . . . But we can contribute many things from our countries, a lot of culture, many things that people [here] don't know."

Her awareness of this position in between and her role as a cultural broker is a characteristic of diasporic citizenship that many of the youths in our study demonstrated, and it renders legible their refusal to identify with any single nationality. Razena had dual citizenship (Spain and the Dominican Republic) but like most of the young people in our study, she did not consider herself Spanish. She identified as Dominican in Spain but also said she did not belong in the Dominican Republic and wouldn't choose to live there again. "I've tried it and it wasn't bad," she explained, "but I don't know, I don't see myself there. Anyway, I adapted very well and I didn't have any problems, but still, I don't see myself living there." Razena's experiences in the Dominican Republic had shown her she could adapt "very well," despite the doubts she had expressed in her reflection two years earlier. But they had also shown her that she didn't belong there. The space in between— "ese espacio que sí, que no" (that space of yes and no), as Enrique put it— was now her home. As Razena said, "I've gotten used to it. I already see it as normal."

Brokering questions and judgments from people in both places was a central role of diaspora youth that shaped their identity formations. This chapter opens by quoting Maritza, born in Spain to Moroccan parents: "Spanish? Moroccan? Born in Spanish lands, judged everywhere." Her reflection continued: "My ears have heard the good and the bad about my roots. So many commentaries, so much instability. Like a child lost in a labyrinth, sometimes I don't know what to think." Maritza's reflection gives voice to the disorienting aspect of negotiating so many conflicting messages and value judgments, of "navigating the multiplicity," as diaspora scholar Nadine Naber (2012) writes. But the youths' narratives demonstrated that they were highly skilled at responding to these judgments and had developed nuanced and astute critiques of the social and cultural dynamics that produced them. Their understanding led them to be both critical and appreciative of their host and home societies. For example, Razena lamented that in Spain people associated Dominicans with gangs and that the police used this as a pretense to treat Dominican youths more roughly, when in fact there were Spanish youths in gangs, too. But she was also fiercely defensive of Spain and Madrid to people in the Dominican Republic who expressed the view that black people would be treated worse in Spain. In spite of her own experience of being targeted and racially profiled by the police in Madrid for being Dominican, she insisted that there was no race-based discrimination (as discussed in chapter 3). This stance becomes more understandable when seen from Razena's perspective, as a defense of her current home from the judgment of persons who have not been there and in the context of the many aspects of life in Madrid she appreciates. As she explained:

> When you arrive here from Santo Domingo, after never having traveled, arriving here really opens your mind because over there you only see Dominicans, Dominicans everywhere. But you get here and you see Colombians, Ecuadorians, from every country—you see Chinese, Japanese—so much diversity, you learn from it all. . . . It's going to open your mind a lot. I think that being there [in the Dominican Republic] with people it's a little bit closed.

Razena's experience of cultural diversity in Madrid gave her a nuanced picture of race and made her unwilling to accept the claims of Dominicans on the island that Spain was a difficult place to be black. Diaspora youths, who were highly aware of how they were viewed in both societies, were adept at challenging stereotypes of their communities in both places, even as they had their own critiques of these communities. It was one thing to critique your community from the inside, but criticism from the outside—from those who had "never traveled" or experienced life in both places—was unwarranted.

A primary example of this, which is explored more thoroughly in the next chapter, had to do with gender roles and relations in Latino and immigrant communities. Mariela and Luisa, sisters born in Spain to a Dominican mother, expressed concern about the Spanish media coverage of immigrants and its disproportionate focus on violence against women. If an immigrant killed or raped a woman it would be all over the news, they said, as if gender violence was a problem only in the immigrant community. They were well aware of the Spanish stereotypes of Latinos as *machista* (macho) men and sexually promiscuous women (see chapter 3). And yet, Mariela and Luisa were also highly critical of what they saw as sexism in the Dominican community. In their representations of themselves, they defended their right to complex identities that drew selectively from their multiple cultural communities. The narratives of Mariela, Luisa, Razena, and many of the youth in our study challenge the assumptions of nationalist integration policies that immigrant youth who maintain ties to their communities and countries of origin would adopt an *anti*-host country identity. Instead, viewing each community from the perspective of the other led them to critique *and* embrace (or defend) different elements of both. As Mariela explained, "Cuando voy a Santo Domingo echo de menos a España" (When I go to Santo Domingo, I miss Spain).

The Presentation: Challenging the Discourse of Integration

The complex self-representations of immigrant youth were on full display in the presentation we made at the Autonomous University of Madrid. At the end of our workshop at ASI, we took a group of youths to the university to share our work with an audience of professors and graduate students. The presentation at the university assumed importance for the youths as an opportunity to engage in the public sphere and recast their identities on their own terms. It also illustrated their struggle to be heard when they name their experiences in ways that defy dominant discourses about immigrants.

During the presentation, the young people shared their findings on the challenges facing immigrants, their multiple connections to Spain and their home countries, and their struggle to belong. In planning the presentation, we (Andrea and Enrique) had suggested organizing the content along the themes of ways they belong and ways they don't belong in Spain and their home countries. However, it became clear that even these categories imposed boundaries that falsely contained their experiences, and the youth presenters took advantage of the floor to disrupt these categories and add nuance. For example, during the discussion of their relationship to Spain and ways they belong in Spain, the presenters listed some of the advantages of living in Spain that we had identified in our research, including safety and security, better educational opportunities, friendships through school and soccer teams, and more jobs with better salaries than in their home countries. But as fourteen-year-old Raquel explained these advantages, she added a caveat. She said that many immigrants who have studied and earned degrees in their home countries cannot practice their professions in Spain. She referred to Mariela's neighbor in Madrid, whom Mariela had interviewed for our project. She had been a dentist in the Dominican Republic but could not practice here because her degree and training were not recognized in Spain. "You arrive here and you have to start from zero," Raquel said. By inserting this story, Raquel diverged from the script and qualified the notion that Spain was the land of opportunity.

Several of the stories the youths shared punctured the myth of the "Spanish Dream." Raquel said that Spain offered "una vida mejor, pero sin descanso" (a better life, but without rest). Raquel was quoting Marilyn's mother, whom Marilyn had interviewed about her experiences as an immigrant in Spain. Marilyn's mother had immigrated from Ecuador for a "better life" and found a steady job as a caretaker for the elderly, but in her words, she "worked without rest from Sunday to Monday, like the circular [metro that circles the center of Madrid]." Raquel then shared the story of her own mother, who worked as a maid cleaning houses. Although her mother had brought Raquel and her siblings from the Dominican Republic to be reunited with them, she did not get to spend any time with them. As Raquel said, "Since I arrived here I have not spent a single full day with my mother." Such stories challenged the myth that immigrants' lives were unequivocally better in Spain and exposed the painful trade-offs that migration entailed.

The youths shared experiences with racism, police harassment, and segregation in their schools. Marilyn explained the challenges of growing up as a black Ecuadorian in Spain and said that she used to be ashamed of being black ("me daba verguenza"). Ana Silvia, from Brazil, said that since she had arrived in Spain she had felt lonely ("me he sentido sola") and that she would like to hang out with Spanish kids but they did not seem to want her. Yet, in spite of these personal testimonies of exclusion, some members of the audience asked questions that challenged the young people's narratives and the existence of racism. The Q&A with the audience allowed us to witness both native Spaniards and immigrant youths wrestling with hegemonic discourses of Spanish benevolence and immigrant integration, and the durability of these discourses in the face of opposing narratives.

Mariela and Luisa insisted on inviting questions from the audience after each section rather than waiting until the end of the presentation. Questions were numerous, impassioned, and long-winded, and several times one of us had to step in to ensure there would be enough time to finish the presentation. Clearly the presentation had touched a nerve. The comment of one young Spanish woman in the audience is illustrative.[3] After hearing about the challenges facing immigrants, the woman said, "I would like to offer an opinion." She suggested that immigrants may be inviting the treatment they receive because of their attitude toward Spaniards; that is, they assume Spaniards will be hostile and so they close themselves off: "Si tú te sientes diferente, tú tambien pones límites" (If you feel different, you also put up barriers). The woman offered three variations on this comment at three points during the presentation, each time emphasizing that "both groups" (Spanish and immigrant) were equally responsible for "cultural prejudices" that caused conflict.

After the second time, Mariela agreed that it was possible that immigrants, because of their "bad experiences" with Spanish people, assume that all Spaniards are like that. The woman seemed happy that Mariela had agreed and responded eagerly, "We generalize, we [Spaniards] do it, too, and that's the problem with society." At the end of the presentation, after other questions had been discussed, Raquel returned to the woman's point, telling her, "You are right, it's not only Spanish people" who are to blame, and "we all have to change." A little later, a young man in the audience was given the last question. He said, "I have noticed that the level of racism has gone down [in Madrid]. A few years ago it was very strong, and the media was full of hostile reports about immigrants, but now that seems to have gone away." Without waiting for the youths to respond he continued, saying that it was not racism but social class that was the problem. "If a black man comes with a suit and tie and a fistful of money, he won't be discriminated against."

After the testimonies and data presented by the youths, the man's comment felt like a violent retort, like salt poured on an open wound. It was the violence of denial, of refusing to see the painful realities of the courageous young people in front of him whose lives mattered less than an idea that Madrid was improving. Such is the violence of the discourse of integration in Spain, where to speak of difference is to challenge the fragile peace, to threaten the social fabric. By insisting that racism was not a problem, that social class and "cultural prejudices" were behind whatever hardships immigrants experienced, audience members held fast to their notion that Spain was an open and tolerant society where ethnic distinctions and inequalities were erased in the name of social cohesion.

Why were Mariela and Raquel so willing to accept this view, against their own experiences and the testimonies they had collected? Their response could be seen as reflecting the precarious citizenship of immigrant youth who have been socialized by the discourse of integration and are not equipped to understand their experiences of marginalization or to confront the structural conditions that limit their lives. Given the silences around race described in chapter 3, it is not surprising that the young people accommodated a metanarrative that race doesn't matter. But from the perspective of the diasporic third space, we argue that their response also illustrates their role as cultural brokers mediating two irreconcilable points of view. By inviting questions from the audience at several different points during the presentation, they showed that they embraced this role of translating and interpreting the distinct worlds of their experience and were eager to clarify public notions about their group. In some ways, agreeing with the woman in the audience that immigrants were to blame for their own plight left intact dominant images of Spanish benevolence and immigrant deficiencies, but in other ways it challenged them. By showing themselves to be thoughtful and open to other views, Mariela and Raquel were also challenging stereotypes of immigrant youth as angry and hostile.

The complexity of their self-presentation was especially apparent in their responses to a question from the audience about music. A young man asked the girls what kind of music they listened to and whether they identified more with music from their countries or from Spain. Marilyn, from Ecuador, answered that at first she had listened only to Spanish music because she was ashamed to be black ("me daba mucha verguenza ser negra"), but over time, as she made more Latino friends, she realized that "it wasn't bad for me to like the music from my country, and Latino music, the music that I grew up with." Raquel, from the Dominican Republic, answered similarly, "I've been here for eight years, and at first I listened to Spanish music to feel like them," but over time she realized that "I like the music from my country better, and I felt more identified with it." She hastily added that it was not that Spanish music was worse or "bad," but she just didn't identify with it. Mariela, born in Spain to a Dominican mother, explained that "we listen to both, music from here and from there." She explained that she used to identify with Dominican music more but eventually realized that it was "too sexist," "all about tits, sweat, and heat"; she drew uproarious laughter from the audience at her evocation of the obscene gestures the dances involve. Her sister Luisa agreed, saying, "Like my sister says, being from two countries you have two cultures (*doble cultura*)." They listened to Spanish music with her father's family and Dominican music like *bachata* when they were in the Dominican Republic or with Dominican family in Madrid. She agreed that Dominican music "*is* a little sexist," but maintained that "it's like that, we listen to both." With their answers, all of the girls insisted on the right to identify on their own terms and to identify selectively with different cultural communities. Their explanations demonstrated complex, hybrid identities that change in different ways over time and are affected by their position as racialized, gendered subjects. Such complexity, highlighting variations even between immigrants from the same national-origin background, defies the logic of linear assimilation over time and its opposite, the threat of unassimilated immigrant youth.

Analyzing diaspora young people's narratives of their identities through the lens of diasporic citizenship reveals the richness and complexity of immigrant experiences and the limits of the nation-state optic with its either/or binaries. Through the public presentation, their poetic writings, and our group dialogues and interviews, these youths gave voice to parts of themselves that were invisible in the public sphere. They challenged dominant images of immigrant youth as disaffected, alienated, and criminally inclined, or culturally backward, in-transition-to-assimilated-Spanish subjects, and they insisted on their right to move back and forth and in between their multiple worlds. As diasporic subjects, the youths in our study demonstrate new forms of thinking and consciousness that Anzaldúa calls *pensamiento fronterizo* (border thinking): "a site of criss-crossed experience, language and identity . . . caught between various hegemonic colonial and postcolonial languages, and subaltern dialects, and vernacular expressions"

(Saldívar 2006, 161–62). It is a *pensamiento fronterizo* that is both within nation-state boundaries and at the same time outside of them, beyond their purview and understanding.

Through our participatory research process, we learned that making young people's in-between location a central object of inquiry and reflection becomes a powerful educational and citizenship tool that contributes to the project of decolonizing citizenship. It allows diaspora young people to capitalize on the insights of their outsider status and create new collective identities that are not tied to the nation-state and its hegemonic social formations. These new identities and citizenship formations may not be visible through dominant nationalist lenses that look for assimilated subjects, but they become visible when we allow diaspora young people, our research participants, to direct the inquiry from their lived experience. In the next chapter, we explore these processes more deeply in the context of activist associations where migrant women drew on transnational cultures and identities as sources of resistance to colonial domination.

CHAPTER 5

Feminists in Transition

Transnational Latina Activists in Madrid

Andrea Dyrness

Yes, it's really strange, Andrea, it's like, not feeling like I'm from any place, feeling sometimes from one place and sometimes from another, but Spanish I will never feel.

—Daniela, Ecuadorian and Spanish

And if going home is denied me then I will have to stand and claim my space, making a new culture—una cultura mestiza—with my own lumber, my own bricks and mortar and my own feminist architecture.

—Gloria Anzaldúa, *Borderlands/La Frontera*

A S WE SAW IN THE PREVIOUS CHAPTERS, the youths in our study who had grown up in Madrid between multiple cultural communities experienced the question of national belonging as an uncertainty, the possibility of their eventual identification with Spain as an open question. They struggled to make sense of their experiences and identities as immigrants in social spaces designed for their "integration" by Spanish educators invested in erasing any aspect of cultural difference. In contrast, migrant women involved in several activist associations in Madrid offer a picture of transnational identity formation that unfolds in social spaces controlled by migrants, where a critical orientation to the state (Spain and others) was often assumed. For these women, not belonging to any place was not only an existential reality but also a defining feature of their identities and a conscious political stance. Latina women who had migrated to Madrid from Central and South America under a variety of circumstances found in feminist associations a place to regularly reflect on their experiences and their relationship to multiple communities. These spaces of collective reflection and the citizenship practices they animated, I argue, reflected and nurtured a transnational, decolonial feminist struggle emerging from a "third space" occupied by the women as transnational migrants at the crossroads between nations, races, cultures, and social movements. Using the lens of transnational feminisms, I analyze the cultural and educative practices in these communal spaces and the ways they drew upon transnational cultures of resistance, including feminist epistemologies of Latin America, to nurture new identities and forms of belonging that were not tied to the nation-state.

In this chapter I detail a participatory research project within one activist association, Asociación de Mujeres de Guatemala (AMG; Association of Guatemalan Women), to illuminate processes of identity formation and belonging among Latin American migrants in Madrid. After beginning our inquiry by focusing on the experiences of the four young Guatemalan women who formed the group with me, we broadened our scope to examine the experiences of migrant women in other activist associations, and then used our findings to engage in a dialogue about what it means to be Latina, and a migrant, in Spain. A central focus in our research became the spaces of *autoformación* that sustain migrant women, including the space of AMG. *Autoformación* means both self-formation and self-directed learning. Exploring the role and meaning of *autoformación* in the lives of migrant activists allows us to examine how transnational women educate themselves to become activists and what meanings they make of their own transnational identities.

The Asociación de Mujeres de Guatemala is a feminist, nongovernmental, nonprofit organization founded by displaced Guatemalan women living in Spain, dedicated to preventing and eradicating gender-based violence in Central America and the world. I was introduced to its director, Mercedes, through a mutual friend when I first moved to Spain in 2013. In one of our first meetings Mercedes emphasized that AMG was not an immigrant organization. She explained that its purpose was to "denounce violence against women in Guatemala and Latin America" and to raise awareness and resources in Europe to combat gender violence, especially femicide, in Latin America. While doing this work, they became inevitably drawn into meeting the needs of Guatemalan women living in Spain, so helping immigrant women in the process of integration became another focus of the organization. Both the phenomenon of *violencia machista* (sexist violence) and the strategies to combat it were necessarily transnational. At the time of my research, for example, AMG was involved in lobbying for a law against femicide in Colombia (which passed in 2015) in partnership with NGOs in Colombia, and providing legal services for immigrant women in Spain who were victims of sexual violence and were applying for asylum. Their transnational activism and their local work with immigrant women became two braided strands of a *glocal* strategy to combat gender violence.[1] AMG's mission reflected its explicitly transnational scope:

> Estamos comprometidas con el desarrollo de la presencia social de las mujeres, tanto en Guatemala como en España, y de su inclusión y representación en los espacios culturales, económicos y políticos; con tal fin, detectamos y denunciamos situaciones de desigualdad e injusticia social que impiden el empoderamiento de las mujeres.

> [We are committed to promoting the social presence of women, both in Guatemala and in Spain, and their inclusion and representation in cultural, economic, and political spaces; to that end, we identify and denounce situations of inequality and social injustice that impede the empowerment of women.][2]

While I was already engaged in research with young people at ASI, AMG's transnational activist focus offered a unique space to explore questions of diasporic citizenship and migrant civic identity formation. I was also drawn to the women by our shared Central American background. As a Costa Rican citizen who had spent most of my career in Central American communities, including conducting research in Guatemala, El Salvador, and with Guatemalan and Salvadoran immigrant women in California, I felt an affinity with the Guatemalan women as Central Americans in Spain, who comprise a small fraction of the Latin American immigrant population.[3]

Latin American migration to Spain has been highly feminized, with women overrepresented largely due to the demand for women to work in domestic service (Hierro 2016). Central American women fall into two main groups: those who come to study at Spanish universities, who tend to be from upper- or upper-middle-class families, and those who come to work, primarily in domestic service and other low-wage jobs. While very few Latin American women enter Spain as asylum seekers, many who arrive as labor migrants or students choose to stay in Spain to escape violence in their home countries.[4] It is these exiled and displaced women who made up the core of AMG's associates. These were first-generation immigrant women who had arrived in Spain in their twenties and thirties on student visas, tourist visas, or as workers, almost all of them fleeing some kind of violence in their home countries.

Mercedes, the director and cofounder of AMG, had fled Guatemala ten years earlier at age twenty-five and arrived in Spain on a student visa, seeking safety and anonymity. She had lived outside Guatemala for short periods before—in Cuba and in the United States—each time for reasons of personal security, but once it became clear that Guatemala was too dangerous for her to return, she decided her new permanent home would be Spain, chosen for the language. From the safety of Spain, she dedicated her life's work to investigating, denouncing, and lobbying for prosecution of crimes against women in Central America, leveraging the resources of Spanish and European institutions and networks. While AMG's principal activities were in the areas of advocacy and legal service, through its psychosocial work it also aimed to "contribute to strengthening the exercise of full citizenship of migrant women, through actions ranging from the first reception, counseling and job seeking, to training for empowerment through courses and workshops."[5] It was in this area, focused on education and support for migrant women in Madrid, that Mercedes saw a role for my research, hoping that it could contribute to the formation of young *socias* (associates) of the organization.

I conducted participant observation and interviews at AMG in 2013 to 2014 and on a follow-up visit in the summer of 2016, and over the course of my research I participated in many of their events from meetings and conferences to protests and festive meals. At the heart of this was a participatory research project with a group of young Guatemalan women who became my interlocutors. Ranging in age from twenty-two to thirty-two, the four women in the group had arrived in Spain in the previous two to eight years and had a variety of immigration statuses; two were on student visas, one was a refugee, and one had spent three years in an irregular status before acquiring legal residence and eventually Spanish nationality. All of them were volunteers for AMG in some capacity. We began meeting in my apartment in Malasaña one fall morning and rotated our meetings between different members' homes over the next few weeks, always accompanying our conversation with coffee and elaborate spreads of food: typical Guatemalan breakfasts with black beans, eggs, fried plantains, home-baked goods, and fruits. In the following discussion of our process, methods, and findings, I show how our research process itself became a space for critical reflection and consciousness raising that mirrored the processes we were studying. As a space of *autoformación* based on collective inquiry and reflection, our research provided a window into and embodied feminist practices of citizenship formation that sustained many migrant women in Madrid.

"It Helps to Make Us Aware"

One morning in the living room of Maria's first-floor apartment in Arguelles, we discussed the poem "Child of the Americas," by Aurora Levins Morales.

> I am what I am.
> A child of the Americas.
> A light-skinned mestiza of the Caribbean.
> A child of many diaspora, born into this continent at a crossroads.
> . . . I am an immigrant
> and the daughter and granddaughter of immigrants.[6]

"That line, 'I am an immigrant and the daughter of immigrants,' that really struck me," Erica shared. Erica had immigrated to Spain from Guatemala eight years before at the age of twenty-four. She went on, "Guatemala is a country made up of immigrants, even though nobody thinks so. The Spaniards were immigrants!" She then highlighted another line, "I am a late leaf of that ancient tree," saying it applied to them (Guatemalans) because "we have so much history, we are indigenous, even though nobody wants to recognize it, we are a mix. We don't want to look back, but that would help us look forward." Twenty-six-year-old Marta jumped in, "It would help us not be so racist." Marta emphatically agreed with Erica on the need to recognize their mixed-race ancestry. "You have no [expletive] idea where your roots come from!" They talked about how many Guatemalans deride indigenous people while denying their own indigenous blood. Then Erica said that the fact of migration made her conscious of this racism: "We are racists in our own country and then we arrive here to experience it in the flesh. It helps to make us aware" (field notes 9/27/13).[7]

This excerpt of our discussion, prompted by a poem by Aurora Levins Morales, a California Puerto Rican Jew, illustrates several features of *autoformación,* which I theorize as a process of collective self-recovery and consciousness raising that is reminiscent of Chicana/Latina and U.S. Third World feminist journeys (hooks 1990; Trinidad Galván 2014). Like Levins Morales, all of the women in our group were children of the Americas with mixed backgrounds whose ancestries included migration pathways spanning Europe, Central America, and North and South America, and all of them, as young adults, had themselves migrated from the Americas to Spain. Their acts of migration and their experiences as migrants in Spain made them more conscious of their personal and collective histories of racial, cultural, and gender violence than they had been before migrating. This coming to terms with histories of conquest, colonization, and hybridity that preceded migration—as seen through the experiences of the migrant—is a decolonizing of the mind that is at the center of Latin American and Chicana feminisms (Trinidad Galván 2014). As Trinidad Galván notes, "Latin American feminists examine the intersection of our European and Indigenous, Black, and Asian roots, and the way in which Whiteness is normalized even in discussion of mestizaje and latinidad" (2014, 136). Similarly, Sofia Villenas (2006) writes, "Like other postcolonial and Third World feminist projects, Latina/Chicana feminisms entail revisiting and interrogating the colonial and imperialist past while remarking on the persistent neocolonial, patriarchal and heteronormative relations within the new world order" (660). In this light, *autoformación* is an educational practice that centers processes of identity formation consciously engaging with multiple structures of domination.

Participatory research informed by a borderlands feminist sensibility is in itself a process of *autoformación*—that is, collective self-directed inquiry, education, and action in which, as Torre and Ayala (2009) have suggested, experiences of multiplicity, hybridity, and the contradictions of life *entremundos* (between worlds) become analytic resources that press us toward liberation. I had learned from my earlier work with Latina immigrant mothers in California (Dyrness 2011) to appreciate Latina feminist or *mujerista* (womanist) epistemologies in which *convivencia,* the relationships built through the sharing of personal experiences, are as important as the formal research activities and products (Dyrness 2008, 2011; Trinidad Galván 2011, 2014, 2015). Spaces of *convivencia* like this one, built on the everyday cultural practices of the participants, become a means of affirming individual experiences, developing a critical analysis, and strengthening group identity. In the sharing of individual experiences of collective oppression, *testimonio*, which has a long tradition in Latin American activism, becomes a key method of *autoformación* that serves the goals of both personal and collective transformation. The Latina Feminist Group (2001) describes *testimonio* as a "crucial means of bearing witness and inscribing into history those lived realities that would otherwise succumb to the alchemy of erasure" (2). Incorporating *testimonio* as a participatory research method offers a way to build on and expand Latina women's own capacities for social critique and transformative resistance (Dyrness 2011, 5).

In this research I adapted the tools of PAR to the schedules and constraints of our group, maintaining the core values of *convivencia* and dialogue. I had initially hoped all members of the team would participate in deciding the research questions and carrying out the research activities, but because of the women's schedules that wasn't possible. All of the participants were both working and studying in addition to doing their activist work with AMG, and they all led extremely busy lives. So we devised a modified PAR project that would respect the women's desires for reflection and *autoformación* in community while being flexible enough to allow varying levels of participation in research activities. We conducted a series of group dialogues in which we explored key questions together as a group and generated questions for further inquiry with other Latin American women. I introduced poetry written by Latina migrant women and identity reflection exercises to prompt our discussion. After each group discussion, I pulled out generative themes (Freire [1970] 1999) for further discussion at the next meeting. Importantly, I participated in these discussions, sharing my own experiences and reflections as they resonated with the themes discussed. With this process, we generated a series of questions for interviews with other activist women that probed the relationship between their experiences as migrant women and their activist work. Beginning with contacts Mercedes suggested from her networks, two of the young women and I conducted interviews with five Latina activists and one Latino activist.[8] These formal, in-depth interviews lasted two hours on average. We then discussed their responses together in our group in relation to our own experiences. In this way, although not all of the women participated in the interviewing, the interviews reflected and contributed to our collective inquiry. On a return visit in the summer of 2016 I used the interview guide we developed to interview three more Latin American activists, and I weave data from those interviews into the discussion below.[9]

In the next section I describe the process by which we reflected on our identities as an example of *autoformación,* in which the collective exploration of experiences became a vehicle for raising critical consciousness. Our research was an iterative process in which each dialogue built on and probed more deeply an issue that had come up in a previous discussion and in turn, generated questions for further inquiry. For example, early on, Erica had said she was interested in the experience of feminist immigrants because "many came to know feminism here [in Spain]." Marta confirmed that she was one of those people, adding laughingly that she was a "feminist in transition!" On multiple occasions, the women discussed their evolving ideas of feminism, comparing notions of feminism they had known in Guatemala with different types of feminisms they were exposed to in Spain. "Feminists in transition" became an apt phrase to describe the process of collective self-discovery that was at the heart of our inquiry. We decided to focus on how the experience of migration affects women's identities and enables them to make change, because that would encompass the role of feminism for those women who identified as feminists. Asking other activist women about their own experiences of feminism and what feminism meant to them became part of a protocol intended to probe the relationship between their various identities and their activist work, as the women in our group continued to explore these intersections in their own lives.

Not Belonging to Any Country: In Limbo

The idea of not belonging, or "being in limbo," as Marta put it, emerged early on in our group dialogues when we completed a flower exercise to reflect on our racial, ethnic, national, and gender identities. The Power Flower exercise has individuals fill in petals for each of their social identities (e.g., race, ethnicity, class, language, nationality) to help them reflect on how they identify in relation to the dominant group in each category.[10] This task immediately brought to the fore the contingent and in-between nature of the women's identities. For example, for language, they noted that "Spanish is the dominant language [in Spain], but not the Spanish we speak. It has to be Castilian." Race presented similar dilemmas because "Latina" was a hybrid category not recognized in Spain. Erica noted that her limbo began even before she migrated to Spain, in Guatemala, where she was "ladino," a hybrid ethnicity that is "neither white nor indigenous" but mestiza. In Spain she identified as Guatemalan even though she had acquired Spanish nationality, because, she said, "I don't feel Spanish *at all*. . . . No matter how long I live here, people will always ask me where I'm from. I will never be Spanish." All of the women spoke of not belonging to recognized identity groups in Spain. Deisy and Maria, whose parents had migrated to the United States, experienced another kind of limbo as Guatemalan Americans. Maria explained, "I was Latina in the U.S. But in Spain, I'm American." She said Spaniards did not understand the category of "Latino" and expected all Americans to be white. Yet even in the United States, where Latina was a recognized identity, she was still on the margins of national identity. "In the United States, I'm from Guatemala. And in Guatemala, I'm from the United States! I am always an immigrant my whole life!" she exclaimed. Marta jumped in, agreeing, "You're in limbo: you're neither from here nor from there." She went on, "There [in Guatemala] they have the perception that you're a traitor because you left. . . . It's like really messed up."

Marta's comment suggests a key element of the third space, this "limbo"—that it is born of multiple exclusions. While the women felt they did not belong in Spain because they experienced rejection and discrimination there, they also no longer belonged to their countries of origin because migration had changed them, making them different in the eyes of their friends and family back home, and also had changed their views of themselves and their home countries. While Marta spoke animatedly about how she was viewed by others in Guatemala, Erica said, "In Guatemala I do not feel at home." She felt that her home was in Spain, even though she believed she would always be viewed as an outsider. What does it mean to feel at home in a place you don't belong? And to not feel at home in a place you always belonged? Over the next few weeks we mined this space of contradiction for insights and possibilities, and in the midst of this probing the women identified that this space, this limbo, "te concientiza" (makes you conscious). Although their outsider status had been thrust upon them, imposed by those who rejected them, the women came to embrace it, owning the features of their difference from both societies as a critical political distance. It was through *autoformación* with a community of similarly displaced *compañeras*, a community of diasporic citizens, that the women could identify, prize, and nurture this critical consciousness as the basis for their activist identities and a resource for change.

"I've Had a Love-Hate Relationship with Spain since the Beginning"

During one of our group discussions Erica explained that she arrived in Spain not wanting to belong, wanting to leave everything behind, to disappear. So she felt liberated when she got here: "Me sentía liberada." She loved the fact that she could dye her hair orange if she wanted to or go out wearing whatever she wanted and "nobody would mess with me." It was not like in Guatemala, where you go out and people check you out from head to toe, where the neighborhood gossip mill polices your behavior more strictly than the army does. She wanted to be anonymous, so she loved Spain. "I've had a love-hate relationship with Spain since the beginning," she said. Spain represented freedom and autonomy and safety, things denied to her as a woman in Guatemala, and yet she would always be a foreigner.

The experience of multiple forms of violence in Guatemala—structural, political, symbolic, and everyday (Bourgois 2001)—shaped all of the women's relationships to Spain. Guatemala has one of the highest rates of femicide (killing of women on account of their gender) and other gender-based violence in the hemisphere, with more than seven hundred women and girls murdered each year.[11] In a 2017 study by UN Women, the National Institute of Forensic Science reported that sixty-two women were killed each month and that violence against women was the most reported crime in the preceding five years—part of a cycle of violence that is the legacy of Guatemala's bloody thirty-six-year civil war.[12] And yet the women in my study often were not aware of the ways this violence had affected them until they arrived in Spain. Menjívar (2011) writes about violence in Guatemala, "The everyday, normalized familiarity with violence renders it invisible" (43). Being afraid was a way of life. As Mercedes explained about growing up in Guatemala, "There you have to grow up really fast because you could literally lose your life if you don't assume the responsibility of what it means to take care, no? To take care in many cases translates to being afraid, simply."

For the women in our group, being removed from the context of immediate violence and experiencing safety and autonomy as women in Spain gave them a critical awareness of women's lack of autonomy in Guatemala. Marta shared, "I didn't realize until I arrived here that I lived in a culture of violence there. It was just normal. People would tell you [as a woman], don't go out on the street late, don't walk in certain areas, and you accept it." When she witnessed the murder that caused her to flee the country and seek asylum in Spain, she was walking with her companion to the bus stop at 8:00 at night. Her friends asked her, "What were you doing out at that hour?" as if she had been at fault for what happened. From the safety of her life in Spain, she was able to able to challenge that view: "The question should have been why are they murdering young men at 8:00 at night? Not why was I out at that hour."

Migration gave them the space to recover themselves from structures of normalized violence in Guatemala, and this motivated their activism. Erica said that the freedom she experienced as a woman in Madrid—where it is customary for people to be out on the streets at all hours of the night, with very little crime—made her concerned about the situation of women in Guatemala. "I started to see that you could really live differently, and that there is this thing that we are not aware of in Guatemala that's called rights!" It was only after coming to Spain that she realized that a functioning state with rule of law and citizenship rights was possible. She learned this, she explained, "by the simple fact of existing in Spain. Because if you go out on the street and get robbed, you can call the police and you can count on the police . . . Little things that you notice, that maybe seem so trivial to people here, or going to a demonstration, that in Guatemala I had never done." Not only did they have the freedom to walk around safely as women in Madrid, but they could participate in protests, which, they discussed many times, would have been impossible in Guatemala where they would have risked their lives.

For the women in AMG, the contrast between their lives in Spain and the realities of Guatemala was a constant tension that motivated their commitment to feminist struggle. As Erica shared, "I have a lot of important women in my life who still live in Guatemala and I would like to believe that they can live a full and safe life and have the basic right of locomotion . . . and not get raped or killed because they are women!" This is why she was involved in AMG: "At least I had the opportunity to see that living in a state of fear is not normal and that it's not natural, that it doesn't have to be that way, and we have to do something to change it." On a broader level, migrating to Spain rendered the conditions in Guatemala as a problem that required critical investigation and intervention. All four of the women said that they became motivated to learn more about Guatemala after coming to Spain, particularly after becoming associated with AMG and other Guatemalan women who were politically active. AMG organized conferences and forums on current events in Guatemala and brought prominent activists and human rights workers to speak at them. Mercedes's twenty-two-year-old niece, Deisy, said that it was in Spain, through AMG, that she first learned about the case of Ríos Montt, the former military general and president of Guatemala who was tried for genocide in spring 2013. On her trips to Guatemala she had never learned about the nation's history; she only learned to be afraid for her personal safety. It took coming to Spain to gain the freedom and curiosity to learn more: "When I came to Spain, it was like, OK, I feel safe here, and then I took interest in learning about Guatemala."

Belonging in Spain was intimately tied to the women's feelings of safety, but it was also associated with their evolving feminism and the new identities available to them. The freedoms in Spain that were denied them as women in Guatemala included not only freedom of movement in the streets but also freedom to live outside the bounds of the prescribed female roles of wife and mother. For Deisy and Erica, who did not want to have children and were seen as "black sheep" by their families back home, the community of feminists at AMG offered a welcoming support. Erica shared that her choice not to marry or have children was a key factor separating her from her friends in Guatemala, and her coming to terms with this was at the heart of her feminist journey. She explained that to her, feminism meant "the ability to not feel strange" for rejecting conventional gender roles, and the liberating recognition that "all of those things" like marriage and childbearing "are things that are imposed on you" by society and are not fundamental to womanhood. She believed that Spain had made this "different focus" possible for her, and "maybe that's why I love Spain." As Erica described her journey of coming to terms with her difference from her friends and family back home, I shared that I had experienced similar feelings in choosing not to have a second child, which I had not before processed as a feminist issue. I explained that in the face of relentless social pressure to have another child, I was ashamed to admit publicly that I preferred my intellectual work over the work of parenting, fearing that this would cause me to be seen as selfish, or worse, as a bad mother to my daughter. In the supportive company of women who were also different, I could see my internal struggle clearly as an instance of gender-based oppression. This is one example of how, through the sharing of experiences of structural violence, *autoformación* elevates critical consciousness and strengthens feminist identity.

Yet, even as they cherished the new freedoms they enjoyed in Spain, the women laughed at Spanish stereotypes of Latino cultures as defined by machismo, as if Spain were a paragon of gender equity. Their own experiences of marginalization as immigrant women defied that. Erica said, "[The Spanish stereotype] is due to ignorance, they don't really know what machismo is. They think a macho is a man with a mustache beating his wife all day! And they don't realize they are just as macho, or more, for the fact of coming and paternalizing us so much!" Erica's words suggest that machismo or sexist violence is not only about physical violence but also about "paternalizing" behavior—patterns of control and domination that the Spanish, as colonizers, established in Latin America. As immigrant women it was possible to experience greater personal safety in Madrid—that is, freedom from physical violence—while still being subject to a range of dominating and demeaning practices intended to remind them of their place as colonized subjects. Their refusal to accept the narrative that Spanish society was "better" for women or inclusive and welcoming of immigrants was based on their own experiences of racism.

As a group, the women involved in AMG had several privileges that should have eased their transitions to Spain, including middle-class family backgrounds, university education, fluency in the Spanish language (although not the dominant variety), and legal status. But in spite of their social and cultural capital, they had painful experiences of exclusion and discrimination that served as regular reminders that they could not belong. Erica spoke of being stopped in the street and asked for her papers by the police. Even though she had obtained her resident's card by then, the incident reminded her that her belonging was in question. Erica worked as an English-language teacher at a local private secondary school. Two years in the United States as a child and a talent for languages had given her impeccable English, but her fellow teachers did not treat her as an equal because she did not have a degree recognized in Spain, and perhaps because of her Guatemalan/Latina identity. She said "making myself understood" by colleagues was a challenge due to language and cultural differences, and it was one of the greatest limitations of her life as an immigrant. Language differences "limited me so much and continue to limit me, because I've lost my sense of humor. . . . I've been here eight years and I continue to be misunderstood!" We spoke often in our group about how it felt to have our varieties of spoken Spanish from the Americas misunderstood and disparaged in Spain.

Erica was close friends with Maria, another member of our group, a twenty-six-year-old Guatemalan American who had been in Spain for four years. Maria had originally come to work as an English teaching assistant in a public school and to accompany her Guatemalan boyfriend, who had found a job in Madrid after failing to get his papers in Los Angeles. Maria was now enrolled in a master's program in a university in Madrid and struggled to belong in a place where American Latina was not a recognized social identity. She explained that the large Latino community where she grew up in Los Angeles had helped her to belong, but in Spain people expected Americans to be blonde and blue-eyed, and she didn't fit this image. Although her English skills brought her social capital and her first job, her right to this capital was questioned because she was not white. She explained that in the school where she first worked in Madrid she had tried to educate them about the category of "Latina" in the United States, but they didn't want to hear it. "Here I don't belong because I'm not what the Spaniards expect." Maria's story shows that the social privileges of a bachelor's degree, a job as an English teacher, and U.S. identity and citizenship were not enough to insulate her from racism; she could not belong in Spain because her phenotype did not match what Spaniards expected from someone with her skills and status. The women learned that their academic skills, talent, and specialized training would not always be recognized by Spaniards determined to discipline them for their Latina ways.

Twenty-two-year-old Deisy, Mercedes's niece, had come to Spain to attend medical school and quickly learned to adapt her Spanish to the Castilian spoken in Madrid. That didn't stop her professors from correcting her; one went so far as to deduct a point from her exam for failing to put an accent mark on her own last name (she didn't use the accent mark in the United States). Deisy was born in California to Guatemalan immigrant parents and then moved to Oregon, where she grew up "not belonging to any group." Completely bilingual in English and Spanish, she was also a strong student, earning *matrícula de honor* in medical school for her perfect score at midterm.

The fourth member of our group, Marta, was an artist who had been studying architecture and modern dance in Guatemala City before violence forced her to flee. She struggled to find support for her artistic identity as a refugee in Spain. Although her refugee status entitled her to help from the Spanish state in the form of vocational training and placement, the only courses available for women were *peluquería* (to become a hairdresser) and nursing—low-status jobs that Spaniards didn't want, the women pointed out. Confronted by these job prospects, Marta felt discouraged and out of place. The Spanish state, like the U.S. state (Ong 1996) and the Canadian state (Ameeriar 2017), disciplined refugee subjects by offering narrow vocational opportunities and refusing to recognize training and degrees from countries of origin, which confined them to jobs in the service sector, where most immigrant women were concentrated.

As they discussed the ways they did not belong in Spain or in Guatemala, the women articulated a critique of the multiple forms of structural violence that permeated both societies. If their awakening to "the reality" of violence in Guatemala was facilitated by their feelings of personal safety in Spain, it was equally prompted by the shock of migration and their experiences of racism and discrimination as Latinas in Spain. As Erica pointed out, experiencing racism "in the flesh" made her realize how racist Guatemalans were against indigenous people. She explained that after coming to Spain she immediately stopped using the derogatory term *indio* (Indian) to refer to indigenous people. "It's like my bubble was burst on arriving here."

Migrating to Spain had both unloosed them from their moorings and made them realize how tenuous their belonging in Guatemala had been. Erica reflected, "Over there I always belonged, and I didn't see the social reality. . . . We lived in the bubble of the capital." As a resident of the capital city, Erica had been sheltered from the realities facing poor, rural, and indigenous communities. Erica directly linked her belonging there with a lack of awareness of "the reality" of injustice; her new awareness made it impossible to belong: "I don't see things the same way anymore." She described her frustration at talking to childhood friends back home in Guatemala City who denied that the war ever happened. Marta, too, said that in Guatemala she didn't learn about the war until she went to university. Growing up in the capital, she said, "you never imagine that there was so much injustice." Her family never talked about the war. "So I couldn't learn it from school or from my family," she said.

As they came to this awareness, they distanced themselves from any national identity and embraced the space in between. The "love-hate relationship" with Spain that Erica described became a metaphor for a tension they all maintained, an animating force in their activist lives. Based on our experience, we made the women's relationship to Spain and national identity a central object of reflection and analysis. We added questions for the interviews with activists, including: How would you describe your relationship with Spain? Do you feel like you belong in Spain? How would you describe your relationship to [country of origin]? What have been the greatest challenges in your life as an immigrant? How have you overcome them?

These questions were as richly provocative for the interviewees as they had been for our group, triggering lengthy and emotional responses. Reflecting on their relationships to Spain, all of the activist women we interviewed—from Guatemala, Mexico, Peru, Venezuela, Colombia, and Ecuador—described similarly complicated, ambivalent, and contradictory relationships. But on the question of whether they belonged, the answer was always unequivocally and adamantly *no*. Nor did they belong, any longer, to their countries of origin. As they described their journeys from forced outsider status to conscious rejection of national belonging, they gave voice to the "love-hate" relationship with the nation and the insider-outsider identities that animate the third space.

Like the women in our group, the activists we interviewed expressed their relationships to Spain in terms of appreciation for the lifestyle in Spain, particularly the personal safety and autonomy as women in Spain in contrast to their home countries. They expressed gratitude for things Spain had given them such as "tranquility," "stability," "peace," and "security." Mercedes's words were illustrative: "Spain has given me many things that Guatemala didn't, and in Spain I've achieved many things I didn't get in Guatemala." Foremost among them: "The ability to have, I never had in Guatemala on the street, the sensation of being at peace. Never. Not once. To be able to feel at peace in the public sphere, which is where you finally develop your life, materially and symbolically, I never experienced that being in Guatemala, and I did experience it here." She suggested that safety meant not just freedom from physical violence but a sense of peace and the ability to dedicate yourself to personal, emotional, and intellectual pursuits as well as a "culture of leisure," which you could only do when "the preservation of life is not so present at every moment." For her, the contrast between her life in Spain and in Guatemala motivated her activist work:

> When you are walking down the street for example, coming home
> at two in the morning, peacefully walking home in Spain, and you
> say, "I can't even dream of doing this in my country, because I
> would lose my life, right?" And . . . that is when you start to think,
> "I too want a country like this for my family that I love back there."
> And if I really want it, well somebody's got to start building it.

To be safe walking in the streets at night, "to go out dancing til 6:30 in the morning and go home safely," "to go out for a beer and come home at three in the morning without anyone having to accompany me," to "wear whatever I want," were all freedoms that had been missing in their lives before— "that was impossible in Bogotá," "incredible, unthinkable in Lima!" This was a common thread in the women's narratives, and it bonded them to Spain. Berta, a radio producer who had immigrated from Mexico City, explained that she had never been in love with Spain or dreamed of moving there, but "I like the way of living here, ok? It allows me not to live the violence that is lived in cities in Mexico." Twenty-one-year-old Laura, an activist with the political party Podemos who had migrated from Colombia, credited the "safety and tranquility" with her belonging to Spain: "Once you live it here, you have it, and you know that there [back home] it doesn't exist.... In those moments I feel very Spanish. I feel very, very much from this city. I feel very much from this country."

Their experience of autonomy in Spain gave the women a critical awareness of the reality of violence in their countries of origin and the ways this violence had limited their lives and continued to limit the lives of their loved ones there. Just as it did for the women in our group, this sharpened awareness created a critical distance between the women we interviewed and their home countries, making it impossible for them to "go back"—to their countries and to who they were before they emigrated. The love-hate relationship with both Spain and their countries of origin emerged as a central feature of the activist identities of all the women we interviewed.

Beatriz, an activist who organized domestic workers, had immigrated from Colombia for economic reasons, but after living in Spain she realized, "I was a victim of violence, too." She explained that migration had given her a new view of her country: "Now I see things in a different way.... I was sure that in my country there wasn't that much violence against women. Imagine! A tremendous ignorance. I come to realize that here. In another country, do you understand? The problematic that exists in one's own country." For Beatriz, like Erica, migration had prompted an awakening: "I don't know if I lived inside a bubble or what, but it's that I didn't realize the reality that was there."

Sara was a thirty-four-year-old woman from Peru who had come to Spain on a student visa at age twenty-five and stayed, eventually acquiring Spanish nationality. Although she maintained dual citizenship with Peru and Spain, in her interview she rejected the Lima society she had left behind while also claiming outsider status in Spain. She described middle-class

Lima society as "superficial, capitalist, patriarchal, consumerist." The fear of violence keeps you behind walls in the same three neighborhoods, she said, and her friends were "not aware because they live in that little world." Her lack of belonging in Lima was directly connected to constricting gender roles and her feminist identity. "A thirty-four-year-old woman without kids," she said, describing herself as an oddity in Lima. "My own friends are like, 'Sara, what are you thinking?'" Sara did not know whether she wanted to have kids, but she cherished the freedom to choose not to, just as the women in our group did.

While the women were deeply and intimately connected to their countries of origin, communicating frequently with close friends and family members there, they did not fully belong there because they were seen as different there and they had different desires for their lives. Many of them said that they refused to fit into the social groups and hierarchies that belonging entailed in highly unequal societies. Daniela, a writer and activist from Ecuador, said she did not identify with the middle class where she came from in Quito: "I have never identified with the values of the Latin American middle classes, I feel that they're racist, classist, sexist, homophobic, and I've suffered it since I was a girl." Similarly, Mercedes explained that both Guatemala and Spain are conglomerations of different ethnic groups and power hierarchies into which she did not fit and refused to be placed. Elena, describing her relationship to an extremely polarized Venezuela under President Hugo Chávez, said she could not belong because she refused to have her Venezuelan identity contingent on "positioning myself more or less within a certain political project or a certain politician's discourse. No, I'm not going to do it." In these examples, the women made it clear that they rejected *the terms of belonging* in their countries of origin.

At the same time, all of the women we interviewed were aware that their position as Latin American immigrants denied them full belonging in Spain; the experience of exclusion and rejection in Spain was a key part of their identity formations. Beatriz said "surviving discrimination" was the most challenging part about migrating to Spain: "You feel like a cockroach, a worm." When asked whether she felt she belonged in Spain, she responded, "How can I belong when they themselves reject me?"

In some cases the racism was overt. Laura shared, "Just recently I tried to rent an apartment and they told me they didn't want to rent it to me because I was Colombian.... That's when you realize that it's racism, pure and simple." Similarly, when Mercedes invited a Guatemalan family she knew to move into a recently vacated apartment in her building, a neighbor told her, "What are you doing, Mercedes, you're bringing problems to this community of neighbors where we've never had them before." In Mercedes's view, "the people of the building were pretty racist." Sara, who had come to Madrid from Peru to begin a graduate program in human rights, indignantly described the mistreatment of immigrants by the authorities that she observed at Aluche, the government processing center where she went to renew her student visa. She said she had filed five or six complaints about mistreatment she had witnessed, only one of which was answered.

Other times, colleagues' comments and job offers communicated more subtle messages about the women's worth and place in society. Sara, who had two master's degrees, described eloquently the challenge of "having to prove your worth" as a Peruvian woman: "Each one of my work experiences went through having to prove, constantly, that I had worth. I mean, just for the fact of being Peruvian, like some form of, 'I don't know if you are qualified even though you have a master's and you've done such and such.'" Sara thought she had found the perfect job at a Spanish foundation involved in international development and solidarity work in Latin America and Africa. However, she soon came face-to-face with what she called a deeply internalized coloniality in her progressive Spanish colleagues. She described the strange "sensation of being with people who were highly educated and even progressive, so to speak, who still had these colonial biases and prejudices very, very internalized." That is, she clarified, they were not able to recognize that people from countries seen as "underdeveloped" "can have the same capacities, expectations, needs, etc., and rights."

Consider the experience of Daniela, who had come from Ecuador at the age of twenty-eight with four years of research and work experience under her belt before pursuing graduate degrees in Spain and Germany. Back in Madrid with a doctorate from Germany and having obtained Spanish nationality (she had dual citizenship with Ecuador and Spain), she learned that her Ecuadorian work experience and nationality would be a liability on the job market. She explained that Ecuadorians are a "very stigmatized group" in Spain—"there is a lot of racism." After several negative reactions to her Ecuadorian background from Spanish professionals, she decided to "hide all of my career and academic trajectory from Ecuador from my CV in Spain." She explained: "I started to realize that it was not working in my favor, you know? Because there's this institutional racism, that's super unconscious, right? So, I opted at some point . . . to erase four, five years' of work and research from my CV." By erasing five years of experience from her CV Daniela was also erasing part of herself; this was a metaphor for how Latinas were seen in the public sphere.

Many activists described the strangeness of interacting with Spanish people who expected all women from their home countries to be domestic workers, who considered it a compliment to say, "You people are so nice, because you clean so well!" (as a woman told Daniela). At times, the job opportunities available to immigrant women reproduced Spanish colonial images of Latin Americans as the exotic, primitive Other. Mercedes's first paid job in Spain was for Iberia Airlines, when they introduced their non-stop flight to Guatemala. After announcing the position through the Guatemalan Embassy, the airline hired Mercedes to dress up in a traditional indigenous dress from the Guatemalan province of Quiché to pose for photographs for a marketing campaign. Mercedes found it strange that she was asked to wear a typical dress "that I had never worn in Guatemala"— although she was born in Quiché, she had moved to the capital city as a child and her family was ladino, not indigenous. Indigenous people were "a tourist attraction" for the Spanish, she said, and they wanted her as a spectacle: "They present you like an animal in the zoo."

"I Don't Belong to Any One Place"

Experiences like these prevented the women from feeling an emotional attachment to Spain and contributed to their critique of Spanish national identity, even though most of them had acquired Spanish citizenship. Like the subjects in Abu El-Haj's (2015) study of transnational citizenship among Palestinian American youth, these women made a distinction between legal citizenship and their sense of belonging. While their Spanish citizenship allowed them to access rights and opportunities they would not otherwise have, their *belonging,* understood as emotional attachment, identification, and commitment, was not with Spain. Berta, from Mexico, described her relationship to Spain as "instrumental" because it allowed her things like safety and opportunities but did not inspire any emotional attachment. When we discussed this in the group, Erica agreed, saying, "I am Spanish because the burgundy passport opens many doors for me, but it's not because I really want to wear the title of Spanish. I'm benefitting from it, it's totally instrumental." At this point Marta teased her, giggling, "Immigrant parasite!" Erica responded, "Not either! Because I also pay my taxes, I'm also contributing many things."

This discussion, echoing many we heard during the interviews, provides an important corrective to populist discourses that position immigrants as "parasites" who drain resources from the state while refusing to adopt (presumed) national cultural values. Latina women made it clear that their not belonging in Spain was due to the exclusion or marginalization of important parts of their identities there, and that parts of themselves were also excluded in their countries of origin. As Sara remarked, "My criticism of Spanish society on issues of immigration, coloniality, gender, I would also make of the French, of the United States, of the Peruvian, of the Afghan [society]."

Furthermore, this robust critique of national identity was tied to empathy for excluded groups, which animated their activism. Elena, a thirty-year-old from Venezuela who had come to Spain as a student five years earlier, believed that being a migrant "makes you really connect with situations of oppression and exclusion . . . [and] generates a kind of solidarity impulse that you can't repress." Elena was the most vocal in her critique of the treatment of immigrants in Spain, at one point sharing, "You see how the police show no mercy with immigrants. . . . I've experienced that myself. I felt . . . horrible, like a nonhuman." But she was also the most articulate about embracing the in-between space of not belonging as a privileged space. Explaining why she did not belong in Spain, she reflected: "This is the interesting thing about the transnational experience. You discover that physically your feet may be in a single place, but your experiences are multiplied by many other places. I mean, you are in many places at once. So I don't belong to any one place." She further described national identity as a form of "permanent emotional blackmail" by the state, suggesting the loss of freedom and autonomy that comes with being subjected to the state's categories.

As we have seen, Latina activists' rejection of national identity was based on a refusal to conform to the structures of inequality embedded in national belonging, born of their lived experience of multiple modes of domination in distinct national contexts. Just as importantly, this rejection staked out a vision of community and belonging based on egalitarian relations, which many of them equated with feminism; this was also nourished by their experience in transnational social fields. In the next section I examine how the women's activist efforts in public campaigns for change and in their collective spaces of *autoformación* drew upon and were nurtured by transnational cultures of resistance. In other words, far from employing a strategy of enlisting "enlightened" and well-resourced European audiences to remedy purportedly "backward" conditions in Latin America, Latina activists used their experience in transnational social fields to critique forms of colonial oppression in both Spain and Latin America and to center the resistance efforts of colonized peoples. As they struggled to overcome their marginality in Spain, they took inspiration from and strove to recreate communal practices of *convivencia* and solidarity from oppressed communities in their countries of origin.

Seeking Association and *Autoformación*

Mexican feminist Suárez Navaz (2008) writes, "The task of decolonization begins from the critical thinking of those who live in the borderlands, in the face of multiple exclusions. The personal experience of pain and marginalization for not fitting into dominant categories is both theory and politics" (cited in Trinidad Galván 2014, 137; my translation). As they sought to make sense of their experiences as outsiders in Spain, Latina women found a sense of belonging in activist associations or NGOs in Madrid, which provided them with a community of friends and support for their own *autoformación*. We first explored this in our group, reflecting on the role of AMG in the women's lives as migrants. Marta described it as "a constant learning . . . where every little thing is for your empowerment." When I asked her how she defined empowerment, she said, "The way in which you assert your worth. . . . You value yourself. . . . You seek your own development, and the struggle you have to develop yourself." For Marta, what she valued in AMG was the combination of support and learning that allowed her to develop herself. Marta often said, "When I first got here, I was like a little animal." We all found this amusing. She explained, "I thought, but I didn't notice that I thought. I had never been aware of my struggle." For her, a consciousness of her struggle was something that migration, and the support of AMG, had given her; it was part of her humanization.

The value of AMG as a consciousness-raising space was emphasized by all the women in our group. Deisy explained that the mission of AMG was to raise awareness about violence against women "and what women have to suffer through on a daily basis," but she clarified that a central part of this was helping women survive and thrive: "It wasn't just women trying to get men in trouble or hating on men . . . it was helping other women, and educating them, I guess, in something that we don't get in school or anywhere else, and it's something that's not given to you unless you look for it." Here, Deisy highlights a key difference between *autoformación* and formal schooling: *autoformación* was about seeking the kind of learning that was denied them in school, the knowledge "not given to you unless you look for it." The women had many criticisms of their formal schooling, but it was clear that the experience of migration had pushed them to seek out a different kind of learning that would help them understand their own experiences of violence and exclusion as transnational migrant women.

AMG itself had emerged from the founding women's intensely personal needs for community and healing. Mercedes, the founding director, explained that what first drew them together, more than the desire to "help my country," was the sharing of their own experiences of gender violence: "We came to the sad conclusion that we didn't know a single woman [in our families] who hadn't experienced violence in the area of their relationship." They realized they needed to reflect on their own experiences and transform themselves in order to be able to work for broader political and social transformation. So the association developed two arms: the psychosocial, which entailed meeting regularly to reflect on their experiences and educate themselves, and the political, which focused on denouncing gender violence and lobbying for change in the public realm. At the personal level, once a month AMG held *tertulias* for all the *socias*. At the *tertulias* the women took turns facilitating discussion and reflection on a chosen text, often on an aspect of feminist theory, in a relaxed environment over food and drink. These discussions allowed the women to process their own experiences and their relationship to feminism.

For example, in one *tertulia* I participated in, the women were discussing the different waves of the feminist movement when we realized that for all of us, our schooling had denied us basic knowledge of feminist history. Erica's teenage niece was the first to bring it up: "See, in Guatemala we don't study any of this, feminism." Alma, a Spanish lawyer who worked with the association's legal aid division, said schooling in Spain was no different. She said it wasn't until she was a thirty-two-year-old law student that she learned about Clara Campoamor, a feminist and suffragist credited with securing the right to vote for Spanish women. I affirmed that my K–12 schooling in the United States, too, had taught me virtually nothing about the women's movement. On this occasion, as important as the "facts" of feminist history that we were discussing was the new kinship that emerged from our mutual indignation at how our schooling, in three different national contexts, had deprived us of empowering knowledge as women. This mutual indignation was a key feature of *autoformación* that enabled women to perceive how gender oppression operated across national boundaries, fueling their commitment to activism. As Mercedes explained, "We are a group for analysis and reflection, a study group, really, from which we never emerge indifferent. We end up indignant all the time and what we have to do . . . is channel that rage, right?"

Although most of the association's visible achievements were in the realm of lobbying, Mercedes maintained, "I would be just as satisfied with the work of AMG if we only met that one day a month, to converse and educate ourselves. . . . The mission will continue to be to work in the microsocial, no? In our political but personal spaces so that our work outside can continue to be sustainable." With this, Mercedes directly linked personal transformation to political activism, claiming the central insight of the feminist movement that the personal is political and underscoring the political importance of AMG's work in *autoformación*.

We heard similar testimonies from the activist women we interviewed, all of whom described rich networks of *convivencia* and *autoformación* without which they would not have been able to survive in Spain. Delgado-Bernal et. al. (2008) define *convivencia* as "everyday practices that become a means to share and affirm individual and collective experiences, as well as contribute to citizenship formation" (40). Such practices, which are at the center of Latina feminist or *mujerista*-oriented spaces of teaching and learning (Dyrness 2011; Trinidad Galván 2006, 2014; Villenas 2005), sustained Latina activists in Madrid.

Sara, who had come from Peru to study human rights at a public research university in Madrid, was disappointed with the training she received there and felt it did not meet her needs. So she started a dialogue group on gender with eleven other women, which they named *gener_ando* (a play on the word *gender*), and it had been meeting regularly for three and a half years. She credited this group with the training (*formación*) that had most helped her as an immigrant woman in Spain. Initially a part of her NGO, the group became autonomous and had its own structure of horizontal leadership and *autoformación*. Sara explained:

We study, we dialogue, we reflect. We have a lot of self-formation [*autoformación*]. Each one of us proposes a theme to prepare a space for reflection and dialogue. So, we are strengthening ourselves and we are educating ourselves at the same time . . . but all based on the idea that knowledge is collectively constructed, that none of us knows more than the other.

Elena, from Venezuela, was also a member of this group, and she described it as her "chosen family" whose "active listening" had helped her overcome the limitations in her life as a migrant: "Out of our mutual indignations, out of our similar experiences . . . we are gradually generating a critical discourse, a human discourse, that allows us to analyze where we are and also how we act. . . . [It is] a journey that is internal, but at the same time, collective. Very powerful. And that is what has allowed me to overcome any barrier." Elena's testimony points to the ways the sharing of similar experiences among a community of similarly displaced women enables a critical analysis and informs their action in the world.

Echoing Mercedes's comments about AMG, Sara believed that this personal exchange was as important as their activism on a grand scale:

I don't discount the big advocacy campaigns and other projects that we carry out in [NGO]. But I do feel that what matters most happens at the personal level. In the everyday and in the collective, right? And from there, go to, how do I deconstruct relationships, how do I find inner peace and reconfigure my identity, right? As Sara, a migrant in this country.

For Sara, her identity formation, necessarily engaging with multiple structures of domination she encountered as an immigrant woman, was at the center of the educational process she most valued, and this process of *autoformación* allowed her to develop her own, third-space identity. Anthropologist Lok Siu (2005) writes, "Being diasporic entails active and conscious negotiation of one's identity and one's understandings of 'home' and 'community'" (11). It is this constant reflection and negotiation that makes the third space a space of creative possibility, insight, and critique. Seen in this light, the women's practices of *autoformación* emerge as practices of diasporic citizenship, enabling the women to reflect on their relationship to multiple communities and to form new affinities that support their critical engagement with the world.

In reflecting on her identity and where she belonged, Sara had this to say:

> I am very aware that I am not Spanish, that I don't want to be Spanish. That I have an identity that I like, that is a very diverse identity. . . . But I am thrilled to have this double, triple perspective, of having had this distinct life experience. . . . It's an interesting process because you are constantly constructing and deconstructing, and remembering what and how you want to live.

Sara could have been describing the process in our own research group, and her reflections spoke directly to our questions about whether the space of unbelonging could be an activist resource. She clearly articulated *la conciencia de la mestiza*: "the consciousness of the 'mixed blood' . . . born of life lived in the 'crossroads' between races, nations, languages, genders, sexualities, and cultures, an acquired subjectivity formed out of transformation and relocation" (Sandoval 2000, 61). As Anzaldúa wrote, "The new mestiza . . . learns to juggle cultures. . . . Not only does she sustain contradictions, she turns the ambivalence into something else" (1999, 101). For Sara, the "double, triple perspective" of life on the margins propelled her to engage in decoloniality, as Mignolo described it: "the analytic task of unveiling the logic of coloniality and the prospective task of contributing to build a world in which many worlds will coexist" (2011, 54).

Sandoval (1998) writes, "Oppositional *mestizaje* occurs when the unexplored *affinities inside of difference* attract, combine, and relate new constituencies into a coalition of resistance" (362; emphasis in the original). Through feminist associations in Madrid, Latina women found commonalities and developed kinship with women of diverse experiences, drawing strength from their intersections. Laura was a twenty-one-year-old activist from Colombia who had recently completed her university studies in Madrid and joined the newly formed Podemos political party, believing it would be a constructive way to work for change. But while membership in the party was an important education for her, she spoke more emotively about her participation in the Latin American Women's Network, a coalition of diverse feminist and migrant associations that met regularly, which she said was "fundamental" to her identity as an activist. Being "surrounded by women" had helped her to develop empathy, to connect with and listen to others, and to realize that "pain is never an alien thing." She explained, "Pain is experienced by different types of people in very similar ways. That was one of the most profoundly important teachings that I've had. Because I've seen myself reflected in many people who I would never have imagined I could see myself in." Laura's words evoke the personal and collective healing that took place in and made possible activist associations.

"We have to work in networks, that's the only way we can survive," said Beatriz, also from Colombia, reminding us that these are survival spaces first and foremost. She told us that she first got involved in activism "to escape that loneliness" that you feel as an immigrant. But if joining activist networks was a survival strategy for Latina migrants, it was one informed by cultures of resistance and collective action they had first experienced in their homelands. As Beatriz explained,

> There are women who bring collectivism, all this work, we bring it in our veins. Yes, because you have to remember that in our countries, I remember when I did my practicum in a rural area, the peasants, they put on festivals to fix the school, festivals to buy desks, for example. In this way everything they did, they worked through festivals, through parties, they raised funds, so we bring that from there.

Beatriz's honoring the peasants from her home country of Colombia for their methods of collective organizing, a cultural resource for transcending poverty, was a theme echoed in many of our interviews and group discussions. And yet it was one that I had missed in my early readings of the data on the women's experiences. Focusing only on their experiences of violence and safety, I did not initially see the cultural resources for resisting violence that they found in communities most affected by exploitation. Drawing on a decolonial feminist perspective, I look back at my data and see in the women's stories not only the wounds of colonialism—including multiple forms of violence—but also their efforts to recover ways of being and knowing that have been subjugated by colonialism. As Ruth Trinidad Galván (2014) writes, "Anti-imperialist research endeavors to reveal forms of exploitation, like the feminicides, as well as alliances, *convivencia*, and glocal challenges to these atrocities" (138).

Transnational Cultures of Resistance

Joaquín Chávez (2017), in his historical analysis of the pedagogy that drove revolutionary mobilizations in El Salvador in the 1960s and 1970s, argues that a "pedagogy of the revolution" drew on deeply rooted cultures of resistance in El Salvador (17). Challenging the dominant history that credits urban intellectuals with forming the Salvadoran guerillas, Chávez argues that urban and peasant intellectuals "incarnated cultures of resistance that drew on memories of indigenous peasant uprisings and civic mobilizations in El Salvador" as well as revolutionary and anticolonial movements from across the globe (30). Recently, scholars have examined how memories of historic violence and resistance take on new meaning in the diaspora, as displaced Salvadorans seek to come to terms with their histories (Coutin 2016). Scholars have documented the ways Salvadoran immigrants living in the United States, Canada, and Costa Rica recall and commemorate historic instances of state violence and indigenous resistance to recover and strengthen their identities as Salvadorans (Coutin 2016; DeLugan 2013; Carranza 2007; Hayden 2003). DeLugan (2013) writes, "Interestingly, however, it is only after leaving El Salvador and grappling with the migration experience of being Salvadoran or Salvadoran American in the United States that some choose indigeneity to inform their identities, subjectivities, and cultural practices" (984). In this light, choosing indigeneity can be seen as part of their *autoformación*.

Similarly, Latin American activist women in Spain strategically drew on cultures of resistance and solidarity from their home countries in building their activist identities. Their efforts to support each other, to educate and mobilize Spanish citizens, and to pressure nation-state institutions in both home and host countries to protect the rights of vulnerable groups drew on memories of indigenous and peasant resistance in Latin America. Specifically, these efforts revived indigenous notions of "the communal" that Mignolo (2011) argues are central to "the decolonial option."

At the public level, AMG organized conferences and forums on current events in Central America and brought activists, lawyers, and human rights experts from Latin America to speak about their ongoing efforts for justice. For example, in a session I attended in June 2014 the executive director of the National Union of Guatemalan Women described the remarkable peaceful resistance to displacement being led by indigenous land rights activists, primarily women, whose actions were being met with violent police repression. She then outlined the details of the ongoing criminal investigation of sexual slavery at the former military outpost in Sepur Zarco. She highlighted the bravery of the women in this town who had been victims of sexual crimes during the war who came forward to give testimony in a Guatemalan court.[13] At AMG's annual conference on femicide in 2017, Karla Salas, a lawyer and human rights activist from Mexico, described her efforts to seek justice for the disappeared women in Ciudad Juárez, where femicide crimes have an impunity rate of 99 percent. She said, "We have organized together with the families of the disappeared, and also with Juárez society, *because transformation is not going to come from the government,* but from organized people" (emphasis added). These public events highlighted countries in Latin America as places with weak democratic institutions and grave human rights abuses, but also with cultures of organized resistance. The speakers invited audience members in Spain to join as partners in the struggle for justice, taking the lead from indigenous leaders in the affected countries.

But equally important was the informal, behind-the-scenes learning that young Guatemalan volunteers with AMG gained from being in contact with activists in Guatemala and learning about community organizing there. Volunteers often dined with visiting activists and accompanied them to and from events. One member of our group, Marta, described learning from a conversation with two indigenous activists whom she had picked up at the airport in Madrid. The two activists from Huehuetenango, where a Spanish hydroelectric company was involved in human rights abuses in the local indigenous community, had impressed her. Marta asked them how they found the courage to resist, since so many in Guatemala (she said) are resigned to the way things are. They replied that their community had to defend itself because they were under attack. They also explained that their life is communal, so it was natural for them to organize collectively. As this example shows, participation in AMG and other activist NGOs exposed Latina women to transnational cultures of resistance. Marta and other members of our group emphasized this learning as formative for their identities.

In daily life, Latina women drew on cultures of solidarity and collectivity from their home countries to survive the hardships of life as an immigrant and to critique what they saw as the Spanish individualist lifestyle and lack of solidarity. Latina women repeatedly expressed the notion that Spaniards had a hard time weathering the economic crisis because they did not know how to live in community or solidarity. In one of our group discussions Marta explained: "There [in Guatemala] we're used to organizing to survive, no? 'We have to eat, so we're going to do this, this, and this.' But the Spanish are like no, 'because I have a degree in [such and such].'" Erica responded, "Exactly! We know what it is like to be really in need. Crisis? What crisis? We have lived in crisis for all of our lives!"

Similarly, Sara, from Peru, put it this way: "In Latin America if we had not known how to be creative and come up with collective social actions, people in Peru in 1984 would have died of starvation." Repeatedly, the women made reference to the cultures of resistance that enabled indigenous and peasant communities in their home countries to survive brutal state repression, poverty, and violence. In doing so they invoked "the communal," which is, in Mignolo's (2011) words, "a type of social organization that was disrupted by European invasion, but that nonetheless subsisted for five hundred years" (320). Mignolo emphasizes that "the communal," as a form of collective management and use of resources, emerges not only from social organizations of the Tawantinsuyu (the Incas) and Anáhuac (Aztec) peoples before the arrival of Europeans "but from five hundred years of experience coexisting under Spanish colonial rule and under nation-states after independence, during the nineteenth century" (319). Thus, it is a survival strategy perfected in resistance to colonization.

Likewise, Latina migrant women emphasized their historical experience with multiple oppressions in developing their collective capacity to resist current "crises." When Mercedes addressed a Spanish public audience on the theme of the economic crisis, she said, "I have been breathing crisis since I was in the womb," referring to the history of state violence in Guatemala. She continued, "Crisis is overcome by networks, by weaving networks of solidarity."

Importantly, women narrated experiences from their home country with indigenous and peasant communities as memories to which they consciously turned in their efforts to build feminist activist identities. This was the case for Laura, the activist with Podemos, who had immigrated to Spain from Colombia as a child but returned frequently to visit her grandfather. She described accompanying her grandfather, an activist professor, on literacy campaigns in the countryside. She was amazed that the peasant women who could not read or write "truly had another kind of relationship far beyond anything I had seen in Europe or anywhere else. Because of course, here in Europe, people are so much more individual ... and when I began to discover feminism, I remembered that."

Similarly, Elena, from Venezuela, described working with indigenous communities in Bolivia before emigrating to Spain and learning from their processes of "engaging in politics from the community." She explained that those experiences "left me very impacted . . . [and] inspired me a lot in what became my future political struggles and even how I thought of myself as a political subject. I learned so much from that contact with the people and indigenous movements." In describing her feminism, she cited Julieta Paredes, an indigenous Bolivian feminist whom she had recently heard speak, who defined feminism as "a form of struggle against all oppressions."

Countering popular stereotypes in Spain that Spanish culture was more "evolved" in terms of gender equality than Latin American cultures, Latina women often recalled experiences of organizing and activism in Latin America to critique social movements in Spain. Daniela, from Ecuador, poignantly described being excluded from the 15M movement—the youth-led antiausterity movement that began with *los indignados* in 2011—because she was an immigrant. She contrasted that with the indigenous uprising in Ecuador in 2000, which was "one of the most beautiful collective acts I have seen in my life" but which also triggered extreme state repression and a wave of Ecuadorian migrants to Spain and other countries. Mercedes, too, faulted the young leaders of the 15M movement in Spain for not knowing how to open space for others. This was "the most highly educated generation, the girls have like five master's, a lot of doctorates, above all a lot of young women who have returned to academic life because there were no jobs for them," but their activism was focused only on "opening space for themselves." Mercedes said that in contrast, the feminist movement in Latin America has "always believed in internationalism." She emphasized that internationalism was strategic because "political articulation is only possible to the extent that they network with each other, that it be regional. And those networks here [in Spain], the Spanish feminist movement has an enormous debt to immigrant women, because it has not been capable of accepting under equal conditions within its ranks women who come from other national origins."

Here, Mercedes frames the inability of Spanish feminists to recognize the contributions of immigrant women as limiting the success of their movement. She shared how her own knowledge and experience were ignored due to assumptions made about her background:

> In spite of the fact that I move in those circles [activist circles], it is a world in which for example national origin weighs heavily. And weighs generally in a negative way: "You are other, you don't know Spain." They're always talking to you about Spain as if you don't know it, when after ten years here I think I know something!

At the same time, she frequently said, if a Spanish woman traveled to a country in Central America for even a short time, she would come back talking like an "expert" on that country and nobody would challenge the basis for her expertise.

As these examples show, Latina women pointed out the contradictions of Spanish social movements based on their own experiences as immigrants and recalled experiences of activism from Latin America in framing their identities as feminists in Spain. Like U.S. Third World feminists, these women used their "outsider/within" status to nurture political critique and strategies for change that were not recognized by the dominant power structure (Sandoval 2000; Collins 2000; Anzaldúa 1999; Hurtado 1989, 2003). However, in this case, Latina women made sense of and made up for their exclusion from activist spaces in Spain by drawing on cultural experiences of resistance to inequality in Latin America that they had learned through their experiences in transnational social fields, before and after migrating. Comparing experiences of social movements in Latin America and experiences of exclusion in Spain compelled them to elaborate a critique of coloniality and to turn to the cultural practices of marginalized communities in Latin America for strategies for resistance.

Sara, who worked at a foundation involved in international solidarity work, pointed out that the most progressive faction of Spanish society had managed to organize against cuts to public health and cuts to education, but not against the mistreatment of immigrants by Spanish authorities. Spanish activists were very good at criticizing human rights abuses around the world, she said, but "very little able to empathize or be in solidarity with immigrant people who are their neighbors." She said that the economic crisis had helped Spaniards develop a little more solidarity, "but not to the levels that we have in Latin America." Returning to the example of Peru during the 1980s, she explained that mass starvation was avoided only by the creative collective acts of women; these women, she noted, "didn't have a master's degree or a diploma and they weren't political activists. But [they acted] out of the need of 'we have to sustain our lives, what can we do?' "

Sara's words echo a critique of formal education that ran through many of the women's narratives. The women criticized the schooling they had received in their home countries and in Spain (those who had pursued higher education in Spain) as being elitist and antifeminist, and they especially criticized the European notion that higher education and degrees made one more qualified to lead social movements. Their experiences of rural organizing in Latin America had taught them the wisdom of indigenous and peasant communities who had little formal schooling but extraordinary capacities to organize collectively for change.

For some, however, it took migrating to Spain and experiencing discrimination as an immigrant for them to recognize and reflect on the wisdom of indigenous and poor communities in their countries. The experience of migration and reflection with other migrant women solidified their political educations. As Sara said, "The vital experience of being conscious of colonialism, of racism; the limiting aspects of migration give you a strength and a clarity. . . . It's a constant reminder of your political responsibility."

As women- and migrant-centered spaces of teaching and learning, activist associations became places for migrant women to find themselves, to process their histories and experiences together with others, and to make alliances across space and time to make change. Processes of *autoformación* allowed the women to draw from the painful experience of not belonging to create a richly educative space where they could not only critique their experiences of exclusion but also mobilize diverse cultural resources for transcending violence and inequality. In terms of diasporic citizenship, these groups were new communities of belonging that allowed the women to resist the hierarchies of nationalism and embrace new third-space identities based on difference and resistance to domination.

For Latina activists, it was these new ways of being and belonging that defined their understandings of feminism. While many of them said they had come to feminism in Spain, their conceptions of feminism were complex and evolving, combining elements of their experience in multiple countries. Their explanations of feminism emphasized new social relations and ways of living based on equality, peace, collectivity, and opposition to all forms of domination and subordination. Elena, who cited Bolivian feminist Julieta Paredes as her inspiration, described feminism as "a political project of profound cultural transformation, a way of living and thinking that bets on equality." Mercedes said feminism is a "culture of nonviolence" that is both "everyday, academic, and political . . . to learn other ways of exercising power." Given the experiences of organizing in Latin America that the women described and supported, it is clear that their visions of feminism were transnational, nurtured by their experiences of violence *and resistance to violence* in Latin America and Spain. Their ideas of feminism were intimately tied to their refusal to conform to national identity and their choosing of the third space as the space of belonging. As Beatriz from Colombia said, what is feminism but nonconformity?

Suárez Navaz (2008) has suggested that we confront the heredity of colonialism in any geopolitical state (Trinidad Galván 2014). It was such a confrontation and the weaving of new affinities in the diaspora that animated spaces of *autoformación* among Latina activists in my study. As Mercedes said, after explaining why she rejected both Spanish and Guatemalan national identities, "In the end you can feel part of a group by the people who comprise that group, and my group continues to be made up of many national origins. . . . They are people with whom I have connected through activism and we are united by social struggle." These are the metaphorical borderlands as articulated by Gloria Anzaldúa, "the geographic and symbolic spaces between countries and differences" (Delgado-Bernal, Alemán, and Carmona 2008, 32).

For Sara and Elena, too, the diversity of their group was important. The women came from various national backgrounds but were united in their quest to understand and transform the structures of domination that shaped their lives. Drawing on Audre Lorde's work, Chela Sandoval (1998) called the "third space" of U.S. Third World feminism a "bridging house of difference": "Our place was the very house of difference, rather than the security of any one particular difference" (358). It was just such a place that the activist women in our interviews described.

At the end of our interviews we asked the activists about their dreams for the future and their ideal world. Their imaginings often blended cultural aspects of communal life in their home countries with the legal support for democratic rights in European states. Mercedes, for example, said she would like to "recover that spirit of living in community" that she felt has been lost in modern capitalist societies. She described creating a "house of women" where women could live safely, express themselves, and do "lo que les diera la gana" (whatever they feel like). And where would this house be?

I asked. She replied, "In an intermediate place in my imagination between Latin America and Europe. A place where the state was as strong as some Nordic countries, for example, but with the natural paradise like the Eternal Spring of Guatemala! Yes, the Finnish state, or the Danish state, or a state like Iceland, with the natural environment and climate of Guatemala." I had to agree that nothing could be better than a Guatemalan paradise with a Danish state. But these imaginings are more than fantasy; they reflect the insights of transnational women who embody the knowledge and experience of multiple landscapes and ways of being and can draw from these varied experiences in their quest to imagine and enact a more humane world. They inspire us to move forward with the confidence that "the healing images and narratives we imagine will eventually materialize" (Anzaldúa 2002a, 5).

Conclusion

Reflections on *Acompañamiento* in the Borderlands

For those of us born and raised transborderly, we are a countryless people, and more and more this does not sadden me.

—Ruth Trinidad Galván

Sometimes what accretes around an irritant or wound may produce a pearl of great insight, a theory.

—Gloria Anzaldúa

DURING OUR STAY IN MADRID our five-year-old daughter, Sofia, attended a public school in the central city neighborhood where we lived. Observing and accompanying her struggles to belong as an outsider, we caught a glimpse of what the immigrant youths in our studies experienced daily, and we connected more deeply with their stories. Although Sofia was an outgoing and social kid who was already conversant in Spanish when she arrived (though in Mexican/Latino Spanish, not the Castilian that is spoken there), everything about her school was foreign and strange to her. The Spanish families all seemed to know each other, and their children, who had been together since the first year of *infantil* (preschool), already had their friend groups. For a long time, Sofia stood with her teacher during recess because she did not know anyone and did not understand the children's games. Language was an issue at the very beginning, but long after fluent Castilian spouted from her mouth, the feeling of being a cultural outsider persisted. And even in a designated "bilingual" school (the school had forty-five minutes of English instruction every day), some kids made fun of her for speaking English. One evening a couple of months into the school year, Andrea read to her *The Upside Down Boy*, by the poet Juan Felipe Herrera. *The Upside Down Boy* is a beautiful rendering of a Mexican migrant boy's experiences starting school taught in English. "Will my tongue turn into a rock?" he asks. Sofia was riveted.

When I jump up
everyone sits.
When I sit
all the kids swing through the air.
My feet float through the clouds
when all I want is to touch the earth.
I am the upside down boy. (Herrera 2000)

Asked if she sometimes felt that way at school, Sofia nodded sadly. Andrea pulled her into a hug and said, "You're my upside down girl!" Then Sofia smiled broadly and said, "No, mami, I'm sideways," motioning with her hand to show herself sideways, flat, parallel to the earth; "I'm más o menos."

Sofia captured better than we could the condition of the insider-outsider. She identified with the Upside Down Boy and found solace in his story, but reinterpreted it to match her sense of partial belonging. Her sense of herself as being sideways, *más o menos* (more or less), evoked both the unique vantage point and the painful strangeness of the migrant child. In claiming this vantage point, she refused the position of the victim. As we witnessed her creative assimilation of new Spanish vocabulary, her astute cultural observations and penetrating questions, and also her tears, we re/membered the pain and poignant beauty that come with this condition. The tears were growing pains as she (and we) evolved into conscious and reflective border crossers. Like all border crossers, she might always be on the margins, but she would have the capacity to penetrate multiple worlds.

Our experiences with Sofia's school not only brought us closer to the experiences of the youths in our study but also brought us into closer relationship with them. The youths at ASI welcomed her warmly and always asked about her if she was not with us, but when they learned about her struggles at school, they demonstrated a compassion and empathy that could only come from the lived experience of unbelonging, a vulnerability they did not often display. Whenever we brought her to the youth center the young women would surround her, put their arms around her, and offer her snacks, paper and pens for coloring, and gentle words. We often ran into Mariela and Luisa or Ana Sylvia on the street in the neighborhood and they would always greet Sofia with a bear hug or high five. A particular memory stands out: one evening Esther, a thirteen-year-old from Nigeria, walked us almost all the way home with her arm around Sofia's shoulder, saying, "Anda, no llores, eres una niña muy guapa" (Come along, don't cry, you're a beautiful girl). While we sought to understand their experiences and accompany them through our research, they accompanied us in our struggle to feel at home in Madrid.

In this conclusion we reflect on lessons we learned from conducting participatory research in multiple locations of the Latino diaspora and the insights we gleaned from our positionality as U.S. Latino/a scholars of race and migration. In particular, we consider how our capacity to recognize, support, and create spaces of *acompañamiento* is nurtured by our own borderlands subjectivities and the intimate connections we have made with others in the borderlands. These experiences provide cultural resources for navigating unfamiliar and hostile terrain and for strengthening our critical responses to forces of displacement. Below we provide two more examples of transborder encounters to drive home the "shared cultural citizenship" of those living in between nation-states (Saldívar 2011; Dyrness and Sepúlveda 2015).

Fieldwork Encounter: Andrea

While the youths at ASI accompanied Sofia on her journey adjusting to a new school, the Guatemalan women at AMG accompanied Andrea in their research group, where her experience at Sofia's school entered into the group's *testimonio.*

One rainy Friday morning I left a particularly tough drop-off at Sofia's school (she had been wailing when I left) and headed to a research meeting at Erica's house in a turmoil of emotions. Climbing the stairs to Erica's third-floor apartment, I was instantly warmed and comforted by the smell of beans and frying onions. Black beans for breakfast was a staple of my childhood, and the smell alone was enough to transport me to what was familiar and "home." I knew it had to be coming from Erica's apartment because who else would be cooking beans for breakfast in Madrid? Sure enough, Erica was in the kitchen preparing a full Guatemalan breakfast: scrambled eggs with onions, peppers, and tomatoes, refried black beans, bread, and strong coffee. Marta and Maria arrived minutes later with juices, yogurt, and donuts, and everyone exclaimed about the feast. As we set up the table and spent the first half hour of the meeting eating and socializing, the wounds of the morning's encounter with the hostile staff member at Sofia's school faded into the *convivencia* of *compañeras.* But this was not the ordinary comfort of friendship. Erica, Marta, and Maria knew intimately what it was like to have their varieties of Central American Spanish misunderstood and disparaged in Spain, to feel out of place even after years in Madrid. Such experiences were a frequent topic of conversation in our group. Spaces of *convivencia* like this one, built on the everyday cultural practices of the participants (including, in this case, Guatemalan breakfast), become a means of affirming individual experiences, developing a critical analysis, and strengthening group identity. They are spaces of solidarity and *acompañamiento* and of critical citizenship formation.

As we shared our own experiences of struggle, we opened ourselves to receive comfort from each other and invited shared critical analysis of the patterns we encountered. On one occasion, my story about an indignant exchange with the male *jefe de estudios* (director of studies) at Sofia's school prompted a critical discussion about gender relations and machismo in Spain. Discussions like this not only garnered insights into how our coresearchers experienced gender, race, and culture in their daily lives but also gave us new perspectives on and ways of making sense of our own experiences. They illustrate the transformative healing potential of PAR when individual and collective inquiry, self-recovery, and action are joined.

Fieldwork Encounter: Enrique

One day on the school grounds at El Rio I came across a group of four male *bachiller* students (between the ages of fifteen and seventeen) outside the boys' bathroom on the second level near the *secundaria* classrooms. It was lunchtime, and the various social cliques were occupying their well-established hangouts while the students from lower grades were in their classrooms. Lucas, the student I came to know best and the most social of the group, immediately acknowledged me. He interrupted his private conversation with a female student and extended his hand to shake mine in a manner that I am accustomed to back home in my California urban barrio. At the time I thought little of this seemingly minor, inconspicuous act of greeting low-income Salvadoran urban youths in a familiar way, but later it came to represent for me that new transnational social space where new citizen subjects experience moments of shared cultural understanding and belonging (Saldívar 2011).

At some point in our conversation the boys noticed my use of *órale*, a common expression in the Chicano/Mexican California lexicon, and wanted to know more about how I talked back home when I was their age.

The discussion especially interested Lucas, who moved away from his female friend and asked me directly if I said "homie" or "homeboy" when referring to good friends. When I said yes, the group immediately became excited and began laughing and engaging in side conversations about urban Latino homeboys and their various linguistic expressions. Some of the boys mimicked California barrio homeboy behavior, playing with and trying on gestures and expressions such as "órale, homes" and "wuz up." Soon the bell rang and lunch was over. We shook hands again, like true homeboys, smiled, and went our separate ways.

As I walked to my classroom a question lingered in my mind: how is it possible that complete strangers can share an intimate moment and bond over familiar subcultural subjectivities and language while having lived thousands of miles apart, separated by three national borders? These youths had a familiarity with both general mainstream U.S. cultural knowledge (e.g., U.S. presidential politics) and the particular, very localized under-standings of Chicano/Latino California barrio subculture. For them, I was a U.S. educator—obviously Latino, but a stranger nonetheless, and from far away. In our brief, initial conversations they picked up verbal cues indexing that I had an intimate understanding of Chicano homeboy language and barrio youth culture, something the average Salvadoran teacher didn't have or understand, much less respect. Homeboy language and identities represent peripheral subjectivities in El Salvador embodied by youth gangs and Salvadorans (gang-affiliated or not) deported from California. As Zilberg (2004) notes, "They reveal a painful rupture between culture and nation, where cultural identity does not correspond to, but is, rather, excluded from national citizenship" (762). As male students in El Rio expressed their affinity with homeboy language and culture, they claimed a marginal social identity in both El Salvador and the United States.

As the above example shows, such processes of subject formation are not simply a question of neocolonized subjects having knowledge of the popular culture and politics of the neocolonial power; rather, these transnational intimacies index profound cultural formations and relation-ships that are not tied to one nation-state. They represent the ways "ordi-nary people 'imagine' their social surroundings" in a transnational field (Saldívar 2011), where Salvadoran homeboys and a Chicano researcher can come to feel a sense of "shared fate" and shared cultural citizenship (Taylor 2004).

Ethnographic Encounters in the Borderlands

A homeboy handshake in a Salvadoran schoolyard; black beans for break-fast in Madrid; thirteen-year-old Esther walking Sofia home and reassuring her, "Anda, no llores." These encounters in the borderlands, when a simple moment of recognition between fellow border crossers invites a human response of connection, fellowship, and accompaniment, open space for different ways of being and new community formations that resist the alienation inflicted by mainstream institutions. These examples under-score a central finding of this book: for migrants in the diaspora, spaces of *acompañamiento* broker experiences of exclusion in national institutions, helping us (re)interpret our experiences in ways that affirm our dignity and wholeness. *The Upside Down Boy*, a book about the migrant experience writ-ten by the son of migrant farmworkers, as well as the children's books by Daniela Ortiz and Junot Díaz discussed in the introduction to this book, the poems we used in our research groups, and the discussions they prompted, reflect epistemologies and pedagogies of the borderlands that excavate and nurture cultural resources for resisting oppression. Building community around shared experiences of difference, they allow us to embrace the in-between, insider-outsider position as a privileged space of critical reflection and identity formation. Gloria Anzaldúa, reflecting on her own ways of cultural production and her role as an artist, calls this space of creation "Nepantla." "Nepantla is the point of contact y el lugar between worlds—between imagination and physical existence, between ordinary and nonordinary (spirit) realities. . . . Nepantlas are places of constant ten-sion, where the missing or absent pieces can be summoned back, where transformation and healing may be possible, where wholeness is just out of reach but seems attainable" (Anzaldúa 2015, 2).

We were reminded of this during a conversation at AFEPA when sixteen-year-old Gabriel said he struggled to remember an older brother in Ecua-dor whom he had not seen in many years. Gabriel had moved to Spain when he was five and returned to Ecuador only once, about five years before our meeting. In our first group discussion he shared that he felt sad that he could not remember much about his native country and he longed to be together with all of his family again. He was able to talk to his sister and his grandfa-ther occasionally through Skype because his sister had a computer and internet access, but his older brother did not. Internet access still could not be taken for granted in all parts of Ecuador. On hearing this, another group member, Paula, suggested that Gabriel talk to his mother about his brother and look at photos of the family. Like the child protagonist Lola in Junot Diaz's *Islandborn,* Gabriel needed help to recall and recreate the land of his birth, and he found encouragement from his compañeros/as in the diaspora. In the space of AFEPA, his fellow migrants accompanied him in his efforts to "summon back" the missing parts of himself.

The urge to know their families, to be connected to the land of their birth, and to make sense of lives that had been fragmented was present for all of the youths before we met them. But they needed a context in which to express it, a safe space to explore what was denied or condemned by the mainstream institutions in charge of their care. Across all the locations of our research, in rural Northern California, San Salvador, and Madrid, young people told us they did not have opportunities in their schools to speak about their experiences of migration or issues of diversity, identity, race, and racism. Without these opportunities, without the space to build community around their shared experiences, they had no support for developing the critical consciousness that was naturally emerging from their experiences in transnational social fields. By and large, as we have shown, the citizenship education they received in their schools and after-school programs focused on personal responsibility and behavior management, suggesting, as Soo Ah Kwon has observed, "the construction of citizenship as a private practice of self-improvement" (Kwon 2013, 16). Implored to take personal responsibility (and more often, blame) for their social predicaments, diaspora youth received little assistance in understanding the larger forces of displacement that fragmented their families and communities. While they lived their lives at the nexus of multiple contradictions—between legal status and lived realities, between democratic rhetoric and racialized and economic processes of exclusion, between nationalist discourses of belonging and their own multiple affiliations, to name only a few—they were largely on their own in making sense of and navigating these contradictions. For some of our research participants, our group provided the first occasion to reflect on and collectively examine these realities; for others, like the Guatemalan activists in chapter 5, our participatory research tapped into and deepened processes of *autoformación* that were already occurring in their associations. In all cases, PAR provided a context that supported the community formation and critical consciousness building that inform and make possible collective resistance.

The teenagers at the youth associations and the young women activists in Madrid shared similar experiences of complex transnational belongings and racialized exclusion as migrants from Latin America in Spain; the only significant difference between them was that the activists had regular exposure to spaces of solidarity and critical reflection in their activist associations, which gave them a language for understanding the intersecting oppressions they experienced. The activists made it clear that it was these spaces of *convivencia* and *autoformación* with other migrants that made possible their participation in social movements for the rights of the indigenous, immigrants, and women. Importantly, they sought out (or formed) these associations to help them make sense of and overcome their experiences of isolation as migrant women, to feed their desire to stay connected to cultural resources from their home countries while leveraging new cultural resources in Spain and critically analyzing the forces stacked against them. Thus, this research underscores the feminist insight that the personal is political; the quest for personal healing and transformation precedes and makes possible more public forms of resistance (Dyrness 2011; Latina Feminist Group 2001; Villenas 2001). It also suggests that the awareness of marginalization can fuel democratic civic engagement rather than alienation and withdrawal.

This inclination to seek out networks of solidarity, to find company and accompany others as a response to feelings of unbelonging, suggests a very different reading of the role of "perceptions of discrimination" from theories of "reactive ethnicity" offered by sociologists. Sociological theories of segmented assimilation and reactive ethnicity, as described by Portes, Aparicio, and Haller (2016), posit that higher perceptions of discrimination slow the process of integration and that immigrant youths who perceive greater discrimination in the host society are more likely to adopt "reactive ethnicity," or assert a foreign identity in opposition to the host country's national identity. Portes and his colleagues present this as a worst-case scenario: "In the worst case, the process leads to reactive ethnicity with youngsters refusing to abandon their parents' nationalities as markers of self-identification" (Portes, Aparicio, and Haller 2016, 137).

One of the most striking findings of their study of the second generation in Spain is their low perception of discrimination: "Just 5 percent of the original sample and just 8.5 percent of our replacement sample reported experiencing discrimination frequently or repeatedly during the preceding three years. . . . These low perceptions of discrimination can . . . be taken as a *prima facie* indicator of a successful integration process" (114). This finding was in marked contrast to that of the Children of Immigrants Longitudinal Study in the United States, which found that perceptions of discrimination among second-generation youth were much higher and actually increased over time. According to this study, immigrant youth in the United States were much more likely to embrace a panethnic label (e.g., Hispanic, Latino, or Asian) in adolescence, reversing "the process of psychosocial integration into mainstream society" (112). Portes, Aparicio, and Haller view this as a response to American racism and rigid ethnoracial hierarchies in the United States that do not exist in Spain.

Based on our research, we offer another possible interpretation of these findings. We suggest that the higher perceptions of discrimination among immigrant youth in the United States reflect a greater level of critical consciousness due to the presence of established ethnic communities and a long, prolific history of people of color activism there. Far from being anti-American, this is the same critical consciousness that fueled the civil rights movement and pushes the United States to live up to its democratic ideals. As we saw in chapters 3 and 4, the reluctance of immigrant teenagers in our study in Madrid to name discrimination and racism coexisted with their lived experiences of racialized violence, which emerged through multiple layers of data collection in the context of a safe space of *acompañamiento*. It was not that they did not experience racism or discrimination, but that in the absence of exposure to immigrant activism, discourses of integration, tolerance, and inclusion in Spain complicated their ability to understand and respond to their experiences. The activists Andrea interviewed (chapter 5) readily named their experiences of racism, sexism, nationalism, and colonialism because their activist work gave them the language to do so; they had developed their critical consciousness about their own experiences of oppression and strengthened their ability to respond.

Certainly, some might argue that these activists are antidemocratic or threats to national security; recall that after 9/11, President George Bush added critics of neoliberalism to the United States' growing list of "hemispheric security concerns" (Grandin 2006, 212). During the trial of former dictator Ríos Montt in Guatemala in 2013, the Asociación de Mujeres de Guatemala (see chapter 5) appeared on a list of "terrorists" released by a Guatemalan foundation against terrorism. The labeling of women's, indigenous, and immigrant rights activists as threats to national security reveals the colonial and imperial underpinnings of national citizenship rooted in

racial hierarchies (Maira 2018). We argue that the Latina feminist activists
described in chapter 5 are in fact decolonizing citizenship, removing democracy from liberal and neoliberal imperial agendas and claiming it for "all of
us," for "anthropos and humanitas" (Mignolo 2011, 92). In their transnational
activist work for the rights of women and migrants, they pushed against
histories of colonialism and toward more democratic futures for Spain and
Latin America. The networks of *convivencia* that sustained them and nurtured their critical consciousness, networks that the immigrant youths in
our study lacked, would likely be condemned as "ghettoes" by scholars of
Spanish integration (Velasco Caballero and Torres 2015; Portes, Aparicio,
and Haller 2016) and Danish policymakers who claim that they arrest the
process of integration by reaffirming "resilient foreign identities."[1] But
this view reflects the binaries of colonial thinking, posing immigrants as
either assimilated into the mainstream (and upwardly mobile, progress-
ing) or oppositional—static, backward, unchanging. It fails to capture the
dynamism of the space in between where diaspora youth carve out their
identities, the third space where "the *affinities inside of difference* attract,
combine, and relate new constituencies into a coalition of resistance" (Sandoval 1998, 362; emphasis in original). Our borderlands subjectivity
frames these as spaces of critical citizenship formation that are essential to
the restoration and revitalization of democracy.

While Western liberal nationalisms presume that individuals must shed
cultural ties to assume the rights of democratic citizenship, research on
transnational and diasporic citizenship shows that it is through group membership that diaspora youth learn to engage civically in a democracy (Abu
El-Haj 2015; Jensen 2010; Flores-González and Rodríguez-Muñiz 2014).
Group membership—including transnational and diasporic identities—
provides young people with the affective ties, social responsibility, motivation, critical consciousness, and skills in collective action that are
foundational for democratic civic action (Dyrness and Abu El-Haj
2019). Flores-González and Rodríguez-Muñiz's (2014) research exploring the relationship between political solidarity and Latino/a identity
formation among Puerto Rican youth in the diaspora found that lived
experiences as racialized minorities *and* close relationships between youth
activists and local Puerto Rican politicians and community leaders generated political awareness among the youth. For both Muslim and Puerto
Rican youth in the United States, the awareness that legal citizenship is
not enough to guarantee equal rights—a critique of Western democratic

citizenship—is a precursor to political identity formation and civic action (Abu El-Haj 2015; Flores-González and Rodríguez-Muñiz 2014). Puerto Rican scholar-educator Eileen Gonzalez (2014) explains that citizenship status was insufficient to shield her from the racism and xenophobia she experienced in schools in the United States: "It was not until I made connections with Puerto Ricans and other Latinos here in the States that I began to feel comfortable" (190). Established Puerto Rican communities helped. Likewise, Lene Jensen (2008) found that immigrants' strong connections to their cultural communities and their motivation to ensure or enhance the welfare of these communities grounded their civic engagement in the United States.

U.S. Latina/o scholars have long pointed out the role of Latino cultural citizenship in U.S. society, how Latinos have expanded democracy by claiming the right to be different and still belong (Flores and Benmayor 1997). This perspective seems to be missing from the debate on integration in Spain. Portes, Aparicio, and Haller note that Spain "has not had time to develop a comparable racial-ethnic framework" like the United States' (2016, 229), and they attribute the speedy integration of immigrant youth to the absence of this framework. On the contrary, drawing on theories of coloniality, we argue that the cultural racism in Spanish educators' discourse about immigrant youth reflects enduring racial hierarchies from colonial times; what is missing is a history of social movements contesting this racism. In the United States immigrant youth come of age amid and often connected to diverse movements of people of color activism that shape their political consciousness (Naber 2012; Negrón-Gonzalez 2014; Flores-González and Rodríguez-Muñiz 2014). Research on the undocumented student movement in the United States suggests that undocumented immigrant students internalize the message of citizen change and invoke the civil rights movement taught by their schools in support of their activism (Negrón-Gonzalez 2014). By contrast, the immigrant youths in our study in Madrid were not aware of anyone who fought for the rights of immigrants in Spain. While there were emerging immigrant rights movements in Madrid such as Brigadas Vecinales, described in chapter 3, and a nascent movement against deportation and detention, these movements had not yet been able to connect with the concerns of immigrant youth or provide support for cultural rights and identity-based inclusion. The second-generation immigrant youths in our study were profoundly disconnected from these movements.

The gravity of this distance between the youths in our study and an immigrant rights consciousness was brought home to us one afternoon when we facilitated a conversation via Skype between a Connecticut Dreamer activist and the students in our group at ASI.[2] Gloria, a Mexicana living in Bridgeport, Connecticut, shared her story and the work of Connecticut Students for a Dream (C4D), a statewide student activist group connected to the national group United We Dream. Gloria's parents had brought her to the United States from Mexico at the age of four, and she never realized she was undocumented until her senior year of high school when she began applying for college admission and employment. She was told she didn't qualify for federal financial aid for college. Then she was offered a job at a prestigious company, but as soon as they found out she didn't have a social security number they retracted the offer. She said that moment changed her life. She was so disheartened she turned to C4D for help. They directed her to local universities that were friendly to undocumented immigrants and offered financial aid, and she began studying at Fairfield University. She also worked as a "core leader" volunteer for C4D because she said she didn't want any other young immigrant students to have to go through what she went through.

The youths at ASI were fascinated by Gloria's story and asked many questions. One in particular stood out: Mariela asked, "Do you think there continues to be racism in the United States?" Gloria answered immediately, "Yes, I think there is still racism, and that is not going to stop. There continues to be a lot of racism." She explained that the targets of racism would change over time; as new waves of immigrants arrived they would always be discriminated against—it used to be the Jews, then the Italians, now it is the Latinos, later it would be some other group. Gloria demonstrated a well-developed political consciousness along with an impressive knowledge of the U.S. political system and immigration laws. She spoke about her Connecticut senators as if she had a personal relationship with them. She explained that C4D was now focused on achieving immigration reform at the national level. She had been part of a delegation that went to the White House the previous summer to meet with senators, and she said it was a wonderful experience.

Gloria's observation of the high level of racism in the United States and her assessment that it was "not going to stop" would classify her as "reactive" in sociological studies of immigrant adaptation. Yet it was clear that her perception of racism was braided into her political consciousness and fueled her civic engagement for democratic social change on behalf of immigrants. Her story of coming to awareness followed a narrative structure common to Dreamer activists: once she had awareness of her exclusion she dedicated herself to pushing for change and helping others so that other young students would not have to experience what she had. It was also clear that C4D, the activist group to which she belonged, had provided the supportive space for her to develop her political consciousness and convert her feelings of despair into positive social engagement (see also Nuñez-Janes and Ovalle 2016; S.I.N. Collective 2007). Nuñez-Janes and Ovalle (2016), drawing on Sepúlveda (2011), theorize these activist spaces as "spaces of acompañamiento" where "undocumented youth accompany each other as they create networks of caring and extend notions of kinship among immigrants and allies" (193).

We argue that it was the absence of these spaces that shaped the difference between Gloria and the immigrant youths in our study in Madrid, especially their differing perceptions of racism and discrimination. Significantly, although the youths at ASI had many questions for Gloria, after we ended the interview and switched off the computer they were less willing to engage in a discussion comparing the conditions in the United States that Gloria described with the conditions facing immigrants in Spain. When Andrea asked them if they saw any similarities between Gloria's experience and what immigrants face in Spain, most of them said no. Yet, some of them had real concerns about their legal status and possible deportation, which they had disclosed in interviews with us. We suggest that students' hesitance to name the vulnerability of unauthorized immigrants in Spain was due at least in part to the absence of an undocumented student movement there, which would have legitimated the identity of the undocumented immigrant. At the next week's meeting we asked the students who had participated in the call with Gloria to share with those who had not been there what they had learned or what had struck them about the conversation. Asked to explain who the "Dreamers" are, they said, simply, "students." "Just students?" we probed. Eventually, Junot said, "immigrant students." But they missed a key aspect of Gloria's identity. We reminded them that Gloria organized as an undocumented immigrant student—*estudiante inmigrante sin papeles*—a political identity category that did not exist in Spain. Finally, Mariela and Raquel offered that Gloria was "very strong" and "very brave." Weeks later, at the end of the workshop as we prepared to share our findings in the presentation at the university, Mariela said that meeting *la*

Soñadora (the Dreamer) was one of the things that most impressed her about our workshop. Perhaps in some small way, meeting a Dreamer activist had shown them that they were not alone.

While sociological studies of adaptation would see the youths at ASI, with their low perceptions of discrimination, as highly integrated, we see young people who are struggling to make sense of their experiences and to give voice to identities that have been silenced in the public sphere, with little guidance from others—mentors or immigrant activists—who have had similar experiences. In their grappling with their contradictory realities there are the seeds of critical consciousness, but these seeds must be cultivated by critical educators to bear fruit. While Gloria the Dreamer would be seen by some scholars and policymakers as reactive and oppositional, a threat to democratic society, we see a critically conscious, politically empowered young person who is exercising her democratic right to participate and to open space for others.

We make the comparison between the Dreamers and the youths in Madrid not to suggest that the United States is a "better" context than Spain for immigrant youth. Rather, the longer presence of diaspora communities in the United States provides a supportive context for critical consciousness raising and decolonial thinking. As Gonzalez (2014) suggests, displacement, creating community, and developing critical consciousness are fundamental to the experience of living in the diaspora. Our research highlights the need for spaces that allow diaspora young people to examine their experiences of displacement, to capitalize on the insights of their in-between position and create new collective identities that are not tied to the nation-state and its hegemonic social formations. Drawing on a borderlands and diasporic citizenship framework, we propose that spaces of *acompañamiento* are cultural resources that help diaspora youth navigate their experiences of exclusion and broker hegemonic discourses that construct them as outsiders. This analysis engages nationalism as an important factor in migrant young people's identity formation but also looks beyond it to capture the agency and creativity of diasporic subjects' practices of belonging in the spaces in between nations. Likewise, it engages the role of ethnic communities (including the presence or absence of them) in young people's identity formation but also looks beyond that to capture the impact of border crossing itself—of life between multiple communities—in the development of democratic citizen identities.

Our principal finding is that diaspora youth's hybrid identities and multiple connections to home and host countries defy the binaries of nationalist discourses that construct unassimilated youth as a problem or a threat to democratic society. On the contrary, their complex relationships to communities in host and home countries give them a unique vantage point from which to understand inequalities and compelling motivations to engage civically for democratic social change. It is precisely their complex, multiple attachments that guard against uniform or knee-jerk aggressive reactions to discrimination in the host society, as predicted by theories of "reactive ethnicity." As we saw in chapters 3 and 4, Afro-Caribbean youth in Madrid could experience racialized police violence *and* still feel fierce attachments to Spain, due to their complex experiences of diversity and belonging in a transnational social field. Guatemalan and other Latina women could articulate sharp critiques of the racial and colonial discourses in Spain that construct them as inferior Others while still embracing the enhanced autonomy, safety, and freedom they experienced as women in Madrid compared to their home cities in Latin America. It was their feelings of belonging and safety as women in Madrid that compelled them to struggle against violence against women in their home countries, and against other forms of exclusion in Spain, that limited women's full participation as citizens.

This ability to distinguish between forms of oppression and belonging that come with any nation-state was a key insight of diaspora that activists articulated most clearly. A final example from Spain captures this. Andres was a twenty-four-year-old activist from Ecuador who worked in a Madrid restaurant with Marta, Andrea's coresearcher from AMG. Marta suggested and arranged the interview with Andres because he was an activist with the Communist Youth League. Over coffee one morning in June 2014, he told us his story. Andres described becoming politicized after a personal experience with police abuse three years earlier, when he was twenty-one. He and a friend were arrested after they opened a fire extinguisher in a metro station at 1:00 in the morning. "Fue una tontería de chavales" (It was a foolish kids' prank), he said, but it resulted in a long ordeal with the police.

They hit us, they pushed me. . . . They handcuffed me, threw me against the wall. And there began that long night. They called me to the station, my friend, too . . . [and there] they hit us, they kicked us, a lot of police passed by, friends who were working the night shift, and they were laughing, "How cute, go back to your country, is this what you came here for?" . . . And we were in handcuffs. . . . It was really a drawn-out thing, the indignation.

At his court hearing, the police testified that he had hit them, which wasn't true, and he was ordered to pay 1,100 euros in damages. It was the first time he realized that immigrants would be treated poorly regardless of their track records. The experience so discouraged Andres that he dropped out of school, but eventually it motivated him to get involved organizing immigrant youth for the Communist League because he recognized "the need to change that reality." His analysis of the conditions of immigrants' lives led him to become civically involved in a political party working to change those conditions. When we asked how he would describe his relationship with Spain, he reflected, "The structure of the Spanish state I hate, for sure. But my relationship with Spain, with the people of Spain, is one of love. Because I can't explain myself without Spain . . . I don't know what my life would be without Spain." As Andres's analysis shows, immigrant youths' responses to discrimination are mediated by multiple forms of belonging and attachment that guard against any singular, violent response. In spite of negative experiences with Spanish authorities, Andres could no more renounce Spain than he could renounce himself. His activism allowed him to distinguish between "the Spanish state" and "the people of Spain" and to work to change aspects of the state that had injured him. Like Andres, all of the Latinx immigrant youths in our research expressed in various ways a love for Spain, "for the things that Spain has given me," as Mercedes put it. But this love coexisted with experiences of injury that prevented them from embracing the Spanish national identity. Given these experiences, their refusal of national identity must be seen as a refusal of oppression, a democratic impulse that citizenship educators might engage rather than shun. As Gloria Anzaldúa (2015) observed, "Sometimes what accretes around an irritant or wound may produce a pearl of great insight" (2).

In our analysis, the ambiguous and ambivalent identities of transnational youth emerge from their democratic yearnings, which are not fully met in any country or context. Their lives in transnational social fields, encompassing multiple experiences of rights-bearing inclusion and rights deprivation across different axes of inequality, provide both a critical perspective on citizenship and deepened yearnings for new forms of belonging that would embrace the multiplicity of their transnational selves. If we care to look, they also provide cultural resources for transcending inequality that are not found within the boundaries of a single nation-state. As Ruth Trinidad Galván (2011), recalling Anzaldúa, reflects, "For those of us born and raised transborderly, we are a countryless people, and more and more this does not sadden me" (553). In her self-reflexive essay Trinidad Galván describes the lessons of *supervivencia* (survival and beyond), *convivencia,* and "new tribalism" that she learned from living and working transborderly between the United States and Mexico as riches that outweighed "the voices of judgmental teachers, unsympathetic peers, [and] a disapproving society" (556). Perhaps the borderlands are not so desolate if one is accompanied. "I can be here and there transing among places," Trinidad Galván continues, "as long as there is a connection to people across space and place" (553).

Like the deeds of the good Samaritans in Mrs. Gonzalez's border-crossing story who left gallons of water in the desert, cultural acts of *acompañamiento*—acts of solidarity, community building, claiming space, and bearing witness—help border crossers navigate the dangerous journey and difficult terrain. Spaces and practices of *acompañamiento* in the borderlands open up new ways of being in our times, ways that resist the fragmentation, alienation, and hostility of our modern global era. These spaces allow young people to examine their own forms of cultural, linguistic, and racial difference as defining their experiences, in defiance of integrationist paradigms that erase their stories, identities, and ways of being in the world. As cultural resources that emerge from the experience of displacement, these spaces and practices answer our deepest human need for connection with others, for finding common ground across distinct experiences of struggle. The children in the stories discussed in the introduction to this book were encouraged to find themselves—to overcome the beast of the immigration office and the anomie of *olvido,* or oblivion—by joining together with others who were displaced and taking inspiration from their stories. They represent the diaspora cultural wisdom that we find our place in the world not by forgetting but by remembering how and why we are different.

Acknowledgments

Our deepest gratitude goes to the youths in all three locations who opened their lives to us and allowed us to accompany them on parts of their journeys toward belonging and making sense of their complex global world. Their thoughtful reflections and spirit of *convivencia* made this work possible and continue to give us hope for the future. In each location, several key people took an interest in our work and facilitated our entry into the community, giving generously of their time and wisdom and going above and beyond duty to make us feel welcome. In California, Enrique thanks the Rodriguez Ulluoa family, particularly Cirenio, Gloria, and Teresa, for their ongoing mentorship of multiple generations of Chicana/o educators and their long-standing activism around educational justice, bilingual education, and political representation, and for supporting his research at Bosque High School. He is grateful to the teachers who allowed him to observe their classrooms; they must remain anonymous. He is deeply grateful to Dr. Karen Watson-Gegeo for her mentorship and inspirational teaching at University of California, Davis, and her pathbreaking decolonial research in the Solomon Islands.

In El Salvador, Haydee Díaz and José Luis Benitez made us feel welcome, connected us to events, conferences, and seminars on migration, and shared their insights in numerous conversations that deepened our thinking and our love and respect for the people of El Salvador. The late Tonny Orellana, education coordinator for the NGO that hosted our research, facilitated our connection to the school in El Rio and received us with a warmth and generosity beyond our expectations. We benefitted from his orientation and insightful conversation on countless rides to El Rio, and we hope our work honors his memory. In the way ethnography often happens, getting to and from the school taught us as much as our formal observations at the school. Tonny and his team of coaches from La Esperanza offered perceptive commentary and cheerful company as we sat in traffic observing the crowds on the streets and sidewalks of downtown San Salvador, the rickety patchwork *puestos* selling everything imaginable—"los hácelotodo, los véndelotodo, los cómelotodo," as Salvadoran poet Roque Dalton referred to his compatriots. On those long rides the coaches shared profound observations that deeply informed our understanding of life in El Rio, and for this we are grateful.

The director and several staff members of the school in El Rio willingly gave us access to students, school facilities, documents, and plans, and they shared their insights with us in countless conversations and interviews. We cannot name them here for reasons of confidentiality, but this research would not have been possible without them. Likewise at the Lincoln School, many teachers and administrators graciously allowed us into their classrooms and meetings, invited us to tag along on numerous school trips and events, and engaged our questions with genuine interest and concern for the topic of Salvadoran citizenship. A few extended their friendship, offering their homes, food, reflections, and fellowship in ways that enriched our lives and this book. We are so grateful. At Trinity College, Andrea's student Claudia Dresser, a 1.5 generation immigrant from El Salvador, skillfully transcribed hours of recorded interviews from El Salvador and engaged in thoughtful discussions that enriched our understanding of the connections between El Salvador and the United States.

In Spain, we are indebted to David Poveda and Marta Morgade for giving us a home at the Universidad Autónoma de Madrid and for collaborating with us on our research in Madrid. David connected us to the two youth-serving NGOs that became our research sites, conducted some focus groups with us, and organized numerous formal and informal discussions about our research at the university, including the presentation with the youths that made its way into this book. For David and Marta's collaboration and *convivencia,* including hours of debriefing over tapas and *cañas,* we are eternally grateful. We thank the staff at both youth-serving NGOs and the Asociación de Mujeres de Guatemala (AMG) for making space for our research and assisting our efforts to better understand the lives of these youths. Mercedes Hernández of AMG welcomed Andrea into her organization from their first meeting and introduced her to the four *socias* who became her research partners in the investigation of transnational feminists in Madrid. Mercedes's activism on behalf of women who cross borders to escape violence, drawing on multiple transnational networks, is an inspiration. That she found time in her dizzying schedule to share so much with us is a testament to her collaborative and generous spirit.

Festive meals in her home are among our fondest memories, and we are so grateful to have been included in her community. Monetary support for the research in Spain came from the Spencer Foundation's New Civics Initiative and from Trinity College's quadrennial leave (for Andrea).

Among colleagues in the Council on Anthropology and Education we owe special thanks to Bradley Levinson, Reva Jaffe-Walter, Thea Abu El-Haj, and Patricia Sánchez for their careful reading and supportive comments on drafts of various chapters in this book, some of which were first presented as papers at meetings of the American Anthropological Association. Ongoing conversations with these scholars and their inspiring research have enriched our analysis. Special thanks to Reva for her careful reading of the entire manuscript. At the University of Colorado, Boulder, doctoral student Ana Contreras, the daughter of immigrants from El Salvador, assisted with interview analysis that enriched (and made possible a timely completion of) chapter 5. Thank you, Ana. And finally, thank you to our families, for supporting us always, no matter what part of the world our research takes us to. Our parents, Romelia Sepúlveda and Bill and Grace Dyrness, modeled the skills of living across borders and offer emotional and spiritual support that sustains us, and our daughter, Sofia, accompanies us joyfully on this journey. We are quite sure that bringing her along on our research in El Salvador and Spain made possible new relationships of trust and solidarity with our young informants and new insights as we saw the world through her eyes. In life and in research she is our greatest teacher.

Notes

Introduction

1. Steve Inskeep, "In Junot Diaz's 'Islandborn,' a Curious Child Re-creates Her Dominican Roots," National Public Radio, March 12, 2018, https://www.npr.org/2018/03/12/591732716/in-junot-diazs-islandborn-a-curious-child-recreates-her-dominican-roots.

2. "State Multiculturalism Has Failed, Says David Cameron," BBC News, February 5, 2011, https://www.bbc.com/news/uk-politics-12371994.

3. Katie Rogers, "Trump Highlights Immigrant Crime to Defend His Border Policy. Statistics Don't Back Him Up," *New York Times*, June 22, 2018; Scott Horsley, "Fact Check: Trump, Illegal Immigration and Crime," National Public Radio, June 22, 2018, https://www.npr.org/2018/06/22/622540331/fact-check-trump-illegal-immigration-and-crime.

4. Ellen Barry and Martin S. Sorensen, "In Denmark, Harsh New Laws for Immigrant 'Ghettos,'" *New York Times*, July 1, 2018.

5. Stephen Gadd, "More Action Needed to Prevent 'Re-education' Trips Abroad, Says Minister," *Copenhagen Post*, February 22, 2018.

6. We recognize that Chicanx persons do not consider themselves to be a diaspora population because they are inhabiting their ancestral lands. However, Mexican migrants display many characteristics of diaspora populations, and in this book we explore the affinities between borderlands and diaspora theorizing. For another analysis of the Mexican diaspora, see Zavella (2011).

7. For a detailed analysis of this, see chap. 6, "English Lessons and Neocolonial Longing," in Hurtig (2008).

8. *Conocimiento* and *La Facultad* are concepts from Anzaldúa (1999) and Anzaldúa and Keating (2002) that will be explained later in the book.

1. *Acompañamiento* in the Borderlands

1. To clarify, I see Mexican identity not as a fixed and static identity but rather as a subject position that is socioculturally produced, complex, and fluid, and always in the making, multivocal, and perspectival. Part of this cultural production has to

do with how Mexican subjectivities are positioned in a historical field of colonial and neocolonial power relations centered around racialized, gendered, and heteronormative arrangements.

2. There were many white mainstream educators who expressed concerns about underachieving students in general. Some went further and expressed deep empathy toward Chicano Mexican students in particular. But very few stepped out of the traditional education box to do something different for this particular student population. Concomitantly, not all Chicano Mexican educators who had border-crossing experiences subscribed to alternative forms of learning. It is equally important to note that there was one white, English-only-speaking teacher, who I call Mrs. Vicky, who stood out. She was a very empathetic individual and concerned about the lack of achievement of her mainly Mexican students, who were classified as long-term ELD students (some staff members referred to them as "lifers" because of their enduring inability to master the English language and then be reassigned to mainstream classes). Mrs. Vicky talked to me about wanting to do something different in her classroom to engage her students about life. She invited me several times to give talks and lectures in her class about my research and ideas about learning and life. At the time, Mrs. Vicky was undergoing a religious conversion to Judaism; although she didn't frame it this way, she was undergoing her own cultural and spiritual border crossing.

3. By and large, these conversations about the various forms of Mexican masculinity did not challenge heteronormative and patriarchal assumptions and the usual order of things.

4. The Spanish word for hugs, *abrazos,* contains the word for arms, giving it a much more evocative imagery.

5. "Coyotes" are guides or smugglers, depending on whom you talk to.

2. In the Shadow of U.S. Empire

1. Pew Research Center tabulations of the 2015 American Community Survey counted 2,174,000 Salvadorans in the United States, surpassing the number of Cubans for the first time (see Flores 2017). However, as early as 2002, official Salvadoran sources from the Ministerio de Relaciones Exteriores de El Salvador estimated the figure to be 2.5 million (PNUD 2005, 37; Asociación Equipo Maíz 2006, 16). Given the high number of undocumented immigrants in this community, it is likely that they are significantly undercounted by U.S. official sources. See Programa de las Naciones Unidas para el Desarrollo (PNUD 2005, 34–38) for an extended discussion of the discrepancies between U.S. and Salvadoran counts of Salvadoran immigrants. Phippen and Boschma (2015) compared the fastest-growing Latino groups through 2013. As this book goes to press, new data compiled by the Pew Research Center shows that the Venezuelan population is now the fastest-growing

Latino group by far, but Salvadorans remain the third-largest group by numbers, at 2,307,000 in 2017 (see Noe-Bustamonte 2019).

2. A total of 67,339 unaccompanied children were apprehended at the southwest border from El Salvador, Guatemala, Honduras, and Mexico in FY2014, according to the Department of Homeland Security, U.S. Border Patrol Southwest Border Apprehensions. See https://www.cbp.gov/newsroom/stats/southwest -border-unaccompanied-children/fy-2014. In 2016, when the crisis had faded from the news, 17,512 unaccompanied minors arrived from El Salvador, and another 24,114 Salvadorans arrived in family units (apprehended by the Border Patrol with at least one other family member).

3. Matt O'Brien, "Salvadorans Now Fourth Largest Latino Group in the U.S.," *Mercury News*, May 26, 2011.

4. All quotations from *ECA* are our own translations.

5. Raúl Gutiérrez, "Dollarisation Backfires, Fuelling Price Hikes," Inter Press Service, February 5, 2008.

6. Comments were reprinted in Menéndez Castro (2008); quotes in the text are our translation from the Spanish.

7. ARENA represented the consolidation of the right wing's political power in the contemporary era.

8. "Congresistas en EEUU: en peligro TPS con FMLN" (U.S. Congressmen: TPS in danger with FMLN) was the headline of *El Diaro de Hoy* on March 12, 2009.

9. "Peligran Remesas y TPS si el FMLN Gana," (Remittances and TPS in danger if FMLN wins), *El Diario de Hoy*, March 12, 2009.

10. Manuel Enrique Hinds, *El Diario de Hoy*, February 27, 2009; our translation.

11. All school and personal names are pseudonyms.

12. Operation by the Jesuit NGO is allowed by an arrangement in El Salvador's education laws.

13. The school did have an assistance fund for the families of current students who had fallen on hard times; to be eligible, students had to have been enrolled at the school for at least two years. When asked whether the school had considered using scholarships to recruit talented low-income students, the president of the board told us they had decided against it because it would be too difficult for low-income students to adjust to the environment of the Lincoln School.

14. For a more detailed description of participatory research theory and method, see Park (1993), Cammarota (2011), and Dyrness (2008, 2011).

15. We arranged to meet when students would otherwise have been in *seminario,* a loosely focused seminar covering research methods, among other things.

16. The cost of the *canasta básica alimentaria,* "basic nutritional basket," in urban El Salvador in 2009 was $167.99. This does not include the cost of clothing, housing, education, or health care for an average family. Data is provided by El

Salvador's Dirección General de Estadística y Censos (DIGESTYC) and available at: http://www.digestyc.gob.sv/index.php/servicios/en-linea/canasta-basica -alimentaria.html.

17. National data show that remittances are seldom used for this purpose; 94 percent of remittance recipients use this money to cover daily consumption expenditures. Other uses, although less frequently mentioned, include expenses related to education and health care. See Keller and Rouse (2016).

18. The oldest private university in El Salvador, most famous for the on-campus killings of six Jesuit priests by the military in 1989.

19. This is similar to the "peripheral vision" described by Zavella (2011), referencing the transnational subjectivity of Mexicans on both sides of the U.S.–Mexican border.

20. Julie Hirschfeld Davis, "Trump Calls Some Unauthorized Immigrants 'Animals' in Rant," *New York Times*, May 16, 2018, https://www.nytimes.com/2018 /05/16/us/politics/trump-undocumented-immigrants-animals.html.

3. Negotiating Race and the Politics of Integration

1. Between 1994 and 2007 the employed population grew by 67 percent, adding 8.2 million new jobs (Actis 2013).

2. Belén Domínguez Cebrián, "La Unión Europea pierde brillo para los inmigrantes de Latinoamérica," *El País*, June 5, 2015. The authors of the report for the International Organization for Migration did not disaggregate data or differentiate between Latin Americans who were returning and Spaniards who were leaving.

3. Most studies report disparities in rates of completion of compulsory secondary education (ESO), enrollment in *bachillerato* (preuniversity), and university enrollment. However, at least one study analyzed results from the Programme for International Student Assessment (PISA), and it found that "non-Spanish-speaking immigrant students have better educational results than those whose mother tongue is Spanish," irrespective of parents' cultural backgrounds (García Castaño, Rubio Gómez, and Bouachra 2015, 42). Spanish-speaking Latino immigrant students thus enjoy no advantages in the Spanish educational system.

4. F. Javier Barroso, *El País*, February 26, 2013, our translation.

5. F. Javier Barroso, *El País*, May 4, 2014, our translation.

6. The second generation was defined in their study as children of immigrants born in Spain or brought to the country before age twelve.

7. Alejandra Agudo, "El 50% de inmigrantes de segunda generación se siente español," *El País*, May 13, 2013.

8. Alejandro Portes and Rosa Aparicio, "Investigación Longitudinal Sobre la Segunda Generación en España: Avance de Resultados," Fundación Ortega-Marañón, May 2013, p. 13, http://blog.intef.es/cniie/wp-content/uploads/sites /3/2013/05/Resultados-ILSEG2013ok.pdf. Our translation from the Spanish.

9. Ibid., p. 13, our translation from the Spanish.

10. This presentation and our interviews were in Spanish; all quotes in English are our translation.

11. Asociación de Servicios Integrales (Association for Integral Services) is a pseudonym. All personal names, too, are pseudonyms, to protect the identities of the participants.

12. Asociación para Familias, Educación y Paz (Association for Families, Education, and Peace) is a pseudonym.

13. "III Informe de las Brigadas Vecinales de observación de los derechos humanos (2012–2014)," Brigadas Vecinales, May 21, 2015, http://brigadasvecinales.org/2015/05/iii-informe-bvodh/. Our translation.

14. The list of problems included their studies, parental separation, violence/fights among youth, racism, health, family conflict, inequality, and the future. We asked them to rank in order of importance their top three problems, by secret ballot so they would not be influenced by peer pressure. Racism got the most votes.

15. The Personal Identity Molecule, adapted from the Anti-Defamation League's A World of Difference Institute.

16. Students had difficulty filling out the molecule this way and were not familiar with the categories of "ethnicity," "race," or "social class." We explained the categories several times in various ways.

4. Transnational Belongings

1. Throughout this chapter, quotes in English are our translation from the Spanish.

2. Historically, Dominican migration to Madrid comes from this region (Barahona), in contrast to Dominican migration to New York City, which has been primarily from Santo Domingo (see Smith and Guarnizo 1998, chap. 8).

3. The entire presentation and the discussion afterward were video recorded; the quotes here are from a transcript of the recording.

5. Feminists in Transition

1. I draw on Trinidad Galván (2014), who uses the term *glocal* to describe the local/global relations in Latina feminist epistemologies and alliances.

2. "Nosotras," Asociación de Mujeres de Guatemala, retrieved September 5, 2013, http://mujeresdeguatemala.org/nosotras. My translation.

3. The largest Latin American subgroups in Spain were Ecuadorians and Colombians, followed by Argentineans and Bolivians (Actis 2013).

4. This has changed somewhat since my research was conducted in 2013, with more asylum seekers arriving and with that, more women from Latin America,

especially (in this order) Venezuela, Colombia, Honduras and El Salvador (Mercedes Hernandez, pers. comm., 2/2/19).

5. "Nuestro Trabajo," Asociación de Mujeres de Guatemala, retrieved August 3, 2015, http://mujeresdeguatemala.org/nuestro-trabajo. My translation.

6. Aurora Levins Morales, excerpt from "Child of the Americas," from Aurora Levins Morales and Rosario Morales, *Getting Home Alive* (Firebrand Books, 1986). Copyright 1986 by Aurora Levins Morales and Rosario Morales. Used with the permission of The Permissions Company, Inc., on behalf of Aurora Levins Morales, www.auroralevinsmorales.com.

7. Names are pseudonyms except when subjects asked me to use their real names. Our conversations were in Spanish with occasional English words thrown in by Erica and Maria, who were bilingual. Quotes in English are my translations from the Spanish.

8. Marta suggested interviewing her coworker, an immigrant from Ecuador, because although he was not a woman, he was an activist with the Young Communist League.

9. All interviews were recorded and transcribed. Many of our group discussions were also recorded and transcribed; others were recreated in my field notes immediately after the meetings.

10. Power Flower exercise adapted from Arnold et al. (1991).

11. Mercedes Hernández, public presentation, University of Murcia, June 15, 2016.

12. "ONU Mujeres: La muerte de 41 niñas es una fotografía del país," La Vanguardia, February 28, 2018, https://www.lavanguardia.com/vida/20180228/4411 51671564/onu-mujeres-la-muerte-de-41-ninas-en-guatemala-es-una-fotografia -del-pais.html.

13. Shortly after this presentation two ex-military officers were arrested in Guatemala in connection with the investigation; the Sepur Zarco trial began, after repeated postponements, on February 1, 2016, and after four weeks of hearings, the court convicted the two former military officers of crimes against humanity on counts of rape, murder, and slavery. It was the first time a national court had prosecuted crimes of sexual slavery and sexual violence during conflict.

Conclusion

1. Barry and Sorensen, "In Denmark, Harsh New Laws."

2. Dreamers are undocumented immigrants and their allies who have lobbied for the passage of the Development, Relief, and Education for Alien Minors (DREAM) Act, which would provide legal status and a path to citizenship to certain undocumented immigrants who graduate from U.S. high schools.

Bibliography

Abrego, Leisy. 2014. *Sacrificing Families: Navigating Laws, Labor, and Love across Borders*. Stanford, Calif.: Stanford University Press.

Abu El-Haj, Thea Renda. 2007. "'I Was Born Here but My Home, It's Not Here': Educating for Democratic Citizenship in an Era of Transnational Migration and Global Conflict." *Harvard Educational Review* 77 (3): 285–316.

Abu El-Haj, Thea Renda. 2009. "Becoming Citizens in an Era of Globalization and Transnational Migration: Re-imagining Citizenship as Critical Practice." *Theory into Practice* 48 (4): 274–82.

Abu El-Haj, Thea Renda. 2015. *Unsettled Belonging: Educating Palestinian American Youth after 9/11*. Chicago: University of Chicago Press.

Abu El-Haj, Thea Renda, Anna Ríos-Rojas, and Reva Jaffe-Walter. 2017. "Whose Race Problem? Tracking Patterns of Racial Denial in US and European Educational Discourses on Muslim Youth." *Curriculum Inquiry* 47 (3): 310–35.

Actis, Walter. 2013. *Impactos de la crisis sobre la población inmigrada: Entre la invisibilidad y el rechazo latente* [Impacts of the crisis on the immigrant population: Between invisibility and latent rejection]. Madrid: Colectivo IOÉ.

Aguado, Teresa. 2009. "The Education of Ethnic, Racial, and Cultural Minority Groups in Spain." In *The Routledge International Companion to Multicultural Education*, edited by James A. Banks, 474–85. New York: Routledge.

Aigla, Jorge H. 1995. *The Aztec Shell*. Tempe, Ariz.: Bilingual Press.

Alarcón, Norma. 2013. "Anzaldúan Textualities: A Hermeneutic of the Self and the Coyolxauhqui Imperative." In *El Mundo Zurdo 3: Selected Works from the 2012 Meetings of the Society for the Study of Gloria Anzaldúa*, edited by Larissa M. Mercado-López, Sonia Saldívar-Hull, and Antonia Castañeda, 189–208. San Francisco: Aunt Lute Books.

Alexander, Meena. 2009. *Poetics of Dislocation*. Ann Arbor: University of Michigan Press.

Ali, Arshad Imtiaz. 2017. "The Impossibility of Muslim Citizenship." *Diaspora, Indigenous, and Minority Education* 11 (3): 110–16.

Ameeriar, Lalaie. 2017. *Downwardly Global: Women, Work and Citizenship in the Pakistani Diaspora*. Durham, N.C.: Duke University Press.

Anzaldúa, Gloria. (1987) 1999. *Borderlands/La Frontera: The New Mestiza*. 2nd ed. San Francisco: Spinsters/Aunt Lute.

Anzaldúa, Gloria. 2002a. "(Un)natural Bridges, (Un)safe Spaces." In *This Bridge We Call Home: Radical Visions for Transformation*, edited by Gloria E. Anzaldúa and AnaLouise Keating, 1–5. New York: Routledge.

Anzaldúa, Gloria. 2002b. "Now Let Us Shift . . . the Path of Conocimiento, Inner Works, Public Acts." In *This Bridge We Call Home: Radical Visions for Transformation*, edited by Gloria E. Anzaldúa and AnaLouise Keating, 540–77. New York: Routledge.

Anzaldúa, Gloria. 2015. *Light in the Dark/Luz en lo oscuro: Rewriting Identity, Spirituality, Reality*. Durham, N.C.: Duke University Press.

Anzaldúa, Gloria, and AnaLouise Keating. 2002. *This Bridge We Call Home: Radical Visions for Transformation*. New York: Routledge.

Argueta, Jorge. 2017. *En carne propia: Memoria poética/Flesh Wounds: A Poetic Memoir*, Houston, Tex.: Arte Público Press.

Arnold, Rick, Bev Burke, Carl James, D'Arcy Martin, and Barb Thomas. 1991. *Educating for a Change*. Toronto: Doris Marshall Institute.

Asociación Equipo Maíz. 2006. *El Salvador: Emigración y remesas*. San Salvador, El Salvador: Asociación Equipo Maíz.

Ayala, Jennifer, Julio Cammarota, Margarita I. Berta-Ávila, Melissa Rivera, Louie F. Rodríguez, and María Elena Torre, eds. 2018. *PAR EntreMundos: A Pedagogy of the Américas*. New York: Peter Lang.

Baker-Cristales, Beth. 2009. "Mediated Resistance: The Construction of Neoliberal Citizenship in the Immigrant Rights Movement." *Latino Studies* 7 (1): 60–82.

Bammer, Angelika. 2005. " 'Between Foreign and Floating Signs': The Language of Migrant Subjects." In *Migrant Cartographies: New Cultural and Literary Spaces in Post-Colonial Europe*, edited by Sandra Ponzanesi and Daniela Merolla, 151–63. Lanham, Md.: Lexington Books.

Barbero, Jesús Martín. 1997. "Descentramiento cultural y palimpsestos de identidad." *Estudios Sobre Las Culturas Contemporáneas* 3 (5): 87–96.

Bartlett, Lesley, and Ofelia García. 2011. *Additive Schooling in Subtractive Times: Bilingual Education and Dominican Immigrant Youth in the Heights*. Nashville, Tenn.: Vanderbilt University Press.

Bhabha, Homi. 1990. "The Third Space: Interview with Homi Bhabha." In *Identity: Community, Culture and Difference*, edited by Jonathan Rutherford, 207–21. London: Lawrence & Wishart.

Bhabha, Homi. 1994. *The Location of Culture*. New York: Routledge.

Bourgois, Philippe. 2001. "The Power of Violence in War and Peace: Post–Cold War Lessons from El Salvador." *Ethnography* 2 (1): 5–34.

Brown, Wendy. 2006. *Regulating Aversion: Tolerance in the Age of Identity and Empire.* Princeton, N.J.: Princeton University Press.

California Department of Education. 2005. "Educational Demographics." http://dq.cde.ca.gov/dataquest/.

Cammarota, Julio. 2007. "A Social Justice Approach to Achievement: Guiding Latina/o Students toward Educational Attainment with a Challenging, Socially Relevant Curriculum." *Equity & Excellence in Education* 40:87–96.

Cammarota, Julio. 2011. "A Sociohistorical Perspective for Participatory Action Research and Youth Ethnography in Social Justice Education." In *A Companion to the Anthropology of Education,* edited by Mica Pollock and Bradley A. Levinson, 517–29. West Sussex, U.K.: Wiley-Blackwell.

Cammarota, Julio, and Michelle Fine. 2008. *Revolutionizing Education: Youth Participatory Action Research in Motion.* New York: Routledge.

Cardoso, Lawrence. 1980. *Mexican Emigration to the United States, 1897–1931.* Tucson: University of Arizona Press.

Carranza, Mirna E. 2007. "Building Resilience and Resistance against Racism and Discrimination among Salvadorian Female Youth in Canada." *Child and Family Social Work* 12: 390–98.

Cellitti, Anarella. 2008. "Beyond Educational Interventions." *Latino Studies* 6 (3): 313–18.

Cervantes-Rodríguez, Margarita, Ramón Grosfoguel, and Eric Mielants, eds. 2008. *Caribbean Migration to Western Europe and the United States: Essays on Incorporation, Identity, and Citizenship.* Philadelphia: Temple University Press.

Chávez, Joaquín M. 2017. *Poets and Prophets of the Resistance: Intellectuals and the Origins of El Salvador's Civil War.* New York: Oxford University Press.

Chavez, Leo R. 2008. *The Latino Threat: Constructing Immigrants, Citizens, and the Nation.* Stanford, Calif.: Stanford University Press.

Chavez, Leo R. 2013. *The Latino Threat: Constructing Immigrants, Citizens, and the Nation.* 2nd ed. Stanford, Calif.: Stanford University Press.

Coates, Ta-Nehisi. 2015. *Between the World and Me.* New York: Spiegel and Grau.

Collins, Patricia Hill. 2000. *Black Feminist Thought: Knowledge, Consciousness, and the Politics of Empowerment.* 2nd ed. New York: Routledge.

Coutin, Susan Bibler. 2007. *Nations of Emigrants: Shifting Boundaries of Citizenship in El Salvador and the United States.* Ithaca, N.Y.: Cornell University Press.

Coutin, Susan Bibler. 2016. *Exiled Home: Salvadoran Transnational Youth in the Aftermath of Violence.* Durham, N.C.: Duke University Press.

De Genova, Nicholas. 2005. *Working the Boundaries: Race, Space, and "Illegality" in Mexican Chicago.* Durham, N.C.: Duke University Press.

Delgado-Bernal, Dolores, Enrique Alemán Jr., and Judith Flores Carmona. 2008. "Transnational and Transgenerational Latina/o Cultural Citizenship among

Kindergarteners, Their Parents, and University Students in Utah." *Social Justice* 35 (1): 28–49.

del Olmo, Margarita. 2010. *Re-shaping Kids through Public Policy on Diversity: Lessons from Madrid.* Madrid/Vienna: Navreme Publications.

DeLugan, Robin. 2012. *Reimagining National Belonging: Post–Civil War El Salvador in a Global Context.* Tucson: University of Arizona Press.

DeLugan, Robin. 2013. "Commemorating from the Margins of the Nation: El Salvador 1932, Indigeneity, and Transnational Belonging." *Anthropological Quarterly* 86 (4): 965–94.

Díaz, Junot. 2018. *Islandborn.* New York: Penguin Random House.

Donato, Ruben, Gonzalo Guzman, and Jarrod Hanson. 2017. "Francisco Maestas et al. v. George H. Shone et al.: Mexican American Resistance to School Segregation in the Hispano Homeland, 1912–1914." *Journal of Latinos and Education* 16 (1): 3–17.

Duany, Jorge. 2011. *Blurred Borders: Transnational Migration between the Hispanic Caribbean and the United States.* Chapel Hill: University of North Carolina Press.

Du Bois, W. E. B. 1903. *The Souls of Black Folk.* Chicago: A. C. McClurg.

Durand, Jorge, Douglas S. Massey, and René M. Zenteno. 2001. "Mexican Immigration to the United States: Continuities and Change." *Latin American Research Review* 36 (1): 107–27.

Dussel, Enrique. 1996. *The Underside of Modernity: Apel, Ricoeur, Rorty, Taylor, and the Philosophy of Liberation.* Atlantic Highlands, N.J.: Humanities Press International.

Dussel, Enrique. 1998. "Beyond Eurocentrism: The World System and the Limits of Modernity." In *The Cultures of Globalization,* edited by Fredric Jameson and Masao Miyoshi, 3–31. Durham, N.C.: Duke University Press.

Dyrness, Andrea. 2008. "Research for Change versus Research *as* Change: Lessons from a *mujerista* Participatory Research Team." *Anthropology & Education Quarterly* 39 (1): 23–44.

Dyrness, Andrea. 2011. *Mothers United: An Immigrant Struggle for Socially Just Education.* Minneapolis: University of Minnesota Press.

Dyrness, Andrea. 2012. "'Contra viento y marea (Against wind and tide)': Building Civic Identity among Children of Emigration in El Salvador." *Anthropology & Education Quarterly* 43 (1): 41–60.

Dyrness, Andrea. 2014. "National Divisions, Transnational Ties: Constructing Social and Civic Identities in Post-war El Salvador." *Journal of Latin American and Caribbean Anthropology* 19 (1): 63–83.

Dyrness, Andrea, and Thea Renda Abu El-Haj. 2019. "The Democratic Citizenship Formation of Transnational Youth." *Anthropology & Education Quarterly* 0 (0): 1–13, online. doi:10.1111/aeq.12294.

Dyrness, Andrea, and Enrique Sepúlveda. 2015. "Education and the Production of Diasporic Citizens in El Salvador." *Harvard Educational Review* 85 (1): 108–31.

Dyrness, Andrea, and Enrique Sepúlveda. 2017. "Between 'Here' and 'There': Transnational Latino/a Youth in Madrid." In *Global Latin(o) Americanos: Transoceanic Diasporas and Regional Migrations*, edited by Mark Overmyer-Velazquez and Enrique Sepúlveda, 139–61. New York: Oxford University Press.

ECA (*Estudios Centroamericanos*). 2007. Introduction to "Migraciones." Special issue, *ECA* 62 (699–700).

ECA (*Estudios Centroamericanos*). 2008. "Un 'siglo americano.'" In "El Salvador y Estados Unidos: Balance de un siglo de relaciones." Special issue, *ECA* 63 (713–14): 147–51.

Eigen, Sara, and Mark Larrimore. 2006. *The German Invention of Race*. Albany: State University of New York Press.

Espiritu, Yen Le. 2003. *Home Bound: Filipino American Lives across Cultures, Communities, and Countries*. Berkeley: University of California Press.

European Commission. 2018. *Public Opinion in the European Union*. Standard Eurobarometer 89. Luxembourg: European Commission. doi:10.2775/00.

Fals-Borda, Orlando. 1996. "A North-South Convergence on the Quest for Meaning." *Qualitative Inquiry* 2 (1): 76–87.

Fals-Borda, Orlando, and Mohammed A. Rahman. 1991. *Action and Knowledge: Breaking the Monopoly with Participatory Action-Research*. New York: Apex Press.

Fine, Michelle. 2018. *Just Research in Contentious Times: Widening the Methodological Imagination*. New York: Teachers College Press.

Flores, Antonio. 2017. "How the U.S. Hispanic Population is Changing." Pew Research Center. September 18. https://www.pewresearch.org/fact-tank/2017/09/18/how-the-u-s-hispanic-population-is-changing/.

Flores, William V., and Rina Benmayor. 1997. *Latino Cultural Citizenship: Claiming Identity, Space, and Rights*. Boston: Beacon Press.

Flores-González, Nilda, and Michael Rodríguez-Muñiz. 2014. "Latino/a Diaspora, Citizenship, and Puerto Rican Youth in the Immigrant Rights Movement." In *Diaspora Studies in Education: Towards a Framework for Understanding the Experiences of Transnational Communities*, edited by Rosalie Rolón-Dow and Jason Irizarry, 17–38. New York: Peter Lang.

Fouron, Georges, and Nina Glick Schiller. 2002. "The Generation of Identity: Redefining the Second Generation within a Transnational Social Field." In *The Changing Face of Home: The Transnational Lives of the Second Generation*, edited by Peggy Levitt and Mary C. Waters, 168–210. New York: Russell Sage Foundation.

Franzé, Adela. 2008. "Diversidad cultural en la escuela: Algunas contribuciones antropológicas." In *Revista de Educación* 345 (Enero/Abril): 111–32.

Franzé, Adela, María Fernanda Moscoso, and Albano Calvo Sánchez. 2011. "Donde nunca hemos llegado: Alumnado de origen Latinoamericano entre la escuela y el mundo laboral." In *Biculturalismo y segundas generaciones: Integración social, escuela y bilingüismo,* edited by Ángeles A. Garrido, Francisco Checa y Olmos, and Teresa Belmonte García, 279–308. Barcelona: Icaria + Antrazyt.

Freire, Paulo. (1970) 1999. *Pedagogy of the Oppressed.* New York: Continuum.

Freire, Paulo. 2001. *Pedagogy of Freedom: Ethics, Democracy, and Civic Courage.* Lanham, Md.: Rowman & Littlefield.

García Castaño, F. Javier, Maria Rubio Gómez, and Ouafaa Bouachra. 2015. "Immigrant Students at School in Spain: Constructing a Subject of Study." *Dve Domovini/Two Homelands* 41:35–46.

García-Peña, Lorgia. 2016. *The Borders of Dominicanidad.* Durham, N.C.: Duke University Press.

Gibson, Margaret A., and Silvia Carrasco. 2009. "The Education of Immigrant Youth: Some Lessons from the U.S. and Spain." *Theory Into Practice* 48 (4): 249–57.

Gilroy, Paul. 1987. *"There Ain't No Black in the Union Jack": The Cultural Politics of Race and Nation.* Chicago: University of Chicago Press.

Glick Schiller, Nina, Linda Basch, and Cristina Blanc Szanton. 1992. "Transnationalism: A New Analytic Framework for Understanding Migration." *Annals of the New York Academy of Sciences* 645 (1): 1–24.

Glissant, Édouard. (1990) 2000. *Poetics of Relation.* Ann Arbor: University of Michigan.

Goizueta, Roberto S. 2001. *Caminemos con Jesus: Toward a Hispanic/Latino Theology of Accompaniment.* New York: Orbis Books.

Gonzalez, Eileen M. 2014. "From 'La Borinqueña' to 'The Star Spangled Banner': An Emic Perspective on Getting Educated in the Diaspora." In *Diaspora Studies in Education: Towards a Framework for Understanding the Experiences of Transnational Communities,* edited by Rosalie Rolón-Dow and Jason Irizarry, 183–91. New York: Peter Lang.

Gonzalez, Gilbert G. 2011. "Mexican Labor Migration, 1876–1924." In *Beyond La Frontera: The History of Mexico–U.S. Migration,* edited by Mark Overmyer-Velázquez, 28–50. New York: Oxford University Press.

González, Roberto. 2016. *Lives in Limbo: Undocumented and Coming of Age in America.* Oakland, Calif.: University of California Press.

González-Enríquez, Carmen. 2014. "Spain." In *European Migration: A Sourcebook,* edited by Anna Triandafyllidou and Ruby Gropas, 339–50. Farnham, U.K.: Ashgate.

Gordon, Lewis R. 2011. "Shifting the Geography of Reason in an Age of Disciplinary Decadence." *Transmodernity: Journal of Peripheral Cultural Production of the Luso-Hispanic World* 1 (2): 95–103.

Grandin, Greg. 2006. *Empire's Workshop: Latin America, the United States, and the Rise of the New Imperialism.* New York: Owl Books.

Grosfoguel, Ramón, Margarita Cervantes-Rodríguez, and Eric Mielants. 2008. "Introduction: Caribbean Migrations to Western Europe and the United States." In *Caribbean Migration to Western Europe and the United States: Essays on Incorporation, Identity, and Citizenship,* edited by Margarita Cervantes-Rodríguez, Ramón Grosfoguel, and Eric Mielants, 1–17. Philadelphia: Temple University Press.

Hall, Kathleen. 2002. *Lives in Translation: Sikh Youth as British Citizens.* Philadelphia: University of Pennsylvania Press.

Haller, William, and Patricia Landolt. 2005. "The Transnational Dimensions of Identity Formation: Adult Children of Immigrants in Miami." *Ethnic and Racial Studies* 28 (6): 1182–1214.

Hallett, Miranda Cady, and Beth Baker-Cristales. 2010. "Diasporic Suffrage: Rights Claims and State Agency in the Salvadoran Trans-Nation." In "Salvadoran Migration to the US." Special double issue, *Urban Anthropology and Studies of Cultural Systems and World Economic Development* 39 (1/2): 175–211.

Harvey, David. 1989. *The Condition of Postmodernity: An Enquiry into the Origins of Cultural Change.* Cambridge, Mass.: Wiley-Blackwell.

Hayden, Bridget A. 2003. *Salvadorans in Costa Rica: Displaced Lives.* Tucson: University of Arizona Press.

Herrera, Juan Felipe. 2000. *The Upside Down Boy/El Niño de Cabeza.* New York: Children's Book Press.

Hierro, María. 2016. "Latin American Migration to Spain: Main Reasons and Future Perspectives." *International Migration* 54 (1): 64–83.

hooks, bell. 1990. *Yearning: Race, Gender and Cultural Politics.* Boston: South End Press.

Huff, James. 2007. "Democratic Pentecost in El Salvador? Civic Education and Professional Practice in a Private High School." In *Reimagining Civic Education,* edited by Bradley Levinson and Doyle Stevick, 69–90. Lanham, Md.: Rowman & Littlefield.

Huntington, Samuel. 1996. *The Clash of Civilizations and the Remaking of the World.* New York: Simon & Schuster.

Huntington, Samuel. 2004. *Who Are We? The Challenges to America's National Identity.* London: Simon & Schuster.

Hurtado, Aida. 1989. "Relating to Privilege: Seduction and Rejection in the Subordination of White Women and Women of Color." *Signs* 14 (4): 833–55.

Hurtado, Aida. 2003. *Voicing Chicana Feminisms: Young Women Speak Out on Sexuality and Identity.* New York: New York University Press.

Hurtig, Janise. 2008. *Coming of Age in Times of Crisis: Youth, Schooling, and Patriarchy in a Venezuelan Town.* New York: Palgrave Macmillan.

Irizarry, Jason. 2011. *The Latinization of U.S. Schools: Successful Teaching and Learning in Shifting Cultural Contexts.* Boulder, Colo.: Paradigm Publishers.

Jackson, Michael. 2002. *The Politics of Storytelling: Violence, Transgression, and Intersubjectivity.* Copenhagen: Museum Tusculanum Press University of Copenhagen.

Jackson, Michael. 2007. *Excursions.* Durham, N.C.: Duke University Press.

Jaffe-Walter, Reva. 2016. *Coercive Concern: Nationalism, Liberalism and the Schooling of Muslim Youth.* Stanford, Calif.: Stanford University Press.

Jensen, Lene A. 2008. "Immigrants' Cultural Identities as Sources of Civic Engagement." *Applied Development Science* 12 (2): 74–83.

Jensen, Lene A. 2010. "Immigrant Youth in the United States: Coming of Age among Diverse Civic Cultures." In *Handbook of Research on Civic Engagement in Youth,* edited by Lonnie Sherrod, Judith Torney-Purta, and Constance Flanagan, 425–43. New York: John Wiley & Sons.

Kasinitz, Philip, John H. Mollenkopf, Mary C. Waters, and Jennifer Holdaway. 2008. *Inheriting the City: The Children of Immigrants Come of Age.* Cambridge, Mass.: Harvard University Press.

Keller, Lukas, and Rebecca Rouse. 2016. *Remittance Recipients in El Salvador: A Socioeconomic Profile.* September. Washington, D.C.: Inter-American Development Bank Group.

Kishi, Katayoun. 2017. "Assaults against Muslims in U.S. Surpass 2001 Level." Pew Research Center. November 15. https://www.pewresearch.org/fact-tank /2017/11/15/assaults-against-muslims-in-u-s-surpass-2001-level/.

Kleiner-Liebau, Désirée. 2009. *Migration and the Construction of National Identity in Spain.* Madrid: Iberoamericana, 2009.

Koliba, Christopher J. 2004. "Service-Learning and the Downsizing of Democracy: Learning Our Way Out." *Michigan Journal of Community Service Learning* 10 (2): 57–68.

Koopmans, Ruud, Paul Statham, Marco Giugni, and Florence Passy. 2005. *Contested Citizenship: Immigration and Cultural Diversity in Europe.* Minneapolis: University of Minnesota Press.

Kramsch, Claire. 2004. "Response to 'Border Discourses.'" In *What They Don't Learn in School: Literacy in the Lives of Urban Youth,* edited by Jabari Mahiri, 99–101. New York: Peter Lang.

Kwon, Soo Ah. 2013. *Uncivil Youth: Race, Activism, and Affirmative Governmentality.* Durham, N.C.: Duke University Press.

Lam, Wan Shun Eva, and Doris S. Warriner. 2012. "Transnationalism and Literacy: Investigating the Mobility of People, Languages, Texts, and Practices in Contexts of Migration." *Reading Research Quarterly* 47 (2): 191–215.

Latina Feminist Group. 2001. *Telling to Live: Latina Feminist Testimonios.* Durham, N.C.: Duke University Press.

León, Luis D. 2004. *La Llorona's Children: Religion, Life, and Death in the U.S.–Mexican Borderlands.* Berkeley: University of California Press.

Levinson, Bradley. 2005. "Citizenship, Identity, Democracy: Engaging the Political in the Anthropology of Education." *Anthropology and Education Quarterly* 36 (4): 329–40.

Levinson, Bradley, and Juan Berumen. 2007. "Democratic Citizenship Education and the State in Latin America: A Critical Overview." *REICE—Revista Electrónica Iberoamericana sobre Calidad, Eficacia y Cambio en Educación* 5 (4): 1–15.

Levitt, Peggy, and Nina G. Schiller. 2004. "Conceptualizing Simultaneity: A Transnational Social Field Perspective on Society." *International Migration Review* 38 (3): 1002–39.

Levitt, Peggy, and Mary C. Waters, eds. 2002. *The Changing Face of Home: The Transnational Lives of the Second Generation.* New York: Russell Sage Foundation.

Lilla, Mark. 2015. "France on Fire." *New York Review of Books,* March 5, 2015.

Lowe, Lisa. 2015. *The Intimacies of Four Continents.* Durham, N.C.: Duke University Press.

Lucko, Jennifer. 2011. "Tracking Identity: Academic Performance and Ethnic Identity among Ecuadorian Immigrant Teenagers in Madrid." *Anthropology & Education Quarterly* 42 (3): 213–29.

Lucko, Jennifer. 2014. "'Here Your Ambitions Are Illusions': Boundaries of Integration and Ethnicity among Ecuadorian Immigrant Teenagers in Madrid." *Journal of the History of Childhood and Youth* 7 (1): 135–64.

Lukose, Ritty A. 2007. "The Difference That Diaspora Makes: Thinking through the Anthropology of Immigrant Education in the United States." *Anthropology & Education Quarterly* 38 (4): 405–18.

Mahler, Sarah J. 1995. *American Dreaming: Immigrant Life on the Margins.* Princeton, N.J.: Princeton University Press.

Maira, Sunaina M. 2008. "Flexible Citizenship/Flexible Empire: South Asian Muslim Youth in Post-9/11 America." *American Quarterly* 60 (3): 697–720.

Maira, Sunaina M. 2009. *Missing: Youth, Citizenship, and Empire after 9/11.* Durham, N.C.: Duke University Press.

Maira, Sunaina. 2018. "Radicalizing Empire: Youth and Dissent in the War on Terror." In *Ethnographies of U.S. Empire,* edited by Carol McGranahan and J. F. Collins, 391–410. Durham, N.C.: Duke University Press.

Marcus, George E. 1995. "Ethnography in/of the World System: The Emergence of Multi-sited Ethnography." *Annual Review of Anthropology* 24 (1): 95–117.

Massey, Douglas S. 2011. "Epilogue: The Past and Future of Mexico–U.S. Migration." In *Beyond La Frontera: The History of Mexico–U.S. Migration,* edited by Mark Overmyer-Velázquez, 251–65. New York: Oxford University Press.

Massey, Douglas S., and Mágaly Sánchez. 2010. *Brokered Boundaries: Creating Immigrant Identity in Anti-immigrant Times.* New York: Russell Sage Foundation.

Mendoza Pérez, Karmele, and Marta Morgade Salgado. 2018. "'Unaccompanied' Minors? Accompanied Foreign Minors, Families, and New Technologies." *Journal of International Migration & Integration* (July): 1–16.

Menéndez Castro, José Rolando. 2008. "Ponencias del foro de intelectuales de El Salvador." *Realidad y Reflexión/Reality and Reflection* 7 (24): 10–43.

Menjívar, Cecilia. 2000. *Fragmented Ties: Salvadoran Immigrant Networks in America.* Berkeley: University of California Press.

Menjívar, Cecilia. 2011. *Enduring Violence: Ladina Women's Lives in Guatemala.* Berkeley: University of California Press.

Menjívar, Cecilia, and Néstor Rodríguez, eds. 2005. *When States Kill: Latin America, the U.S., and Technologies of Terror.* Austin: University of Texas Press.

Mignolo, Walter D. 2000. *Local Histories/Global Designs: Coloniality, Subaltern Knowledges, and Border Thinking.* Princeton, N.J.: Princeton University Press.

Mignolo, Walter D. 2002. "The Zapatista's Theoretical Revolution: Its Historical, Ethical, and Political Consequences." *Utopian Thinking* 25 (3): 245–75.

Mignolo, Walter D. 2007. "DELINKING: The Rhetoric of Modernity, the Logic of Coloniality and the Grammar of De-coloniality." *Cultural Studies* 21 (2): 449–514.

Mignolo, Walter D. 2011. *The Darker Side of Western Modernity.* Durham, N.C.: Duke University Press.

Miller, Arpi. 2011. "'Doing' Transnationalism: The Integrative Impact of Salvadoran Cross-Border Activism." *Journal of Ethnic and Migration Studies* 37 (1): 43–60.

Morrell, Ernest. 2006. "Youth-Initiated Research as a Tool for Advocacy and Change in Urban Schools." In *Beyond Resistance: Youth Activism and Community Change,* edited by Shawn Ginwright, Pedro Noguera, and Julio Cammarota, 111–28. New York: Routledge.

Moscoso, María Fernanda. 2009. "Perspectivas de padres y madres (ecuatorianos) sobre el contrato pedagógico entre la institución escolar y la familia en un contexto migratorio." *Papeles de Trabajo sobre Cultura, Educación y Desarrollo Humano* 5 (1): 1–40.

Naber, Nadine. 2012. *Arab America: Gender, Cultural Politics, and Activism.* New York: New York University Press.

Nabudere, D. W. 2008. "Research, Activism, and Knowledge Production." In *Engaging Contradictions: Theory, Politics, and Methods of Activist Scholarship,* edited by Charles R. Hale, 62–87. Berkeley: University of California Press.

Negrón-Gonzalez, Genevieve. 2014. "Undocumented, Unafraid, and Unapologetic: Re-articulatory Practices and Migrant Youth 'Illegality.'" *Latino Studies* 12 (2): 259–78.

Ngai, Mae. 2004. *Impossible Subjects: Illegal Aliens and the Making of Modern America.* Princeton, N.J.: Princeton University Press.

Noe-Bustamonte, Luis. 2019. "Key Facts about U.S. Hispanics and Their Diverse Heritage." Pew Research Center. September 16. https://www.pewresearch.org/fact-tank/2019/09/16/key-facts-about-u-s-hispanics/.

Nuñez-Janes, Mariela, and Mario Ovalle. 2016. "Organic Activists: Undocumented Youth Creating Spaces of *Acompañamiento*." *Diaspora, Indigenous, and Minority Education* 10 (4): 189–200.

Ogbu, John. 1987. "Variability in Minority School Performance: A Problem in Search of an Explanation." *Anthropology & Education Quarterly* 18 (4): 312–34.

Ogbu, John. 1991. "Immigrant and Involuntary Minorities in Comparative Perspective." In *Minority Status and Schooling: A Comparative Study of Immigrant and Involuntary Minorities,* edited by Margaret A. Gibson and John Obgu, 3–33. New York: Garland.

Ong, Aihwa. 1996. "Cultural Citizenship as Subject-Making: Immigrants Negotiate Racial and Cultural Boundaries in the United States." *Current Anthropology* 37 (5): 737–51.

Ong, Aihwa. 1999. *Flexible Citizenship: The Cultural Logics of Transnationality.* Durham, N.C.: Duke University Press.

Ong, Aihwa. 2006. *Neoliberalism as Exception: Mutations in Citizenship and Sovereignty.* Durham, N.C.: Duke University Press.

Ortiz, Daniela. 2017. *There Is a Monster under My Bed! A Tale about the Beast of the Immigration Office.* N.p.: printed by author.

Oso Casas, Laura. 2008. "Dominican Women, Heads of Households in Spain." In *Caribbean Migration to Western Europe and the United States: Essays on Incorporation, Identity, and Citizenship,* edited by Margarita Cervantes-Rodríguez, Ramón Grosfoguel, and Eric Mielants, 208–31. Philadelphia: Temple University Press.

Overmyer-Velázquez, Mark. 2011. *Beyond La Frontera: The History of Mexico–U.S. Migration.* New York: Oxford University Press.

Overmyer-Velázquez, Mark, and Enrique Sepúlveda, eds. 2017. *Global Latin(o) Americanos: Transoceanic Diasporas and Regional Migrations.* Oxford: Oxford University Press.

Padilla, Genaro M. 1993. *My History, Not Yours: The Formation of Mexican American Autobiography.* Madison: University of Wisconsin Press.

Paris, Django, and H. Samy Alim, eds. 2017. *Culturally Sustaining Pedagogies: Teaching and Learning for Justice in a Changing World.* New York: Teachers College Press.

Park, Peter. 1993. "What Is Participatory Research? A Theoretical and Methodological Perspective." In *Voices of Change: Participatory Research in the United States and Canada,* edited by Peter Park, Mary Brydon-Miller, Budd Hall, and Ted Jackson, 1–19. Westport, Conn.: Bergin & Garvey.

Pérez, Emma. 1999. *The Decolonial Imaginary: Writing Chicanas into History.* Bloomington: Indiana University Press.

Periódico Nuevo Enfoque. 2008. "Foro de Intelectuales." *Periódico Nuevo Enfoque* 40 (Segunda Quincena de Octubre).

Pew Research Center. 2017. "U.S. Muslims Concerned about Their Place in Society, but Continue to Believe in the American Dream." July 26. https://www .pewforum.org/2017/07/26/findings-from-pew-research-centers-2017-survey -of-us-muslims/.

Phippen, J. Weston, and Janie Boschma. 2015. "The Three Fastest-Growing Latino Groups Will Surprise You." *Atlantic Monthly,* July 23.

PNUD (Programa de las Naciones Unidas para el Desarrollo). 2005. *Informe sobre el Desarrollo Humano 2005: Una mirada al nuevo nosotros, el impacto de las migraciones.* San Salvador, El Salvador: PNUD.

Pollock, Mica. 2004. *Colormute: Race Talk Dilemmas in an American School.* Princeton, N.J.: Princeton University Press.

Portes, Alejandro, Rosa Aparicio, and William Haller. 2016. *Spanish Legacies: The Coming of Age of the Second Generation.* Oakland: University of California Press.

Portes, Alejandro, Luis E. Guarnizo, and Patricia Landolt. 1999. "The Study of Transnationalism: Pitfalls and Promise of an Emergent Research Field." *Ethnic and Racial Studies* 22 (2): 217–37.

Portes, Alejandro, and Rubén G. Rumbaut. 2001. *Legacies: The Story of the Immigrant Second Generation.* Berkeley: University of California Press.

Portes, Alejandro, and Rubén G. Rumbaut. 2005. "The Second Generation and the Children of Immigrants Longitudinal Study." *Ethnic and Racial Studies* 28 (6): 983–99.

Portes, Alejandro, Erik Vickstrom, and Rosa Aparicio. 2011. "Coming of Age in Spain: The Self-Identification, Beliefs, and Self-Esteem of the Second Generation." *British Journal of Sociology* 62 (3): 387–417.

Portes, Alejandro, and Min Zhou. 1993. "The New Second Generation: Segmented Assimilation and Its Variation." *Annals of the American Academy of Political and Social Science* 530:74–96.

Poveda, David. 2012. "Literacy Artifacts and Semiotic Landscape of a Spanish Secondary School." *Reading Research Quarterly* 47 (1): 61–88.

Poveda, David, María Isabel Jociles, and Adela Franzé. 2009. "La diversidad cultural en la educación secundaria en Madrid: Experiencias y prácticas institucionales con alumnado inmigrante latinoamericano." *Papeles de Trabajo Sobre Cultura, Educación y Desarrollo Humano* 5 (3): 1–42.

Poveda, David, María Isabel Jociles, and Adela Franzé. 2014. "Immigrant Students and the Ecology of Externalization in a Secondary School in Spain." *Anthropology & Education Quarterly* 45 (2): 185–202.

Poveda, David, María Isabel Jociles, Adela Franzé, María Moscoso, and Alabano Calvo. 2012. "The Role of Institutional, Family, and Peer-Based Discourses and Practices in the Construction of Students' Socioacademic Trajectories." *Ethnography and Education* 7 (1): 39–57.

Quijano, Aníbal. 2000. "Coloniality of Power and Eurocentrism in Latin America." *International Sociology* 15 (2): 215–32.

Ravitch, Sharon, and Matthew Riggan. 2016. *Reason and Rigor: How Conceptual Frameworks Guide Research.* 2nd ed. Los Angeles: Sage.

Reed-Danahay, Deborah, and Caroline B. Brettell. 2008. *Citizenship, Political Engagement, and Belonging: Immigrants in Europe and the United States.* New Brunswick, N.J.: Rutgers University Press.

Ríos-Rojas, Anna. 2011. "Beyond Delinquent Citizenships: Immigrant Youth's (Re)visions of Citizenship and Belonging in a Globalized World." *Harvard Educational Review* 81 (1): 64–95.

Ríos-Rojas, Anna. 2014. "Managing and Disciplining Diversity: The Politics of Conditional Belonging in a Catalonian Institut." *Anthropology & Education Quarterly* 45 (1): 2–21.

Rodríguez, Ana Patricia. 2005. "Departamento 15: Cultural Narratives of Salvadoran Transnational Migration." *Latino Studies* 3 (1): 19–41.

Rolón-Dow, Rosalie, and Jason G. Irizarry, eds. 2014. *Diaspora Studies in Education: Toward a Framework for Understanding the Experiences of Transnational Communities.* New York: Peter Lang.

Rubin, Beth. 2007. "'There's Still Not Justice': Youth Civic Identity Development amid Distinct School and Community Contexts." *Teachers College Record* 109 (2): 449–81.

Rumbaut, Rubén G. 2002. "Severed or Sustained Attachments? Language, Identity, and Imagined Communities in the Post-Immigrant Generation." In *The Changing Face of Home: The Transnational Lives of the Second Generation,* edited by Peggy Levitt and Mary C. Waters, 43–95. New York: Russell Sage Foundation.

Rumbaut, Rubén G. 2008. "Reaping What You Sow: Immigration, Youth, and Reactive Ethnicity." *Applied Developmental Science* 12 (2): 108–11.

Saldívar, Ramón. 2006. "Américo Paredes and the Transnational Imaginary." In *Identity Politics Reconsidered,* edited by Linda Martín Alcoff, Michael Hames-García, Satya P. Mohanty, and Paula M. L. Moya, 142–51. New York: Palgrave Macmillan.

Saldívar, Ramón. 2011. "Social Aesthetics and the Transnational Imaginary." In *A Companion to Latina/o Studies,* edited by Juan Flores and Renato Rosaldo, 406–16. Oxford, U.K.: Blackwell.

Sánchez, Patricia. 2007. "Urban Immigrant Students: How Transnationalism Shapes Their World Learning." *Urban Review* 39 (5): 489–517.

Sánchez, Patricia, and G. Sue Kasun. 2012. "Connecting Transnationalism to the Classroom and to Theories of Immigrant Student Adaptation." *Berkeley Review of Education* 3 (1): 71–93.

Sandoval, Chela. 1998. "Mestizaje as Method." In *Living Chicana Theory,* edited by Carla Trujillo, 352–70. Berkeley, Calif.: Third Woman Press.

Sandoval, Chela. 2000. *Methodology of the Oppressed.* Minneapolis: University of Minnesota Press.

Sassen, Saskia. 2006. *Territory, Authority, Rights: From Medieval to Global Assemblages.* Princeton, N.J.: Princeton University Press.

Seif, Hinda. 2010. "The Civic Life of Latina/o Immigrant Youth." In *Handbook of Research on Civic Engagement in Youth,* edited by Lonnie R. Sherrod, Judith Torney-Purta, and Constance A. Flanagan, 445–70. Hoboken, N.J.: John Wiley & Sons.

Seif, Hinda. 2011. "'Unapologetic and Unafraid': Immigrant Youth Come Out from the Shadows." *New Directions for Child and Adolescent Development* 134:59–75.

Sepúlveda, Enrique. 2011. "Toward a Pedagogy of *Acompañamiento*: Mexican Migrant Youth Writing from the Underside of Modernity." *Harvard Educational Review* 81 (3): 550–73.

Sepúlveda, Enrique. 2018. "Border Brokers: Teachers and Undocumented Mexican Students in Search of *Acompañamiento*." *Diaspora, Indigenous, and Minority Education* 12 (2): 53–69.

Shirazi, Roozbeh. 2017. "When Schooling Becomes a Tactic of Security: Educating to Counter 'Extremism.'" *Diaspora, Indigenous, and Minority Education* 11 (1): 2–5.

Simpson, Leanne B. 2017. *As We Have Always Done: Indigenous Freedom through Radical Resistance.* Minneapolis: University of Minnesota Press.

S.I.N. Collective. 2007. "Students Informing Now (S.I.N.) Challenge the Racial State in California without Shame . . . *SIN Vergüenza!*" *Educational Foundations* (Winter/Spring): 71–88.

Sirin, Selcuk, and Michelle Fine. 2007. "Hyphenated Selves: Muslim American Youth Negotiating Identities on the Fault Lines of Global Conflict." *Applied Development Science* 11 (3): 151–63.

Siu, Lok C. D. 2005. *Memories of a Future Home: Diasporic Citizenship of Chinese in Panama.* Stanford, Calif.: Stanford University Press.

Smith, Michael P., and Luis E. Guarnizo, eds. 1998. *Transnationalism from Below.* New Brunswick, N.J.: Transaction Publishers.

Spring, Joel. 2018. *The American School: From Puritans to the Trump Era.* 10th ed. New York: Routledge.

Stoll, Steven. 2017. *Ramp Hollow: The Ordeal of Appalachia.* New York: Hill & Wang.

Suárez Navaz, L. 2008. "Colonialismo, gobernabilidad y feminismos poscoloniales." In *Descolonizando el Feminismo: Teorías y Prácticas desde los Márgenes,* edited by L. Suárez Navaz and R. A. Hernández, 31–73. Madrid: Ediciones Cátedra – Grupo Anaya.

Suarez-Orozco, Marcelo. 1987. " 'Becoming Somebody': Central American Immigrants in U.S. Inner-City Schools." *Anthropology & Education Quarterly* 18 (4): 287–99.

Taylor, Charles. 2004. *Modern Social Imaginaries.* Durham, N.C.: Duke University Press.

Taylor, Lucy. 2013. "Decolonizing Citizenship: Reflections on the Coloniality of Power in Argentina." *Citizenship Studies* 17 (5): 596–610.

Torre, María Elena, and Jennifer Ayala. 2009. "Envisioning Participatory Action Research *Entremundos.*" *Feminism & Psychology* 19 (3): 387–93.

Trinidad Galván, Ruth. 2006. "Campesina Epistemologies and Pedagogies of the Spirit: Examining Women's *Sobrevivencia.*" In *Chicana/Latina Education in Everyday Life: Feminista Perspectives on Pedagogy and Epistemology,* edited by Dolores Delgado-Bernal, C. Alejandra Elenes, Francisca Godinez, and Sofia Villenas, 161–79. Albany: State University of New York Press.

Trinidad Galván, Ruth. 2011. "Chicana Transborder *Vivencias* and *Autoherteorías*: Reflections from the Field." *Qualitative Inquiry* 17 (6): 552–57.

Trinidad Galván, Ruth. 2014. "Chicana/Latin American Feminist Epistemologies of the Global South (within and outside the North): Decolonizing *El Conocimiento* and Creating Global Alliances." *Journal of Latino/Latin American Studies* 6 (2): 135–40.

Trinidad Galván, Ruth. 2015. *Women Who Stay Behind: Pedagogies of Survival in Rural Transmigrant Mexico.* Tucson: University of Arizona Press.

Trueba, Enrique (Henry) T. 2004. "Immigration and the Transnational Experience." In *The New Americans: Immigrants and Transnationals at Work,* edited by Henry Trueba, Pedro Reyes, and Yali Zou, 35–69. Lanham, Md.: Rowman & Littlefield.

Trueba, Henry T., Cirenio Rodriguez, Yali Zou, and José Cintrón. 1993. *Healing Multicultural America: Mexican Immigrants Rise to Power in Rural California.* Washington, D.C.: Falmer Press.

UNHCR (United Nations High Commissioner for Refugees). 2015. *Children on the Run: Unaccompanied Children Leaving Central America and Mexico and the Need for International Protection.* Washington, D.C.: UNHCR.

Valencia, Richard R. 2010. *Chicano School Failure and Success: Past, Present and Future.* New York: Routledge.

Valenzuela, Angela. 1999. *Subtractive Schooling: U.S.–Mexican Youth and the Politics of Caring.* Albany: State University of New York Press.

Velasco Caballero, Francisco, and María de los Angeles Torres. 2015. *Global Cities and Immigrants: A Comparative Study of Chicago and Madrid.* New York: Peter Lang.

Villenas, Sofia. 2001. "Latina Mothers and Small-Town Racisms: Creating Narratives of Dignity and Moral Education in North Carolina." *Anthropology & Education Quarterly* 32 (1): 3–28.

Villenas, Sofia. 2005. "Latina Literacies in *Convivencia*: Communal Spaces of Teaching and Learning." *Anthropology & Education Quarterly* 36 (3): 273–77.

Villenas, Sofia. 2006. "Latina/Chicana Feminist Postcolonialities: Un/tracking Educational Actors' Interventions." *International Journal of Qualitative Studies in Education* 19 (5): 659–72.

Villenas, Sofia. 2007. "Diaspora and the Anthropology of Latino Education: Challenges, Affinities, and Intersections." *Anthropology & Education Quarterly* 38 (4): 419–25.

Warren, Kay. 1998. *Indigenous Movements and Their Critics: Pan-Maya Activism in Guatemala.* Princeton, N.J.: Princeton University Press.

Warren, Kay. 2001. "Indigenous Activism across Generations: An Intimate Social History of Antiracism Organizing in Guatemala." In *History in Person: Enduring Struggles, Contentious Practice, Intimate Identities,* edited by Dorothy Holland and Jean Lave, 63–91. Santa Fe, N.M.: School of American Research Press.

Westheimer, Joel, and Joseph Kahne. 2004. "What Kind of Citizen? The Politics of Educating for Democracy." *American Educational Research Journal* 41 (2): 237–69.

Wike, Richard, Bruce Stokes, and Katie Simmons. 2016. "Europeans Fear Wave of Refugees Will Mean More Terrorism, Fewer Jobs." Pew Research Center. July 11. https://www.pewresearch.org/global/2016/07/11/europeans-fear-wave -of-refugees-will-mean-more-terrorism-fewer-jobs/.

Willis, Paul. 1977. *Learning to Labor: How Working Class Kids Get Working Class Jobs.* Lexington, Mass.: D. C. Heath.

Wiltberger, Joseph. 2014. "Beyond Remittances: Contesting El Salvador's Developmentalist Migration Politics." *Journal of Latin American and Caribbean Anthropology* 19 (1): 41–62.

Wimmer, Andreas, and Nina Glick Schiller. 2003. "Methodological Nationalism, the Social Sciences, and the Study of Migration: An Essay in Historical Epistemology." *International Migration Review* 37 (3) (Fall): 576–610.

Wolfe, Patrick. 2006. "Settler Colonialism and the Elimination of the Native." *Journal of Genocide Research* 8 (4): 387–409.

Zavella, Patricia. 2011. *I'm Neither Here Nor There: Mexicans' Quotidian Struggles with Migration and Poverty.* Durham, N.C.: Duke University Press.

Zilberg, Elana. 2004. "Fools Banished from the Kingdom: Remapping Geographies of Gang Violence between the Americas (Los Angeles and San Salvador)." *American Quarterly* 56 (3): 759–79.

Zilberg, Elana. 2007. "Gangster in Guerilla Face: A Transnational Mirror of Production between the USA and El Salvador." *Anthropological Theory* 7 (1): 37–57.

Zilberg, Elana. 2011a. "Inter-American Ethnography: Tracking Salvadoran Transnationality at the Borders of Latina/o and Latin American Studies." In *Companion to Latina/o Studies*, edited by Juan Flores and Renato Rosaldo, 492–501. Oxford: Blackwell.

Zilberg, Elana. 2011b. *Space of Detention: The Making of a Transnational Gang Crisis between Los Angeles and San Salvador.* Durham, N.C.: Duke University Press.

Zúñiga, Victor, and Hamann, Edward T. 2009. "Sojourners in Mexico with U.S. School Experience: A New Taxonomy for Transnational Students." *Comparative Education Review* 53 (3): 329–53.

Index

ANDREA DYRNESS is associate professor of educational foundations, policy, and practice at the University of Colorado, Boulder. She is author of *Mothers United: An Immigrant Struggle for Socially Just Education* (Minnesota, 2011).

ENRIQUE SEPÚLVEDA III is assistant professor of ethnic studies at the University of Colorado, Boulder. He is coeditor, with Mark Overmyer-Velázquez, of *Global Latin(o) Americanos: Transoceanic Diasporas and Regional Migrations.*